Child of War

Child of War

....

*A Memoir of World War II Internment
in the Philippines*

Curtis Whitfield Tong

Foreword by Samuel Hideo Yamashita

University of Hawai'i Press
Honolulu

Library of Congress Cataloging-in-Publication Data

Tong, Curtis Whitfield.
Child of war : a memoir of World War II internment in the Philippines /
Curtis Whitfield Tong ; foreword by Samuel Hideo Yamashita.
p. cm.
Includes bibliographical references.
ISBN 978-0-8248-3464-7 (hardcover : alk. paper) —
ISBN 978-0-8248-3539-2 (pbk. : alk. paper)
1. World War, 1939–1945—Prisoners and prisons, Japanese.
2. World War, 1939–1945—Personal narratives, American.
3. World War, 1939–1945—Concentration camps—Philippines.
4. Prisoners of war—Philippines—Biography. 5. Prisoners of
war—United States—Biography. 6. Tong, Curtis Whitfield.
I. Yamashita, Samuel Hideo. II. Title.
D805.P6T66 2011
940.53'161—dc22
[B]
2010032645

University of Hawai'i Press books are printed on
acid-free paper and meet the guidelines for permanence
and durability of the Council on Library Resources.

Designed by Janette Thompson (Jansom)
Printed by Sheridan Books, Inc.

Dedicated to my parents

Margaret Whitfield and Walter Curtis Tong

. . . . .

They devoted their time, energy, and love
to the downtrodden of Mindanao
and the needy of our world

Peg and Walter aboard ship en route to their first missionary posting in Davao, Philippines, 1931.

Contents

Foreword by Samuel Hideo Yamashita ix

Preface xiii

Acknowledgments xv

CHAPTER 1 Davao, 1931–Aug. 1941 1

CHAPTER 2 Baguio, Aug. 1941–Dec. 1941 19

CHAPTER 3 Camp John Hay, Dec. 1941–April 1942 43

CHAPTER 4 Camp Holmes I, April 1942–Nov. 1942 81

CHAPTER 5 Camp Holmes II, Dec. 1942–Dec. 1944 141

CHAPTER 6 Bilibid Prison, Dec. 1944–Feb. 1945 199

CHAPTER 7 Homeward Bound, Feb. 1945–April 1945 239

Afterword 250

Bibliography 253

Foreword

Curtis Whitfield Tong was born in 1934 at the southwestern edge of the American imperium, in a town called Davao in southern Mindanao in the Philippines, where his American missionary parents ministered to local aboriginal tribes. He and his two sisters grew up playing with the local children and speaking a combination of Visayan, a local language, and pidgin English. In August 1941, his parents decided that the children would move with their mother to Baguio City in Luzon, the northernmost island in the Philippines, so they could attend the well-regarded Brent School. Tong was a first grader at this school when Japanese aircraft attacked nearby Camp John Hay and other Allied installations in the Pacific on December 8, 1941, initiating hostilities between the United States and Japan.[1] Two and a half weeks later, Japanese forces reached Baguio, and the Japanese civilians who had been imprisoned at Camp John Hay on December 8 were released, and several hundred American and British citizens took their place, with the newly released Japanese now guarding them. War had turned this seven-year-old's world upside down.

Curt Tong's *Child of War* is a moving account of his family's thirty-seven months of incarceration and what they did to survive, both physically and emotionally. Tong's memoir is reminiscent of Agnes Newton Keith's 1947 book *Three Came Home*, the story of another family's incarceration by the Japanese in Borneo. In fact, *Three Came Home* became the model for this genre and had a huge impact on the general public, owing largely to the 1950 film it inspired, starring Claudette Colbert, Patric Knowles, and Sessue Hayakawa.

Keith received special treatment from the commandant of her camp because he had read her first book, but Tong's mother Margaret, was not so lucky. Not only was she just one of several hundred internees living in

---

1. The date of the Japanese attacks on Allied installations in the Pacific and the Philippines is December 8 west of the international date line and December 7 east of the date line.

squalid conditions, first at one camp and then two others, but she also had to be both mother and father to her children because the Japanese had imprisoned her husband in Davao. She had to endure this and was often ill for the more than three years until her husband was reunited with the family. Conditions in the camps were primitive, and by the time American forces liberated the camp in February 1945, Tong's mother was in failing health.

Child of War is valuable to anyone interested in the Pacific War for three reasons. First, Tong has been able to recover the voices of his fellow internees. It is not surprising that the Christian voices are dominant, since so many of the internees were missionaries who, like his parents, had come to save the souls of Filipinos and now struggled to maintain their own faith under difficult conditions. These included Anglicans, Disciples of Christ, Evangelical United Brethren, Methodists, Seventh-Day Adventists, and a few Catholics. A beloved family friend's advice to Tong's mother, offered just a few days before Japanese forces reached Baguio, was typical: "I know only that Japanese are human and, therefore, children of God. Let's treat them with respect." His mother repeated these words in 1943 when she urged her children not to use the terms for the Japanese enemy favored in camp: "Jap," "Nip," "yellow-belly," "slope eyes." Indeed, the Christian voice is heard over and over as Tong remembers his fellow internees' acts of kindness and warmth. He even praises some of the Japanese commandants for their willingness to grant the internees a few precious freedoms—such as family "commingling," classes for the children, evening programs, walks outside the camp, and Christian services. Also cited for their unexpected acts of kindness are a few of the ordinary Japanese and Formosan guards. Thus, he concludes, they "were not too different from us."

Tong also has been able to recreate the voices of the families of the American and British businessmen and engineers that companies like General Motors and petroleum and mining enterprises sent to the Philippines. They were in Baguio at the start of the war because that city was "a favorite escape for foreigners . . . employed in the Manila area." Some of them had come to surrender to the Japanese in chauffeur-driven cars, and these members of the privileged foreign elite felt the humiliation of their incarceration even more acutely, believing as they did in their racial superiority to the Filipinos and Japanese. Tong describes them as speaking in "authoritative tones" and adopting a "no-nonsense" approach in their dealings with "those Japs." When their many requests and demands were not met, they would "explode" in anger, "blow their stacks," "fume," "cuss," and mock their captors, who were "obstinate," "angry," "up to no good," "defensive," "intimidated," and "vengeful." Sometimes even the Christians acted and spoke in this way, too—even the usually patient and reasonable Reverend Carl Eschbach ("Uncle B"). Tong thus captures perfectly the language and the implicit worldview of the Americans and others who had come to the Philippines early in the twentieth century to bring its population firmly into the American imperium.

Finally, Tong reproduces the voices of the servicemen, who were an important part of the American presence in the Philippines. They were there to sustain and protect American military interests in the southwestern Pacific as its chief rival, Japan, advanced southward. Theirs were predictably the angriest voices in camp, muttering "uppo yo assu" instead of *ohayō gozaimasu* at the morning roll call and always referring to the "f——g Nips." When two of them, Richard Green and Herbert Swick, slipped away on April 4, 1944, to join the guerillas in the mountains, they endangered everyone left behind, and their action led to the arrest and torture of four of their friends. Their escape was unsettling to both the Japanese and the internees because it revealed that American and Filipino guerillas were operating nearby. The military voice reemerges most strikingly at the end of Tong's account, when the Americans had liberated the internees and after the Japanese surrender: Tong and his father encounter a serviceman with a Japanese POW on a leash who is made to crawl on all fours and respond to commands and tugs on his leash, a scene that anticipates the more recent American mistreatment of captured Iraqis.

Child of War also reveals much about the way that Tong remembers painful events. We find snippets of what Holocaust survivor Charlotte Delbo called "deep memory." For example, Tong's fear that Major Mukaibo, one of the camp's early commandants, would kill him; his attachment to his toy car and tank; his pleasure at eating scrambled eggs and other foods; his understandable longing for his father and the immense joy he feels once he was returned to the family. At the same time, however, Tong is careful to place these memories within a broader narrative of the sort that Delbo called "common memory" and that scholar Lawrence Langer sees as the product of "an effort to reconstruct a semblance of continuity in a life that began as, and now reassumes what we would consider, a normal existence."[2]

Tong's explicit recognition of his Japanese captors' humanity reaffirms the Christian faith that informed his family's life before and after the war. But there is more here than just Christian forgiveness and triumphalism. As Langer described it, "One effect of common memory, with its talk of normalcy amid chaos, is to mediate atrocity, to reassure us that in spite of the ordeal some human bonds were inviolable," with the result that "atrocity" and "order" exist in "a permanently disrupted suspension."[3] This may be the real meaning of this memoir and why Tong wrote it.

Samuel Hideo Yamashita, Pomona College

---

2. Lawrence L. Langer, *Holocaust Testimonies: The Ruins of Memory* (New Haven, CT: Yale University Press, 1991), 2–3.

3. Ibid., 9.

Preface

In 1994 I reunited for the first time with fellow Americans who as children had been imprisoned by the Japanese military in the Philippines. As I registered in the lobby of a Long Beach hotel, I spotted Reamo, my close boyhood buddy, whom I hadn't seen in fifty years. Though he was dressed in coat and tie, I saw him as my shoeless and shirtless trusted playmate during the war. We shared remembrances, tears, and hugs, and I felt reborn. Other internees were there, too. Their faces had changed, but their voices had not. Those emotional moments rekindled memories of my life as a child of war. Reliving yesteryears with friends gave me the strength to think the unthinkable and write out my story.

Following the war, I focused on my schooling and enjoyed the freedom to play. In the company of schoolmates, in homes or classrooms, or in play areas outdoors, I put aside my memories of the war. I leaned toward silence, piping up to chatter only about comfortable topics like the Boston Red Sox.

As an adult, my life revolved around marriage, children, graduate study, military service, and my career as a college coach, athletic director, and professor. I dedicated summers to competitions in tennis and baseball, travel with our children, and visits with my parents. During my parents' annual get-togethers with their internee friends, I listened with fascination to their clear recollections of prison life—some laughable incidents, but mostly anxious moments of sickness, hunger, torture, and pain. Those gatherings strengthened my memories and etched new ones. Yet with so little time for personal reflection, I continued to suppress my nightmarish recollections of the war.

After the 1994 reunion with Reamo and fellow internees, however, historians at the Pacific Basin Institute in Claremont, California, asked me to share oral accounts of my imprisonment as a child. Another request from the MacArthur Foundation in Norfolk, Virginia, followed. By the time oral history archivists at Williams College requested my wartime recollections, I had begun jotting down notes of my life in prison.

In 2000, my sons Kyle and Kurt—eager to learn about my childhood experience—planned a trip to the Philippines. A Foreign Service officer at the time, Kurt arranged our Baguio stay in the Ambassador's Residence—a stone's throw from Camp John Hay, where I was first imprisoned. North of Baguio we explored Camp Holmes, now known as Camp Dangwa, where I had been a captive for most of the war, witnessing torture and experiencing starvation. As my sons and I walked past the guardhouse next to the sunken garden, I saw a marker commemorating our internment. Looking out over the garden, my eyes grew teary. I again felt the love, hope, and support I had known throughout the war.

After touring Baguio, my sons and I visited Manila's Bilibid Prison, my last site of incarceration. From a rooftop adjacent to the prison, we observed Filipino prisoners milling about the courtyard, as my fellow internees and I had milled about years before.

Although unprepared for the emotional peaks and valleys of this trip, returning to the Philippines sharpened my memories and renewed my commitment to record my story for others.

I have benefited from many resources in the preparation of this book. Being a young confidant and bashful bunkmate of the civilian camp chairman for most of our internment, I was in a position to observe many of the challenges and incidents he faced. The conversations at summertime internee gatherings helped me add detail to my memoir. I also used many of my mother's wartime notes and sketches as well as our postwar chats to help jog my memory. Over time, I perused many documents, books, and personal reports, all of which are listed in the bibliography. My visits with older internees, and even memorable visits with the former commandant Tomibe at his home in Japan, have contributed unique perspectives to my account.

Thus, this memoir is written with love and admiration for those who shared so many trials and hardships with me during my life as a child of war in the Philippines.

Acknowledgments

I extend my profound gratitude to a host of friends, professional colleagues, student-athletes, family members, and others who have lent support and guidance in putting together my story.

Special thanks go to wartime friends, many now deceased, whose encouragement, materials, and recollections aided my writing efforts. They include Frank Cary, Natalie Crouter, Reverend Carl Eschbach, Ruth Zimmerman Eschbach, James Halsema, John Ream, Marilee Scaff, Father Robert Sheridan, Joseph Smith, Katie Ream Sobeck, Rokuro Tomibe, and Evelyn Whitfield.

I also acknowledge my indebtedness to professional colleagues from Otterbein College, Ohio State University, Williams College, Pomona College, International Christian University (Mitaka, Japan), and the University of Massachusetts for their encouragement, guidance, and technical counsel in assembling this manuscript. They include Drs. Bruce Bennett, James Macgregor Burns, Stewart Burns, John Chandler, Carl Furuya, Thomas Kerr, Mika Marumoto, Richard Minear, Yoshio Niwa, James Wood, and Samuel Yamashita.

I owe my immediate family volumes of thanks. They have not only been supportive of my writing, but have unselfishly devoted time to assist with research, photography, and organizing data. They include my parents Margaret and Walter Tong (deceased), my sisters Eloise Purdy and Annarae Hunter, my children Karinne Rae Tong Heise, Kyle Kumler Tong, and Kurt Walter Tong. My wife, Wavalene "Jinx" Tong, has been an immense source of support, providing guidance, patience, research, and love throughout. Unless otherwise credited, all photos are from the Tong family collection in Williamstown, Massachusetts.

Jean Donati, Irene Gresick, Mika Hirai, and Deborah Varnum Tong were all extremely resourceful and supportive in detailing and refining the manuscript.

To each one, I offer my sincere thanks.

Our Modapo Hill home overlooking Davao holds memories of our life in the Philippines before the war. My Filipino friends often joined me in play on the hillside. Dr. Brokenshire is standing on the porch.

CHAPTER 1

Davao

1931–Aug. 1941

. . . .

My Parents' Mindanao Mission

The Philippine archipelago stretches over one thousand miles and has seven thousand islands that extend from Namuao on the north shore of Luzon to Davao on Mindanao's southern coast. Many of the islets are uninhabited but stunningly beautiful beacons of splendor. The entire archipelago, commonly known throughout Asia as the "Pearls of the Orient," retains that title today, despite the long, bitter war with Japan, destructive volcanic eruptions, catastrophic earthquakes, and vicious typhoons.

After its victory in the Spanish-American War at the turn of the twentieth century, the United States assumed territorial rights in the Philippines. There America inherited a population of assorted Asian peoples; most had migrated from Malaysia to the archipelago centuries earlier and settled in regions accessible by sea. Following the war, the many American soldiers who remained integrated themselves into island life. Most married Filipinas. For decades after the American takeover, aborigine settlements in the mountains and along the coasts went largely unbothered.

One exception to this rule, the Davao region, had attracted American, Asian, and European executives and investment as early as the 1930s. The Great Depression in the United States prompted many Americans from the U.S. to seek jobs on plantations or with companies like General Motors, General Electric, and Colgate-Palmolive, which had come to the Philippines, drawn by the fertile soil and ore-rich mountains. The natural harbor made Davao easily accessible, and the puppet Philippine government supported and even encouraged foreign business ventures of all kinds.

The largest populations of newcomers, the Japanese and Chinese, led the migration, and they created great wealth in the agricultural mecca of southern Mindanao. They also became commercially active, founding banks, clothing outlets, and large-scale plantations. The primary export was the highly valuable coconut oil, a derivative of copra.

Foreign investors profited from these economic pursuits, but their takeover of aboriginal lands unsettled the Atas, Bagobos, and Moros, native tribes that had occupied the area for centuries. Some aborigines eventually took on the project of getting rid of the intruders. Over a three-decade

The Philippines

period, approximately two thousand Japanese and Chinese land barons were beheaded.

This politically unstable but beautifully lush land became our home. My sisters and I were born in the Davao Mission Hospital in the years following the arrival of our young, vigorous, and adventuresome parents, Walter and Margaret (Peg) Tong, in 1931. They came to the Philippines at the invitation of the American Board of Commissioners for Foreign Missions (ABCFM) in Boston, an organization which had its informal beginning in 1806, when a group of Williams College students dedicated their lives to serving the world at the "Haystack Prayer Meeting" in Williamstown, Massachusetts. Initially, my parents were assigned to the Davao mission and hospital. The board could not have sent a more perfect duo to Davao. Soon afterward, the board encouraged Dad's explorations into the mountainous aborigine regions, where he introduced more productive farming practices. Indeed, his athleticism, handsome features, broad smile, and warm persona opened many doors across southern Mindanao.

The entry of my sisters and me into multicultural Mindanao took place in the Davao Mission Hospital over a six-year span. Dr. Herbert Brokenshire delivered both Eloise (Wezer), my older sister, and Annarae (Rae), my younger sister. In the late summer of 1934, Doctora Baldomera Esteban Sexon, a diminutive and lovable Filipina surgeon, with the assistance of visiting Dr. Walter White, brought me into this world.

My mother enjoyed telling me about how in the nursery two Filipina babies and I were decked out in matching blue diapers in adjoining woven bamboo baskets. She called us the "Cosmopolitan Choir" as we sang out "praises of joy" to our excited fathers.

Our family home on Modapo Hill in Davao was my paradise. The hillside, a natural botanical garden, featured flowering trees, wild orchids, and bougainvillea vines of varying shades. My Filipino playmates lived on the bank of the hill in squatter shelters constructed with any available materials. We spoke either the common dialect of the province, Visayan, or Pidgin English and regularly gathered assorted fruits from the surrounding hillsides: mangos, papayas, guavas, durians, and so on.

Around the time of my third birthday, Matsumoto Katsuji, a devoted family friend, brought to my parents' attention a leaflet from the marketplace with the heading, "The Orient for Orientals." A supporter of aborigine interests, Matsumoto was an active Japanese Christian in Dad's mission church, a fifteen-year resident of Davao, and head of the huge

Philippine-sponsored Ohta Plantation. His croplands differed from most others in that they had been legally purchased and were located within the greater Davao boundaries. Matsumoto had seen a number of these leaflets in Manila. Noting that identical leaflets had been distributed to Filipino business people in Davao in recent days, he cautioned my parents that the leaflet had a menacing "war gods" smell to it. "Let's keep our eyes open," he said.

Soon after Matsumoto's warning, I accompanied Dad to a missionary meeting in Zamboanga on Mindanao's western peninsula. There Reverend Henry Mattocks, an Anglican missionary from Great Britain, handed Dad a leaflet identical to the one Matsumoto had shared with him and informed Dad that Japanese residents of the province were circulating them. At breakfast, I was startled to hear Mrs. Mattocks challenge her daughter Cecily to clean her plate. "You'll be glad to have it when the Japanese come," she said. Dad learned in that exchange and subsequent conversations during the meetings that the foreign community in Zamboanga expected a Japanese takeover of the peninsula.

Throughout the early years of my childhood, persistent rumors of a coming war filtered into Mindanao. Threatening words in the form of radiocasts and leaflets out of Tokyo lent credence to the rumors and interrupted the peaceful routine of life in the Davao community. War conversations were as common as flies in the Davao City marketplace.

Still, correspondence from the Whitfield family in America only gave a hint of concern in Washington, D.C. about events in Europe and imparted no sense of threat about a possible war in America's Pacific territories.

Furlough to America: 1937–1938

In the fall of 1937, my parents prepared for their ABCFM-required furlough to the United States, a respite from mission work for them and an occasion for my sisters and me to meet our American family and experience snow.

We departed from Manila on the German liner, *Hamburg*, stopping in Singapore and Colombo, Ceylon (Sri Lanka) in the Indian Ocean prior to passage through the Suez Canal and the Mediterranean Sea to Genoa, Italy. There, Dad and I temporarily separated from "the girls." Mom was suffering from an inflammation of bone marrow in her left leg and continued the journey with Wezer and Rae on the *Hamburg* to Rotterdam, Netherlands.

"The boys" (Dad and I—then a curious three-year-old) boarded a train in Genoa and chugged through the Simplon Pass, the famed cut through and beneath the majestic Alps, to Basel, Switzerland. There, we boarded an inland ferry cruising northward on the Rhine River through Germany. I remember being scared when a pair of military customs officials at the German border harshly interrogated Dad. Fear made me attach myself like a barnacle to my dad's sleeve throughout the remainder of our European passage.

During those days on the Rhine, I heard incessant martial music, especially the "Horst Wessel" (the Nazi anthem) whenever the boat approached a village stopover. In Mannheim, huge portraits of Adolf Hitler were displayed throughout the city. Swastika symbols appeared on the entryways of commercial buildings. Throughout the river voyage, the mesmerizing "Horst Wessel" so obsessed me that I began humming it in idle moments. Dad fully understood, but encouraged me to "keep it at a soft hum."

At the German-Dutch border station in Köln, we were again held up for hours as troopers grilled Dad on his credentials. They insisted that he admit his real business in Germany. Their treatment so outraged my exasperated father that he, momentarily, put aside his pastoral vows and delivered a tongue-lashing of the two troopers in Visayan all the while maintaining a calm countenance. After much debate, the lead officer categorized him as an American tourist and waved us through the gate. I felt relief only when we reunited with the girls in Rotterdam.

For my sisters and me, the passage across the Atlantic was marred by boredom. Mom curbed our impatience by reciting the names of her sisters and brothers, as well as Dad's siblings. She woke us early on the day of our arrival in New York so we would see the famed Statue of Liberty. Mom had told us the story of Miss Liberty many times during the voyage. As the sun rose over the Atlantic, Lady Liberty stood beautifully silhouetted against the New York skyline. The scene brought tears to Mom's eyes, as did the dockside introductions of her three children to grandparents, uncles, aunts, and cousins.

From New York City, we traveled to Hackettstown, New Jersey, to stay with our grandparents, Richard and Mercy Whitfield. We met more Whitfields and Tongs days later in New Haven, Connecticut. I especially enjoyed my rides in Uncle Nathan Whitfield's Lincoln car. Only his constant discourses about the economic failings of former President Herbert Hoover dampened the fun of those rides around New Haven.

Grandpa Tong made corrections to my grammar during our walks to the Yale baseball field, which helped my broken English considerably. Sadly, Grandpa died suddenly just a couple of months before our scheduled return to the Philippines. Contemplating what to do after losing her husband, my grandmother, Evelyn (Nana), volunteered to assist our family in any way she could. My parents considered Nana's offer and invited her to accompany us back to the Philippines. She eagerly accepted.

A major question facing my parents and the American Board, though, was whether it would be safe for us to return. The board wired the State Department in Washington, asking for news of Japan's intentions in the Pacific. The Philippine emissary in Washington responded, "Japan has no designs on American territories in the Pacific." My parents were relieved at the good news, for they very much wished to return "home," but not at the price of being caught in a war zone with three children and an aging grandmother.

In the spring of 1938, my parents acquired a second-hand Chevy. They planned to drive across the country to the Port of Vancouver in Canada and board the *Empress of Russia.* Ever the disciplinarian, sharp-tongued Nana kept order in the back seat as we drove through America's "amber waves of grain" and "purple mountain majesties," which awed all of us. Dad, much impressed with the condition of the highways, jokingly shared his wish to bring the road crews to Mindanao for a furlough.

For me, the highlight of the trip was seeing bears, moose, and elk in Yellowstone National Park. According to Dad, my sisters and I hollered "Stop!" every time we saw one of those animals. Nana was so taken by the hourly eruption of the Old Faithful geyser that it filled several pages of her diary and picture album. Yellowstone was a magnificent experience for all of us, and stories about the park became a prominent part of our family lore.

The *Empress* was dockside awaiting us in Vancouver. Memories of that sea voyage have brought me many bad dreams over the years. A storm in the North Pacific rocked the *Empress,* rolling waves over the deck. The crew ordered all passengers to go below deck and hang on to the safety hatches in the cabins. As I ran toward the stairwell, I looked back to see an elderly passenger swept overboard. Those on the bridge saw it, too, but it was too late to attempt a rescue. My childhood memories of a man being swept overboard have kept me from choosing travel by sea as an adult.

Following the custom of ocean voyages in the Pacific, the *Empress* dropped anchor at each major port in Southeast Asia. We stopped for several days in Yokohama, Japan, a peaceful place where the Japanese were extremely gracious in their offers of rickshaw rides and other pleasures. The ambiance so impressed Mom and Dad that they forgot any thought of war with Japan. It seemed to them that Japan had no malicious intentions to intervene with the American protectorates, Hawai'i and the Philippines. Nana and Mom became so taken with the lovely Japanese china that they made purchases to adorn our dining room table in Davao. (Within three years, a turn of fate would put that prized china back in Japanese hands.)

Only in Shanghai, China, where Japan had taken full control of economic interests and the Japanese Navy had "accidentally" sent the USS *Panay* to the bottom of the harbor, did my parents' earlier concerns about Japan's ambitions in East Asia come into focus again. Several American missionary families from Nanking boarded the *Empress* with us, hoping to find safe haven in the Philippines. They related how Japanese troops had slaughtered and raped thousands of Chinese women and children. Those conversations were my introduction to a world where people, when driven by forces of instinct, emotion, and greed will resort to killing innocents, even children. Once again, doubts about the safety of the Philippines crept into my parents' thoughts.

Return to the Philippines

All of us were thankful when the *Empress* finally dropped anchor in Manila harbor. The following morning, before departing our hotel for a stroll, Dad gave his petite mother strict instructions about how to protect her valuables on Manila streets. Yet within seconds of stepping out of the hotel, Nana lost her handbag to a purse-snatcher. Mom, directly behind her, witnessed the theft and immediately gave chase, tackling the thief in an empty lot of canna plants, severely gashing her leg in the process.

An American soldier who witnessed Mom's chase and reclamation of the purse, followed in a military two-seater. He apprehended the purse-snatcher and turned him over to a city police officer called to the scene. The soldier paged Dad at the hotel and then drove Mom to the hospital where she received multiple stitches. The attending police officer informed Dad and me that the thief would remain in jail for a two-week period. The next morning, however, Nana spotted the same thief on the sidewalk across the street from the hotel looking for new prey. It was a reminder of the rampant corruption in the islands' urban areas.

Nana got a broader taste of life in the Philippines during our four-day journey on the *Mactan,* an inter-island freighter that took us from Manila to Davao. Bedding down at night in the extreme heat of the *Mactan*'s lower bowels was a nightmarish experience for her, but she bravely maintained her composure in the company of cockroaches, fleas, lice, and rats—our nightly bedmates. Each of the four nights aboard was the same. During our voyage, we ate only food and beverages purchased in Manila, Mom's formula for survival aboard ferries. Her plan saved us from the dreaded dysentery. Almost all other passengers were stricken with diarrhea and worse. Inter-island vessels also had poor safety records. Sinkings due to overloading, unpredictable currents, and stormy seas were commonplace.

The loyal and loving Dr. Herbert Brokenshire stood tall as he met us at the Davao pier. He was the lead surgeon at the Mission Hospital and Dad's strong ally in serving Davao. Doctora Sexon and Mr. Matsumoto also greeted us upon our arrival. In our newly assigned home on the hospital grounds, our "house girl" Leonie and amah Sixta had prepared a bountiful supper for us all. Afterward, the adult guests updated us on changes in the area during our absence.

They also told us about the large numbers of Japanese civilians who had swept into Davao during our absence. Most were officially tied to local plantations or commercial enterprises in the city. Especially worrisome to Mr. Matsumoto was the fact that a similar swelling of Japanese ranks was occurring in Manila, Baguio, Cebu, Iloilo, and Zamboanga. He found the sudden growth of the Japanese presence in the region suspicious. Matsumoto reported that almost every ship anchoring in Davao Harbor was unloading Japanese nationals by the hundreds; almost all of these were young men with no prearranged employment. He guessed that most were émigrés, not immigrants, and his conversations with various groups of the newcomers supported his suspicions.

Both doctors, Brokenshire and Sexon, spoke of the increase of Japanese patients in the hospital. Numbers had more than doubled during a six-month period. Sexon, in particular, worried aloud about the safety of our family should Japanese military incursions in nearby Asian countries spread to the Philippines.

The following day, with increasing concern for our safety, Dad forwarded a wire to the emissary of the U.S. Diplomatic Mission in Manila. He cited the immense growth of Japanese presence in Davao and other observations shared by Brokenshire, Sexon, and Matsumoto. He was very curious as to the emissary's current position on the topic of a Japanese threat. The wire in response was immediate, simple, and reassuring: "Reverend Tong: There is no cause for concern. We have been assured that Japan respects American territories in the Pacific."

With that official pronouncement, Dad began preparations to reacquaint himself with the several Bagobo tribes with whom he had developed a warm relationship prior to our furlough in the States. Mom worked on matters related to the Davao church, and Nana became involved with Filipina women's groups in the city and started a knitting club, which within months had a hundred women knitting socks and gloves for shipment to the needy in China and England.

Nana also agreed to oversee my energetic and curious play. As I looked for ways to amuse myself, I often ended up getting into trouble. One escapade involved chasing some newborn chicks. Unfortunately, I stepped on one chick and killed it, resulting in my first severe scolding by Nana—but it would not be the last.

Wezer assisted in my next adventure. We placed a praying mantis we wanted to keep as a pet in a jar with jacaranda blossoms on the dining room table. The next morning we discovered a multitude of hatchlings praying all over the house. Nana was furious!

Finally, one morning while Nana was leading a crochet class at the Davao Community Church, Leonie had granted permission for a neighbor boy and me to look for frogs in a shallow marsh behind the hospital. The first frog we came upon was noisily attempting to escape the jaws of a baby boa. Together, we carried the boa to the house to show Leonie. (It truly was only a grass snake, but to a couple of five-year-olds, all snakes on Mindanao were "boas.") After hearing our dog Army barking, the serpent escaped my grasp and slithered into Nana's bedroom. Our frantic efforts to retrieve the snake failed. My dad eventually located and captured the snake, but I still felt Nana's wrath.

That evening, Dad informed me that soon I would be traveling north with him for a week of visits to aboriginal barrios in the mountains of Mindanao. In part, he made this decision to free Nana from watching over me. I was excited that Dad had decided to rekindle our Rhine River partnership and take me on an adventure.

Mom was less keen about the plan. Only after Dad had pledged that our trip would not exceed a week did she agree. For all Nana's desire that her son spend more time with me, the idea of my going with Dad to

Bagobo country did not sit well with her either. She had never seen a Bagobo, but the name sounded sufficiently frightening to prompt a nay vote from her. Nevertheless, Dad took me with him.

Adventure in Bagobo Country

We set out toward Cotabato in the Chevy that had arrived with us from America. The drive on deeply pockmarked roads took more than five hours. I noticed as we neared a village that many of the wooded foothills were afire. Dad explained that the fires were set by Filipinos to make room for constructing huts and planting crops. The scene was a reminder to Dad to discuss the impact of such burns with leaders in Cotabato on his next visit there. He felt strongly that continued burning of the forest would cause massive hillside erosion and could be catastrophic to the area over time.

We reached the Cotabato River in mid-afternoon only to discover the wooden bridge had been washed away. The two young Bagobo men who would be our guides waved at us from the trail on the other side of the river. They were clad in the traditional knee-length pants of woven hemp, and they signaled for us to wait. Then, using their sharp bolos, they cut logs to size and bound them together with vines. Their construction took several hours, but thanks to their genius with the forest materials at hand, a raft was born. During our wait on the opposite shore, Dad secured the Chevy at the nearby home of a Filipino pastor. Using two huge "paddle pokers" (a long wooden pole with a broad flattened edge on one end and a dulled point at the other), the men overcame the strong current and pulled the raft to where we could jump aboard.

The Bagobo crew helped load our two burlap bags onto the raft, then pushed off into the swollen waters, angling toward the opposite bank about fifty yards away. The river was not rocky, so Dad was not worried about my safety. But as we neared midstream, two crocodiles, common to the rivers in central Mindanao, took an interest in our raft and its cargo. "Jumping Jehosaphat!" muttered Dad, using his favorite expression of surprise. He nudged me toward the middle of the floating platform. With the pokers, the Bagobos splashed water in front of the curious crocs to slow their advance. When the raft stopped abruptly against a large tree root at the edge of the opposite bank, we waded quickly ashore.

On shore, Dad and I realized we had dozens of leeches clinging to our legs. We quickly picked them off each other. As the two Bagobos dragged the raft up the embankment, I could see that neither of them had any leeches on their bodies. I curiously stared at their leech-free bodies. They smiled broadly at me, and I noticed that their four front teeth were like v-shaped saw blades. One had black teeth, the other red. Dad explained to me that the coloration depended on whether they chewed black or red betel nut. Bagobo men chewed betel nut like children on Coney Island chewed gum. Over time, the betel nut juice permanently stained the tooth enamel. Upon our arrival at the barrio (village) late that afternoon, I was amazed to watch two women filing their own teeth into the traditional v-shape.

Hiking with our guides over bolo-cleared paths was arduous. The narrow trails were damp, overgrown, and like the river's edge, home to leeches. It was near sunset when we entered a small clearing. The whole village, anticipating our arrival, met us at the trail's end. I was astonished by the excitement Dad caused among the Bagobos, the women especially. They wore broad smiles and made wild welcoming gestures when they saw his rugged figure and warm smile again. Dad had told me what to expect, so I was not alarmed when the giggling women and children took turns touching my hair, which was bleached almost white from the Davao sun. My white hair was as much a novelty to them as their red v-shaped teeth were to me. Their curiosity and friendly fondling eased my dad's earlier anxieties about their reception to a strange-looking child in their midst.

I was surprised to see that the young boys wore no clothing and that the girls wore only a triangular pubic shield held in place by a string around the waist. The women were fully dressed in brightly decorated hemp cloth, and huge ivory earrings about the size of a tin can lid hung from their earlobes. Like the men, they wore beaded necklaces. Our late arrival in the barrio had put us behind schedule at the very outset of our trip. Dad, therefore, readily accepted their invitation to stay overnight. They fed us supper, a sticky gumbo soup with hard bread made of cassava flour, which I found filling but not tasty. Then we joined one of the families in their hut for the night.

The village's seven nipa huts with their banana-leaf roofs stood elevated eight to ten feet above the ground on bamboo poles buried in the baked soil. We climbed a bamboo ladder to an open room, the sleeping quarters for the entire family—altogether fourteen people, counting Dad and me. Dad and I slept on a mat of woven hemp. Most others slept directly on the tightly woven, stripped bamboo floor. Even though we filled the room to overflowing, I heard no conversation, giggling, or human movement until the roosters below the hut crowed in the new day. The roosters below us seemed in cahoots with their cousins under the other huts as all the birds chimed together in a morning chorus. Dogs, cats, chickens, and a noisy pig joined in the choir.

As we prepared to depart the village, I followed Dad to the toilet, a shallow pit in the ground at the clearing's edge. Then we had an early breakfast of a sort of bacon and porridge. Before we left, an elderly man showed me his family treasures: two human skulls displayed as decorative items on a shelf near the stove. Dad, having seen the skulls previously, had forewarned me that they would be proudly pointed out to me. Although he had not asked, Dad surmised that the skulls had once been attached to Japanese or Chinese necks, since years before, settlers from Japan had taken over large tracts of fertile Bagobo land with the support of the Philippine government, which shared in the profits from copra and sugar. It took twenty years and the accumulation of about four hundred such skulls displayed on Bagobo shelves before the theft of aboriginal lands came to a halt.

Narrow paths through the forest connected the small Bagobo barrios, which sat five to eight kilometers apart. We walked about forty kilometers during our journey, stopping at five barrios. I found the hikes more difficult with each passing day. The extreme heat, unforgiving terrain, and unusually heavy undergrowth infested with leeches had me counting the days until we would return to Davao. At one hamlet, our guides obtained a potion of some kind which, when applied to our skin, thankfully lessened the number of leeches that attached themselves to our bodies.

It was late afternoon when we trudged into our next-to-last hamlet. As darkness fell, Dad lifted me onto a high-hanging outdoor hammock for the night. After spending some time demonstrating to several Bagobo men how to dry pig manure before applying it to the soil, Dad climbed onto a high stool and joined me in hammock heaven.

Our guides rose early, carrying hardened bread for our travels. Foremost on Dad's mind was completing the visits on schedule, so as not to worry our family in Davao. The guides led us on a long walk to a hamlet near the river we had crossed by raft a week earlier. At noontime, the red-toothed Bagobo, stick in hand, drew a circular path in the dirt for me, which mapped the river's location and where we had been. I realized then that our eight-day venture had simply taken us on a long circuitous route.

Several hours later, as we approached a cluster of huts in a clearing, strange wailing sounds coming from a group of women and children standing under one of the huts startled us. One of our guides translated an elderly woman's frenzied explanation into Visayan. Between loud sobs and pointing toward a hut where a group of women were standing, she related that shortly before our arrival a huge python swallowed a week-old infant lying unattended on a mat under the hut. The baby's older sister had seen the final moments of the attack and the python slithering away, but her shouts came too late. The young girl pointed to where the snake had reentered the forest and the men of the barrio gathered their bolos and within minutes disappeared into the heavy foliage in search of the snake.

Long hours passed and Dad decided to remain in the barrio overnight to help console the stricken mother and family until the return of her mate and the hunters. Well past sundown, the search party returned carrying a headless twenty-foot python stretched over their shoulders; the meat would feed the barrio for several days.

I spent that night in a hut with other restless children. The thought of a baby in a snake's belly shook me. Sleep came only intermittently as I replayed over and over again thoughts of a baby inside a python. Dad stayed up until nearly midnight trying to comfort the group of men and women who sat around a fire in the clearing. Morning could not come soon enough for me! Shortly after daybreak, our guides led us from the bereaved Bagobos, and together we walked in sad silence to the river.

At the river's edge, we noted that the water level was down considerably. No crocodiles were visible, and the guides easily poled the raft across to where our Chevy was waiting. Dad opened the trunk and handed the two men a large box of shirts for distribution in the barrios. Lightweight shirts were very popular among the Bagobo men.

The six girls of our Davao household were noticeably relieved at the sight of the Chevy pulling up beside the house near suppertime. I was happy to be home, too.

Growing Fears of War

Soon after our return, Mom alerted Dad to growing war concerns Mr. Matsumoto had shared with her. Dad agreed to meet with him the following morning. Matsumoto spoke of Japanese "businessmen" who had recently arrived in Davao gathering "valuable tactical information about the area for use by Japanese generals." He advised Dad to send his mother and family back to the States "before it is too late."

Dad asked Matsumoto to explore travel options for Nana on one of the ships transporting Japanese nationals to Davao. Matsumoto was repeatedly denied a booking. Months passed. Then, in the spring of 1940, he informed my parents that the Japanese freighter *Kitano Maru* would soon arrive in Davao and could take on two additional passengers. Five days later, Nana was on her way to Australia. She arrived in the States almost six weeks later on a Swedish vessel out of Brisbane.

It was a difficult good-bye for Nana because she had come to love Davao and her Filipina friends. But she had also concluded that she should return to America. For the first time, she offered no challenge to Dad's strong recommendation. In the days following Nana's departure, I had an empty feeling when I awoke each morning.

Shortly after she left, Dr. Brokenshire told our family that he had received orders to report immediately to the United States Subic Bay Naval Base in Manila. He was given the rank of lieutenant commander and assigned the role of chief surgeon. His was yet another sad farewell that foreshadowed difficult days ahead in the Philippines.

Following Nana's counsel to spend more time with the family, Dad arranged for several outings with my sisters and me. I became his right-hand man on our first venture to an aborigine village north of the city, where Dad had frequently dug for artifacts with several Bagobo friends. There we gathered broken pieces of ancient earthenware, which Dad enjoyed piecing together into their original shapes.

Soon afterward, Dad, Wezer, and I boarded a small fishing boat to Kiamba in southern Mindanao along the Celebes Sea. Kiamba is a mountainous area known for its colorful birds. While Dad attended meetings, a young Filipino couple he knew well took us on a hike to a site where we might see large monkeys. We enjoyed chattering back and forth with the monkeys as they showed off their acrobatic talents in the treetops. The monkeys seemed far more noisy and inquisitive than those at home on Modapo Hill. We also spotted a few brightly colored birds called "peenees." I was thrilled to watch wild creatures cavorting in their natural habitats. Unfortunately, Dad's meetings kept him from sharing in the excitement.

A few weeks later on a sparkling clear day, Mom and Dad drove my sisters and me to the village of Calinan along the Davao River. From there the view of the Philippines' highest mountain, Mt. Apo, was breathtaking. Dad spoke often of his wish to climb the conical shaped volcano one day. That dream was realized when, with his young handyman pal, Bob

Crytser, he managed the steep and rugged climb to the summit in the spring of 1941. At the nearby Philippine Eagle Conservation Area, we saw two eagles perched atop a tree overlooking the river. One performed a graceful dive into the smooth waters, emerging with a fish firmly held in its beak. On our ride home, Dad's reflections on our eagle sighting stimulated his nagging worry about war, "I hope that the American eagle is as attentive to movement in the Pacific as that Philippine eagle is to the fish in the river."

In March 1941, Dad drove to Midsayap to meet Alvin and Marilee Scaff. Both were young and adventuresome missionaries stationed in Dansalan on the north shore of Lake Lanao in northern Mindanao. The Scaffs returned with him to Davao to acquaint themselves with the mission programs in the southern regions. They immediately noticed the large Japanese presence in the city, and it stunned them. Marilee, noting the abundance of natural resources in the area, wrote in a letter to her mother: "If the United States should get into a war with Japan, Mindanao . . . with no single army base on it . . . would be juicy meat. I think Japan could have it at the taking." The Scaffs would later be captured and imprisoned in the Los Baños prison camp after hiding out for months with other missionary friends in the hills of Negros Island, which lies north of Mindanao and is home of the American Board's Silliman University. One family was more fortunate and managed to rendezvous with an American submarine after a late-night escape by *banca* (a wide rowboat) from Negros.

In the summer of 1941, my parents decided that my sisters and I needed a change from the school and social scene in Davao. The peculiar behavior of Wezer's lone playmate and neighbor, Arcella Zamora, encouraged their decision. Dad described Arcella as "emotionally unstable and as full of superstitions and fears as Army (our dog) has fleas." To my parents' further annoyance, Wezer was regularly urged to join the Zamora children's ritual of "plucking gray hair from their father's head," a common practice in many Filipino homes because gray hair was considered unattractive. I, too, was called upon to pluck Mr. Zamora's hair, but I refused. My parents, having learned that Brent School in Baguio served many missionary children in the islands and had a reputation as a challenging educational institution, decided to enroll us there.

To my delight, only days prior to our planned departure from Davao, the USS *Langley,* a small aircraft carrier, dropped anchor in the harbor. We watched excitedly from the pier as twelve fighter-bombers took off from

Langley's deck in a display I had never before seen. Wezer wondered aloud if that flyover was a message to Japan to stay away from the Philippines.

Matsumoto informed Dad the following day that Tokyo's public radio response to the *Langley's* aggressiveness was a warning to the United States. The very presence of the carrier in Davao represents a "violation of American rights in the Orient," said the announcer. This was a clear indication that Japan held no respect for America's claim to possession of the Philippines.

With enrollment at Brent School arranged, my parents decided that Mom would accompany us to Baguio in August and remain with us through the school year. This decision was extremely difficult for both of my parents. Having to leave my father in Davao, eleven days distant from Baguio, created stress and anxiety in all of us.

I was pained at the mere idea of leaving Dad. Our adventures together had forged a strong and binding love. Even knowing that he planned to join us in Baguio for Thanksgiving, I struggled to hold back tears as we waved farewell from the boat deck. We left Dad on the pier standing with our devoted house girls, Sixta and Leonie, and our dog Army.

*I am happily standing under the pine trees with my sisters and Dad
for this photo taken during my father's Thanksgiving visit only
days prior to Japan's attack on the Philippines in 1941.*

CHAPTER 2

Baguio

Aug. 1941–Dec. 1941

. . . .

Moving to Baguio for School

The freighter ride to Manila was little different from earlier voyages on the inland sea. Again, we fought off seasickness, extreme heat, insects, and rodents. Dr. Brokenshire greeted us at the dock in Manila in his handsome white naval uniform. He spoke of the tension among American civilians in Manila. Many felt trapped after discovering that passage to the United States was unattainable. Like Matsumoto, Brokenshire had come to believe that conflict with Japan was inevitable.

In Baguio, a smiling, bespectacled Reverend Carl B. Eschbach, "Uncle B" as we had known him from earlier visits, was easily recognizable towering above the cluster of dark-haired Filipinos gathered at the bus stop. On prior family visits, Bob (Uncle B's son) and I played "cars" together almost daily. But when we arrived at the Eschbach home Bob was not there, and I missed his companionship very much. He had returned to the United States with his mother Ruth, sister Margaret, and brother Jim. Bob's deteriorating eyesight necessitated immediate medical attention, and the Eschbach family, also sensing danger lurking in Southeast Asia, had been forewarned that a later return to America might be impossible. Uncle B had scheduled a departure from Manila to join his family in the fall of 1941, but by then all bookings had been canceled.

Baguio City had long been a favorite haven for foreigners and wealthy Filipino business people employed in the Manila area. Missionaries stationed on Philippine islands such as Mindoro, Negros, Cebu, or Mindanao, and even those employed in other East Asian countries, often sought out Baguio for their holidays. It was a small cosmopolitan city offering cool clean air and gorgeous mountain views, two very fine hotels, a magnificent golf course on the grounds of Camp John Hay, and fine restaurants. Americans attached to the gold mines or the lumber industry had settled in the area years earlier and lived in luxury.

The expatriate community in Baguio, well removed from military targets like the Subic Bay Naval Base, Clark Air Base, and Nichols Field, was less apprehensive about an outbreak of hostilities with Japan than were our Western friends in Mindanao and Negros. While Japan's incursions across Southeast Asia had been headline news in Davao and Manila, Baguio news sources rarely identified conflict with Japan as probable.

Mom immediately noticed an increased Japanese presence compared to our earlier visits to the city. Japanese now significantly outnumbered Westerners. In a very un-Japanese manner, the newcomers quickly entered the Baguio social scene as members or participants in clubs, community activities, and even churches. Uncle B had also identified those trends. Interestingly, very few Japanese women migrated to Baguio, and this fact lent further credence to premonitions of a coming military takeover.

For understandable reasons, the Chinese population had grown, too. Many of the Chinese worshipping at Uncle B's church were escapees from Nanking, Shanghai, and other cities in southeast China. Almost all had sought refuge in the Philippines after seeing the atrocities perpetrated upon Chinese civilians on the mainland. More than other communities in Baguio, the Chinese feared again becoming possible targets of invading Japanese soldiers.

A small group of Americans representing the Disciples of Christ Board, former missionaries in China, had also arrived in Baguio. They established a Chinese Language School (CLS) there to continue the study of Mandarin they had begun in China.

The Chinese we had known in Davao possessed a centuries-long hatred of the Japanese, and the Japanese returned that animosity. In Baguio, the Chinese closely followed radio reports of Japan's military advances in the Pacific and rumors of spy infiltrations in northern Luzon.

Uncle B had arranged a rental home for us across the street from Burnham Park, a perfect site for three very active children. The house was also within walking distance of Brent School and was especially convenient for Rae, since her kindergarten teacher lived and conducted a small class on the top floor of our new residence.

During our daily family strolls to the Baguio marketplace, I enjoyed watching the indigenous peoples of Luzon. Igorots left their adobe abodes in the dawn hours of each day and walked barefoot for miles to peddle their homegrown fruits and vegetables. The men wore G-strings and Western suit jackets, which looked funny to me. The women were attired, top and bottom, in woven material from plants native to the area. I was most amazed by the women's ability to balance heavy baskets of produce on their heads while sporting long cigars jutting straight out from their mouths. My efforts to emulate the "basket-on-the-head" practice met with little success, and Mom discouraged any thoughts of putting a cigar in my mouth. The Igorots in the Baguio marketplace were friendly toward Westerners, but not to the Japanese. And they did not welcome any outsiders to their barrios.

Ilocanos, who lived in hamlets south of Baguio, also sold their wares in the city markets. The women frequently came adorned in decorated gowns and, like the Igorots, carried fruits and vegetables in baskets balanced on their heads. They regularly toted very thin dogs in bamboo cages to be sold for food, mostly to Igorots who were extremely fond of dog meat. In response to his house girl Marci's query, "What would you like for supper, sir?" Uncle B would often joke in response, "Bring back a dog."

Wezer, Rae, and I always enjoyed our shopping excursions in town. They offered opportunities to visit the toy store and buy fruit, a prominent part of our daily diet in Baguio. The variety of fruits was amazing: *lanzones*, guava, varieties of melon, papaya, mangoes, star apples, durian, mangosteen, pomelo, lychee, monkey bananas, cooking bananas, other varieties of bananas, and more. All topped my list of the tastiest fruits I had ever eaten.

In September 1941, Wezer and I began classes at Brent School, walking each day from our Burnham Park home. We loved the cool mountain air and the regimen of daily classes. Each morning began with prayer, and then we sang to our teacher, "Good morning to you, good morning to you, we're all in our places with sunshiny faces, good morning to you." Our teacher would then respond, "And, good morning to you."

Phyllis Gibbons, one of the teachers at Brent, worked diligently on correcting my heavily accented "Davao dialect" during tutoring sessions. She found my English difficult to understand, but Miss Gibbons was patient and did make some inroads in correcting my peculiar expressions. She took particular exception to my frequent use of the word *qua'an*. In

Visayan *qua'an* meant something not easily defined or described. She also reminded me almost daily that I lacked concentration. (Within weeks she and our class would learn a new definition for the word "concentration.") Four years later, Miss Gibbons became the private tutor of Arthur MacArthur, the son of General Douglas MacArthur.

Charles Henry Brent, then the Episcopal bishop of the Philippines, had founded Brent School in 1909. He was deeply committed to education and found in Baguio a wonderful place that was "never hot and never cold." In his book, *Bishop Brent's Baguio School,* James J. Halsema, son of Baguio's mayor Eusebius Julius Halsema, wrote of Bishop Brent's vision for a school: "Education without religion is a house without foundation, an accompaniment without a song." Brent School truly met that vision. Its headmaster, Father Art Richardson, an Episcopal pastor, was a respected leader in the Baguio community.

Our family spent Sunday mornings at the Evangelical United Brethren Church where Uncle B served as pastor. I preferred the adult service in the sanctuary to Sunday school, because I delighted in the formal manner in which the morning offering was received. Each Sunday, uniformed Filipino cadets from Camp John Hay marched in cadence down the aisles and stopped at each pew. They clicked their heels, bowed, and then carried the offering plate to the next pew of waiting worshipers.

On Saturdays, Rae and I and local Filipino boys played with toy cars in Burnham Park. We occasionally explored some of the adjacent hillsides looking for wild orchids. From the summit of nearby Mt. Santo Tomas, a favorite family climb on clear days, we enjoyed watching ships moving across Lingayen Gulf.

Thanksgiving 1941 was a very special day because Dad surprised us with his promised but otherwise unannounced visit. His two days with us seemed to fly by. We shared tearful good-byes as he boarded a bus back to Manila to connect again with the woebegone vessel *Mactan* and return to Mindanao. Mother, sensing future trouble, seemed more visibly pained than on previous separations. Dad, too, showed the strain as he hugged Mom and my sisters. With moist eyes, he held my head tightly to his chest and whispered softly into my ear, "Take care of our girls." It was a sad goodbye for everyone.

A week later, Dad wired us from Cagayan de Oro on the north coast of Mindanao that he would be heading overland to Davao in a couple of days. That evening we heard on a Manila newscast that public transport on Mindanao Island had been terminated. It was reported that sabotage had destroyed the telephone and telegraph lines to Davao and Japanese infiltrators were raiding foreigners' homes in Zamboanga. Mom was terribly shaken. Dad's message from Cagayan was the last we received from him for nearly two and a half years.

Attack on Our Islands—December 8, 1941

On the morning of December 8, I walked with Wezer into Brent School at 8:00 a.m. in time for my first-grade class to begin. Moments later, all hell broke loose in Baguio.

As the class was singing "Good morning to you . . ." a chilling rumble shook the surrounding valleys. The din grew in volume and my heart thumped. The culminating burst of sound seemed to swallow the rooftops. I clasped my hands over my ears and put my head on my desk in anticipation of a crash into the building. Suddenly, the roar passed and it was quiet.

Our teacher immediately instructed us to line up for a fire drill and in quickstep ushered us into the pinewoods. The trees stood straight and tall like soldiers protecting my secluded spot along the hillside. Minutes later, another crescendo of sound made me flatten my body against the embankment as a second wave of planes flew directly overhead. Peeking upward, I could see the distinctive markings of the Japanese Rising Sun flag under the plane's wings. The second salvo of bombs on the city was even louder than the first. Two more formations followed, each depositing its ordnance near Camp John Hay. The Japanese had arrived like an airborne tsunami.

Following the two raids, the skies quieted. We could hear birds again. After waiting a long time for more planes, the teachers ushered us back to our classrooms and announced that parents would come to pick us up. When Mom arrived, she informed Wezer and me that our house was still standing even though a bomb "spinner" (rudder casing) had fallen on the roof over Rae's kindergarten classroom. No one was hurt. Mom also told us that Uncle B had called and that she was considering a temporary move to the Eschbach home, which was more camouflaged by trees and farther away from where the bombs fell at Camp John Hay. The following day only one flyover resulted in bombing (at Camp Hay), other flights seemed only to be surveying the area, so Mom chose not to move. Manila radio reported that only hours before the Japanese bombed the Philippines, they had struck Pearl Harbor in a similar manner.

On the afternoon of December 9, Baguio became quiet. Local radio broadcasts confirmed that bombs had fallen on Camp John Hay. Located only a few miles from Brent, Hay was a Filipino training base and a retreat for American military personnel stationed in the Philippines. Popularly called "The West Point of the Philippines" by the local chamber of commerce, the military installation was clearly the primary Baguio target. The evening news reported that hikers atop Mt. Santo Tomas had counted at least twenty-five Japanese planes in the first raid. A later broadcast announced that air attacks had also devastated Aparri on the north coast of Luzon. Colonel John Horan, the American commander of Camp Hay, told Uncle B that the Japanese planes were twin-engine bombers launched from Formosa (Taiwan).

We heard the first news of tragedy in Baguio's American community the evening after the first bombs fell. Uncle B told us that the home of American Baptist missionaries, the Paul Collyer family, located near the entry gate of Camp John Hay, had been directly hit by one of the bombs and an occupant on the lower floor was killed. Miraculously, the family's infant son Paul and his amah had survived.

Anticipating more air strikes the next morning, Mayor Halsema decided to post lookouts atop Mt. Santo Tomas. The peak offered a clear view of Lingayen Gulf and the northern hills. The mayor asked Hugo Culpepper, Rufus Gray, and several others of the CLS to serve as lookouts. Their spotting duties made it possible to sound sirens over the city before attacks, alerting everyone to possible bombing raids. Baguio was like a sunken garden with mountains on all sides. Without spotters, Japanese planes could not be heard or seen until they were almost over the city.

Awaiting the Enemy

With school closed in the aftermath of the air strikes, Mom made diligent efforts to keep our family together and prepare us for whatever conditions we might face. She wanted us to experience some good times, knowing in her heart that pleasures would soon be in short supply. Rather than sitting at home, listening to the all-day radio accounts of bombings and enemy landings in the Philippines, we retreated from the city every few days to picnic at playground sites.

Mom tried to hide her deep concern from us. We had heard nothing from Dad since his wire from Mindanao before the first bombings, so he was constantly in our thoughts and prayers. On those picnics, imagining Dad to be with us, I often "talked" with him.

For a number of days after the first bombings, smaller Japanese planes dropped propaganda leaflets on Baguio. Joseph and Winifred (Winnie) Smith, former Disciples of Christ missionaries to China, had been given one of the leaflets by a Filipino friend. The Smiths had been reassigned to the CLS in Baguio a year earlier following Japan's pitiless incursions into China. Initially, they thought the leaflet was a warning against resistance. But the message was simply notice that the Japanese were coming as Asian friends "with the common goal of freeing Asia of American domination and building a greater East-Asia co-prosperity sphere."

From Baguio friends, we learned that large numbers of American travelers had unfortunately docked in Manila only days before the Japanese attacks. Some were missionaries on furlough from other Asian countries; others were only stopping over in Manila en route to job assignments in East Africa. Almost all of those caught up in the ugly mayhem in Manila chose not to risk a makeshift escape on small boats. Warnings of hostile submarines in the waters surrounding the Philippines overrode that temptation.

Long-term American residents of Manila desperately sought safety from the regular bombing raids on the city. Newcomers who had just planned to pass through the islands faced an unfamiliar country and people. Their days were havoc-filled and emotionally overwhelming. Blessed were the few with ties to Manila missionaries. The common counsel they received was to seek passage to Baguio, which was recommended not only for its temperate climate, but also as a site that might be passed over by the Japanese military because of its non-strategic location. Regrettably, Baguio too became a target.

Rumors began to fly around the American/British community in Baguio. The bombings on December 8 and in the following days had stirred up peoples' thoughts and imaginations; some responses were intelligent, others emotional or instinctive. Small groups of Americans and Brits gathered regularly to talk of options other than surrender. Initially, hearsay pointed to Camp John Hay and American military evacuation routes north, like the mountain trail to central Luzon, as the primary targets of the bombings. Several stray bombs had damaged homes on Hay's periphery, but in the Baguio area, Camp John Hay and the *Baguio Post* news office turned out to be the only objects of direct attack.

The December 8 attack on Camp Hay prompted the Filipino cadets stationed there to disappear quickly. Some joined guerilla groups in the hills. Most, however, shed their military uniforms and migrated back to their barrios, disguising themselves as civilians.

Almost all of the American military personnel left Camp Hay to lead guerilla bands in the mountain provinces of central Luzon. A few went south to share foxholes with American forces in Bataan. Those departures left only a couple of American officers at Camp Hay, prompting the city's foreign intelligentsia to dismiss Baguio as a site for future raids. Bombings did become less frequent, but never ceased altogether. Still, many in the city remained optimistic that the "business over Baguio" had been only a message and not the forerunner to a Japanese invasion of the area.

From the first bombings, however, Uncle B foresaw an eventual Japanese Army presence in Baguio. "Count on it," he advised doubters. He believed the Japanese would need to keep an eye on Baguio because of American ties to the guerillas. Whether occupation would mean internment for civilians, he was not certain. Uncle B saw no reason for imprisoning American and British civilians and held high hopes that the enemy would not confine them, certainly not the women and children.

Although Uncle B's demeanor was usually calm, he never shied from expressing his feelings on matters of importance. He was the highly respected pastor of the Evangelical United Brethren Church and had been a community activist in Baguio for years. He knew the city, its leaders, and most of the foreign community well. Most thought Uncle B's suggested plan to encourage and organize the community toward a common surrender was a wise one. The missionaries in the area strongly applauded the surrender plan. Uncle B felt especially justified in proposing the plan once the American and Filipino defense forces had evacuated Camp John Hay.

Surrendering, Uncle B believed, would cause city officials to declare Baguio an open city (that is, no resistance offered). With the blessing of Arthur Richardson, the Brent School headmaster, and Mayor Halsema, Uncle B announced that Brent would be the gathering site for those choosing surrender. Most agreed that the likelihood of Baguio becoming a battle zone would be reduced if it were an open city. The foreign community also hoped that the Japanese would not engage in vengeful action against Western civilians if they surrendered.

Uncle B believed that dodging surrender would only pressure Japanese troops to go house to house, increasing the possibility of ugly confrontations. Not everyone agreed to use Brent School as a gathering place for surrender, but most did. A few chose to remain in the comfort of a hotel. "The Japs will find us there," offered one regular Baguio visitor.

Advocates of a wait-and-see position found themselves pressed into hurried decisions. News that Japanese troops were moving northward on the Kennon Trail nudged more toward surrender. A few families familiar with the mountain areas decided to "take to the hills" and did so within days. Others who had considered that option eventually chose surrender.

As the bombing subsided and Japanese troops moved unchallenged toward Baguio City, citizens planned for the realities that lay ahead, such as the potential unavailability of essential commodities. Another concern brought to Mayor Halsema's attention was the possibility of the Japanese setting fire to the city. That disquieting thought prompted planning escape routes to safe zones north and west of the city. There were few options.

Many American, British, and Chinese women shared profound anxiety about being raped. Particularly fresh on the minds of the Chinese who had resided in Southeast Asia were the real-life horror stories of wholesale rape perpetrated upon Chinese women by Japanese invaders in Nanking. Troubled, too, were the parents of teenaged daughters.

Leora Nagel, a close companion of Mom's, confided to her that fears of rape tempted her not to surrender. Tales out of Nanking led her to believe that all would be killed. After talking with Uncle B, Leora changed her mind and committed to surrender.

Pregnant women feared carrying a child into captivity. They worried about their own health, the prospect of giving birth in confinement, and then raising a baby in a prison environment.

The availability of milk, food, and medicines for babies was another serious concern. Consequently, many hoarded critical supplies. Mothers worried about the welfare of their husbands and their availability to assist with child care. All hoped and prayed that the Japanese would live up to their reputation of having a high regard for children and act kindly toward them.

People also worried about how to protect their valuables. Many Americans who had resided in the Baguio area for many years had accumulated precious objects and put considerable thought and planning into how to keep their treasures from being confiscated or stolen. While rings or jewelry could be buried easily, other possessions like locally crafted water buffalo (*carabao*) figures carved from the aromatic woods like *narra*, mahogany furniture, antique artifacts, and expensive china would be difficult to hide. Entrusting them to Filipino servants posed some risk, but proved the most doable option.

Ultimately, though, the primary focus was on the necessities: safety, food, water, and medications. Knowing little of Japanese culture or language, all questioned how to interact with Japanese soldiers. There was no easy answer to that query. Mom's suggestion was a simple one—"smile."

Christmas 1941

Uncle B seemed to sense that the Sunday morning service on December 21 at his Baguio church would be the last for some time. The church was packed. Even people who were apt to be on the Camp Hay golf course on a Sabbath morning attended.

Two new faces were in the pew behind us, young men decked out in the handsome white uniforms of the U.S. Navy, an unusual sight in Baguio at the time. Mom introduced us to them and we commenced conversation. They seemed eager to talk and related a gripping story about how they came to be there. Both had arrived in Baguio for a short R & R (rest and relaxation) leave on December 6. They had been stationed at the Subic Bay Naval Base and were staying in a barracks at Camp John Hay.

On the morning of December 7, the sailors had played a round of golf on the Camp Hay course. That afternoon a British couple relaxing on the clubhouse porch had shared a drink with the sailors and invited them to their home the next evening, December 8. Like everyone in Baguio, the sailors were awakened in the morning by bombs falling on and around their quarters. Neither was injured, and in spite of the morning raids, they kept their dinner date. They had tried to call the naval base immediately following the first bomb runs that morning and again in the afternoon, but there had been no answer. After dinner with their hosts, a third call for instructions finally reached Subic Bay. The duo was told to remain in Baguio and stand by for further instructions.

Days passed. A Subic superior then informed them that any attempt to return to the naval base would be too risky because of enemy movements along the only access routes to Manila, the sharply curved Naguilian and Kennon trails.

Sharing their dilemma after the church service, they told us that their last order from Subic was to "hold tight." They explained to us that, at first, there was some humor in their dilemma. However, the situation had turned serious when they learned that return to their base was not an option. They seemed forlorn and bewildered.

Only days after we heard the sailors' tale of woe, Mom learned from their British golfing friends that their last encounter with the sailors had focused on the question "What shall we do?" The Brits had suggested that they consider disposing of their navy dog tags, playing civilian, and surrendering with the other Americans at Brent, or taking to the hills. There were no other options. The preoccupations of the days that followed so consumed the British couple that their concern about the whereabouts of the sailors was temporarily put aside. We never did learn what became of them, but they likely joined the guerillas in the hills.

On Christmas Day, a group of friends gathered with their children to share lunch and exchange gifts at the Eschbach home. While the children played, the adults talked seriously. Later, Mom shared with Wezer and me Uncle B's advice about how to relate to Japanese soldiers. "I know only that Japanese are human," he said, "and therefore, children of God. Let's treat them with respect."

Uncertainty about whether to flee the city or surrender to the enemy persisted. Many wanted assurance that they would have company if they were to surrender. All were anxious about the future, especially the parents of young children. Everyone wanted to know where the Japanese troops were and sought out Uncle B for answers. He only knew what Filipino informants had told him after the Sunday service. "They are south of Rosario, on the Kennon Trail and walking northward," he said. If that were true, the enemy was only short days out from Baguio.

Following the children's gift exchange in mid-afternoon, Mom gathered my sisters and me in a bedroom. She reminded us of our Christmases in Davao: the mix of nationalities that came to our house each Christmas stopping by to sing carols around the piano and dine on the potluck of Filipino foods, and the joy of sampling the fruit-flavored desserts created by Leonie and Sixta. I cried as we prayed for Dad's safety. We had received no mail or calls. Rae and I then went outdoors to play with my new toy cars, the last occasion for some time that we would play so freely.

Mom told us that a cultural collision was about to occur in our lives, but she could only guess what it would be. Not yet physically imprisoned, we felt as if we were. Radio reports of developments in Manila presented a picture of almost certain defeat for the American military. Nevertheless, everyone maintained a stoic face and tried to make Christmas, if not merry, then at least meaningful for all of us.

Later in the afternoon, Uncle B and Mayor Halsema met with Headmaster Richardson at Brent School to prepare for the large migration of Americans committed to surrender. The three men formed an unofficial committee to secure food and to perform tasks such as placing "men" and "women" signs on lavatory doors and arranging spaces for the newcomers.

After Uncle B returned home, he advised Mom to have us report to Brent as soon as possible. We walked to the school early the following morning, December 26, after Mom mailed an envelope containing a short birthday poem to her mother, Mercy Whitfield, in New Jersey. (Grandma Mercy never received it, but Mom read it to her when we celebrated Grandma's birthday in Hackettstown, New Jersey, in 1945.)

> 'Tis the day after Christmas, and all through the valley
> Hearts have stopped stirring, yet hope waits to rally.
> The kids are fine, Walter, too, we do pray.
> Keep us in prayers, and we'll see you someday.
> Happy Birthday dear Mother

Surrender at Brent School

Mom led us to Brent after breakfast. We discovered that a number of other families, mostly missionaries, had spent the night on floor mattresses in the boys' dormitory. They told us the sleeping accommodations were restful, but only under mosquito netting. Most had arrived in the late afternoon of Christmas Day. "They must have thought the Japanese were sprinting to Baguio," Mom offered in an obvious effort to dispel some of the tension we felt. Children were playing on the grass-covered grounds beside the front gate of the school.

One couple already positioned at Brent was the British twosome who had befriended the sailors. As more families arrived, the noise of unsettled babies became deafening and the crowded conditions suffocating. On top of that confusion, the city siren sounded, signaling an air attack. Parents assisted their children in a race to the pine grove. Wezer and I led Mom and Rae to the spot where I had hugged the protective embankment weeks earlier. We could hear planes, but they were not directly overhead. We returned to our mattresses after the all-clear siren had sounded. A man walking next to me, exasperated, blurted out loudly to his wife, "Grab your damn bags out of that stinking madhouse. We're going back to the hotel."

Mom had us place our belongings in one corner of the boys' dormitory adjacent to a classroom. That afternoon she and my sisters walked to downtown Baguio. I remained at school to cavort with the other boys playing baseball on the Brent lawn. Mom and the girls returned soon afterward with some items they felt would be useful during our time at Brent. Mom purchased a sleeve of nourishing if small monkey bananas, her favorite. They also brought toothbrushes and a pair of khaki shorts for me. I wore those shorts daily for the duration of our internment. Most importantly, the girls brought bedding and mosquito netting from our Burnham Park house. "But no more toys," announced Wezer.

Mom reported no sign of any Japanese, civilian or military, during their walk through downtown. They had found City Hall closed and the streets spookily empty of vehicles. Many stores were shuttered. The only visible activities were groups of Filipino looters hurriedly moving down alleys with bags on their backs. The downtown scene was one of disorder and panic looting. The normally commonplace police presence was missing.

That evening we had a liverwurst sandwich for supper. The blankets, which the girls brought to soften the wooden floor of our space, were a godsend. It was fortunate, also, that they had returned with a couple of mosquito nets to place over the four of us. Those nets, indeed, saved us from battling the "devils of the night." Still, the constant humming of the pests made it hard to sleep. Those without netting were miserable. Mosquitoes by the thousands forced them into a hands-clapping and cursing mode.

A number of the men abandoned attempts at sleep. They found respite outdoors where they lit cigars as a mosquito deterrent. Those men became the unofficial greeters for late-arriving Americans, some of whom had been driven from hotels and private homes by uniformed Japanese. The greeters directed the incoming families to the remaining classroom spaces so as not to disrupt the "sleep" of those already settled on the floor of the dormitory. I recognized one couple as the same pair who earlier had angrily fled the Brent scene for the Pines Hotel after the air raid. The latecomers to Brent took up the remaining floor space. Their loud conversations kept me awake much of the night.

Most of their chatter centered on the loud shouts of jubilation they had heard in the late night hours emanating from the Japanese school where Japanese locals and their liberators had gathered. This was the first confirmation that the Japanese Army had entered Baguio City.

I woke well before dawn on December 27 to find a substantial increase of new faces at Brent. A friend of Mom's, Harriet Raymond, walked by my mat, stopped a moment, and told me she wanted to talk with Mom when she awoke. Mom interrupted, "Good morning, Harriet." Still shaken, Harriet told Mom her story of "fear beyond anything I could imagine."

At her home, near midnight, a Japanese soldier with a rifle in hand walked into her room and ordered her out of bed. "Dress," he said. She resisted and he repeated his order. With trepidation, she complied by removing her nightclothes as he watched. She quickly dressed. The soldier then rubbed his lips, suggesting she apply lipstick. She did. Then, with a sinister grin, he picked up her already-packed suitcase and ordered her to an awaiting car. Harriet told Mom of her relief that the experience had not taken a more dreaded turn. Mom rose and embraced her, suggesting, "We're past the worst part."

A young man, who with his young boy, Don, had quietly dropped down next to our mats around 2:00 a.m., woke early, and introduced him-self as Harry Taylor to Harriet, Mom, and me. Harriet, familiar with most Americans in Baguio, curiously questioned Harry about his past, and he commenced to tell us his story.

The Taylors had arrived from war-torn Cambodia to locate tempo-rarily in the Philippines, known for its more modern and well-equipped hospitals and superior nursing care. The move was important for Harry, who was suffering from a severe case of malaria, and Miriam, nearing the delivery date of their second child. However, the stifling heat of Manila prompted them to seek respite in Baguio's cooler climate only days before the first bombs fell.

They knew no one in Baguio, had little money, and relied on acquain-tances in Manila for counsel. After the December 8 bombings, the Taylors—like other foreigners—stocked up on canned goods, toiletries, and a large supply of Klim, a common powdered milk staple for infants and children in Asia. The early bombings and unfamiliar surroundings created a sense of panic in the family.

On Christmas Eve, labor pains forced Miriam to enter Notre Dame Hospital. Japanese planes again screamed over Baguio, signaling the imminent arrival of their ground troops. Fortunately, they dropped no bombs on Notre Dame. Harry spent the next two nights at the hospital with Miriam, and the four-year-old Don spent time with a newfound friend. At dawn on Christmas Day, Miriam presented Harry with a lovely present, Janice Allaine.

That afternoon, Harry introduced Don to his baby sister. The next day, December 26, Harry and his son moved into the missionary compound, Doane Rest, near the Baguio Japanese School and a short walk to the hospital. They left all the supplies they had recently purchased along with their remaining funds in Doane. That evening, father and son watched a bonfire on the grounds of the Japanese school and listened to celebratory shouts of *Banzai Nihon!* (Long live Japan/long live the Emperor.)

Sleep came with difficulty. Minutes after midnight, Harry was awakened by pounding on his door. He opened it to see rifle barrels only inches from his face. He and Don were ordered to an awaiting car. They were forced to leave their belongings behind and were driven directly to Brent School.

In the darkness of an unfamiliar building crowded with sleep-seeking prisoners on the floor, the two Taylors, without food, a change of clothing, a mosquito net, or a peso in their pockets, had found a place next to our mats where they lay down until daybreak. Harry's story touched us. We felt his tension. Mom bowed to him and said, "Welcome."

Moments after we listened to Harry's harrowing tale in the early morning of December 27, Mayor Halsema came on the radio to confirm that Baguio was under the control of the Japanese Army. By then, that was old news at Brent School. All who had gathered there were well aware that Japanese troops were in the city. Like Harriet and Harry, a number of Americans had already experienced disrespect, anger, or physical abuse as they were ordered from their homes during the night.

As my sisters wakened, khaki-clad Japanese soldiers stomped into our quarters. They peered down at still prone Americans on floor mats just as Mayor Halsema completed his official announcement on Baguio radio. The sounds of bayonets poking through private belongings startled many to quick alertness. A couple of women near us were alarmed by one guard's insistence that he accompany them to the latrine. They returned to their mats in a rage. One protested loudly that she had never before felt so intruded upon. Her friend cautioned Mom, "Don't go, you'll just become constipated."

More prisoners continued to be trucked into Brent. Conditions and spirits deteriorated. Mom gave the Taylors two bananas and one each to my sisters and me. Mid-morning, two Filipinas who were associated with Brent School distributed very welcome cups of water. Three hundred empty stomachs appreciated their thoughtfulness. I was so hungry later that day that when I was served a cup of watery stew, I considered it delicious, as did the Taylors.

While we waited apprehensively at Brent for the imminent arrival of more enemy troops, conversations among adults who arrived during the night centered on the Japanese intrusions into their homes. They learned from English-speaking Japanese soldiers that on December 8, Japanese civilians had been confined in Camp John Hay. None of us, including Uncle B, knew anything about this. However, one British latecomer told Uncle B that a Japanese resident of Baguio—now a soldier—mentioned that he and scores of others had been interned at Camp Hay for two weeks. That bit of information raised fresh concerns about what level of retaliation we might expect when we became Japanese hostages.

The internment of Japanese civilians by the Filipino militia took place immediately after the first air raids. Americans familiar with Camp Hay believed that Colonel Horan was responsible for the detention and later release of the Japanese prisoners. Their release coincided with Horan's disappearance from Baguio, probably to join the guerilla fighters. Japanese planes continued to bomb Camp Hay, while the Japanese men were detained there, and in fact, one corner of the barracks where they were held, which later served as our women's barracks, had been struck. We never learned of any Japanese deaths from the bombing, however.

Clearly, the deprivation of food and water imposed upon us was in retaliation for the hardships the Japanese prisoners in Camp Hay had suffered. Our captors, some of whom had been interned at Hay, provided no food during our few days at Brent School, and Mom's bananas and bread Uncle B brought with him were our only rations during that chaotic period.

Only afterward did we learn that Mayor Halsema and Elmer Herold, a mechanical engineer and long-time general manager of the Heald Lumber Company, had driven to the Hay barracks and discovered that the food supplies for the Japanese prisoners were indeed meager. The two men immediately arranged for them to be fed. Halsema and Herold hoped that their tardy gesture of human kindness would soften any retribution. Many of our guards had been civilian residents of Baguio and short-term prisoners at Camp Hay, but they now were uniformed overseers of our lives at Brent School. One guard claimed that Horan had left the Japanese under the control of Filipino soldiers and confined without water or food for five days. If true, that was a violation of international law.

Regardless of the circumstances which preceded our surrender at Brent, many prayed that if internment were in the offing, women and children, at least, would escape incarceration. Such were the regulations established by the Geneva Convention. But those internationally accepted rules of war were not to be followed in Baguio. That decision infuriated Uncle B.

Throughout the day, a steady flow of American and British citizens continued to arrive at Brent, some in trucks, most in chauffeur-driven cars. The cars were driven away at once by Japanese soldiers, and the Filipino chauffeurs were ordered from the school grounds. The shanghaied cars soon became the personal property of Japanese officers. For weeks afterward, I frequently saw the vehicles parked in front of our confines. Needless to say this angered their original American owners.

The stories of how American families were discovered and brought to Brent fascinated me. One woman, who bedded near us, whined, "Do you suppose our Filipino servants were paid off for information about us and the location of our homes?" Ever loyal to the Filipinos, Mom responded, "More likely, maps of such details were forwarded to Japan months before by Japanese residents of Baguio." Some of the late arrivals to Brent who had homes on remote forested hillsides also expressed astonishment at having been identified so quickly. The rounding up of Western families at private homes was carried out with remarkable speed and efficiency.

Floor space had become so crowded that newcomers found room for their bedding only in hallways or in adjoining classrooms. The student desks rigidly secured to the floor obstructed any hope for even minimal comfort. By noon on December 27, the population at Brent had risen to more than three hundred and people kept pouring in like water through a sieve. New and growing problems developed. Lines formed at the faucets and lavatories, the only sources of water. The toilet area, teeming with people, caused considerable humiliation, stench, and frayed nerves.

My family had resided in Baguio for five months. During that time, I only knew the Americans at Uncle B's church, some adult students from the CLS, and my friends at Brent School. The large numbers of fresh children's faces entering Brent, therefore, totally surprised me. Soon enough, though, those children became my friends. I learned about where they had lived, the schools they had attended, and the businesses—like gold mining—that had brought their families to Baguio.

Other than a couple of Japanese military police stationed at Brent's main gate and the truck drivers who continued to bring loads of prisoners into the school, the soldiers suddenly and strangely disappeared from our confines in the late morning of December 27. Where had they gone? Their absence was a surprising development; we had expected to have a large detail of guards overseeing our movements during the daylight hours. A few Americans actually slipped out of the school grounds in the afternoon to pick up more needed items from their homes. One family discovered that intruders had already emptied their home of valuables. As darkness fell, however, the soldiers reappeared in force.

Our second night at Brent was even more chaotic than the first, as new arrivals sought places to bed down. In spite of the bedlam, Mom made every effort to get my sisters and me to sleep. But it was virtually impossible.

Shortly before midnight, we were suddenly ordered from our sleeping quarters to a large room in the Brent administration building. In the hallway, I waited in a long line with Mom and my sisters for over an hour to be interrogated. Tired, restless children fussed as their parents tried to calm them. Seated behind a large desk in the interrogation room, an impeccably dressed, mustached Japanese officer appeared to be in charge. The officer spoke in accented but understandable English. He and a subordinate asked for names, nationalities, occupations, places of residence, etc. A small gold cross was pinned on his lapel, and the badge on his jacket revealed his name to be Mukaibo, his rank that of major. (I later learned that Japanese chaplains in the Philippines were not spiritual advisors to Japanese troops. Their assignment was rather to interact with Filipinos, winning their friendship by supporting the large number of Roman Catholic churches in the islands.)

People in line ahead of us quietly shared bits of information with those waiting behind them. When a missionary woman in front of us whispered to Mom that the major had introduced himself as a Christian, Mom responded quietly, "How lucky we are." It seemed to Mom that he was trying to assuage anxieties. It became apparent that only those with a "Reverend label" on Mukaibo's roster of names heard mention of his Christianity. His only query of Mom focused on Dad, "Where is he?" he asked. Mom answered that she thought him to be in Davao. A smile never crossed Mukaibo's face throughout the questioning. Inside the interrogation room, several more soldiers stood with fixed bayonets. They paid no attention to us as we passed them. Armed soldiers stood stonelike by the doorway as we departed the room. An officer at the exit informed each passerby to report to the tennis court at 2:00 p.m. the next day, December 28.

Long-term American residents of Baguio recognized a number of the khaki-clad guards as former civilians. One of them, in fact, was the concierge at the Baguio Hotel. But the guards maintained stoic faces and made eye contact with no one; they showed no sign of recognition. All were dressed in military uniform.

Following the chaos of the midnight interrogations, we were ordered back to our sleeping quarters. There I discovered that new arrivals had placed their bags wherever an open space was available. Guards demanded that everyone bed down in the same dormitory that night. Confusion reigned. Few, if any, could find space to stretch out their mats, much less fall back to sleep. Hearts pounded, babies cried, sobs echoed throughout the night. Soldiers entered the sleeping area every half-hour or so with heavy boots stomping down the foot-wide aisle in the middle of the room. Before dawn, as I rose to go to the toilet, a passing guard pushed me back onto the mat, causing our mosquito net to collapse and adding to the chaos.

When dawn of December 28 finally arrived, Americans continued to trickle into Brent School. Japanese trucks deposited their human cargo, and then went back to pick up the remaining Americans at hotels. During that turbulent morning, we got our first real taste of confinement. Our rational selves rapidly unraveled into emotional and instinctive behavior. Everyone was exhausted, hungry, and in a state of anxiety. Tempers flared, tears flowed, and one elderly man openly sobbed. Mothers of infants held their children tight. The suffering inflicted upon each of us in various ways seemed clearly intentional.

Wherever people had arranged bedding on the floor, guards upended mats in search of personal belongings. They focused primarily on cameras, tools, canned goods, watches, flashlights, and even some children's toys. A few of us were told that the items taken would be placed in temporary storage and returned later. Guards destroyed many personal possessions as they probed with their bayonets, but I managed to hide the two toy cars I had received for Christmas in the pocket of my shorts. Mom struggled to hold back tears from fatigue, thoughts of her dear Walter, and fear of what lay ahead. The harsh treatment and destruction of belongings took its toll on the besieged families. One elderly man seated on a bench outside the lavatory said to a passing guard, "Mr. Bastard, please shoot me." Thankfully, he was not understood.

Early in the afternoon, we were all herded onto the school's tennis court adjacent to the main building. It was the first time I had set foot on the tennis court. Mom led us through the gate to the court enclosure where we joined more than four hundred other anxious internees. For no apparent reason, my sisters and I were suddenly ordered away from Mom. We soon realized that all the children were being separated from their parents. The young people were led to an area along one baseline of the court. The elderly and handicapped were grouped near the gate entrance on the opposite baseline. I stared across the court at a dear family friend, Alice "Ma" Widdoes, looking very stooped, frail, and old. She seemed to have aged since I saw her a week earlier. Women and infants stood along one sideline, and the men stood on the opposite sideline.

The tennis net had been removed and a small portable platform was erected at mid-court. Uniformed Japanese soldiers were positioned a few paces apart inside the fence surrounding the court. All stood with rifles held diagonally across their chests, bayonets fixed. Four machine guns were directed at the mass of prisoners, two atop the platform at center court. Wezer stood between Rae and me, squeezing our hands. Her gesture very much typified her motherly manner. A couple of teenage boys stood behind us. One named David whispered, "We're going to be shot." I looked over at where Mom was standing, partially obscured by other women. She caught my eye, winked, and smiled reassuringly. I felt better.

Major Mukaibo, the same Japanese officer who had directed the interrogation during the night hours, stepped onto the portable platform. After surveying the assembly of prisoners, he began to speak. During the midnight interrogation scene, he had worn a spiffy dress uniform jacket. Now, on the platform, he wore the traditional Japanese billed khaki cap with flaps hanging in the back, and a sword hung at his side. His loud, spiteful, and menacing opening remarks belied his earlier claim to be a Christian. The guard corps around the periphery of the tennis court lent an ominous aura to the scene and heightened my anxiety about what might lie ahead.

Mukaibo's forceful, angry message detailed the retributions that would befall violators of orders. There were frightening threats of death to anyone who failed to report or turn in a weapon, or attempted to escape, and death to others in retaliation for any attempted escape. At the end of each sentence, he emphatically shouted, "Or you will be shot!" He certainly got my attention. While I felt relieved that the death threats did not apply to the present moment, I suffered from thoughts of eventual death. I had never felt such fear.

March to Camp John Hay

Mukaibo's final pronouncement was that everyone had to gather immediately all the belongings that they could carry, and form a line on the road leading to the school's main gate. He did not say where we were going, but I was ready to march anywhere to escape that court and the scene inside Brent. Yet, I could not put Mukaibo's fearful words out of my mind. During those terrifying minutes, I am certain Mom was not feeling the optimism she had felt the night before when informed about Mukaibo's Christian chaplain status.

His tone and threats were unlike any Christian message I had ever heard. Soon afterward, still reflecting on that day, a young teenage boy from Great Britain told me that he hoped American soldiers would never come to free us. "If they come," he said, "we'll probably be shot." For some time, those words crushed my dreams that our family would ever go home to America.

With Mukaibo's menacing words still ringing in my ears, I quickly helped Mom and Wezer gather our belongings to join the growing line of internees. In a very short time, we had all assembled on the driveway leading from the Brent campus. Some parents, wisely but uncomfortably, wore several layers of clothing to lessen the weight of items to be carried. Major Mukaibo, standing by a three-wheeled motorcycle at the main gate, oversaw the order of the march. Seeing him immediately brought his threatening words to my mind. Others, I am sure, felt similarly. Certainly, no one was tempted to break out of line and make a run to freedom. Men were ordered to the front of the line; the women followed. My sisters and I and a large number of other children gathered behind the women, and the elderly followed us. Japanese soldiers flanked the long line. Awaiting the order to walk, all thoughts of play and hunger vanished.

A short while after beginning the march from Brent, I asked Wezer if she had been afraid of being shot on the tennis court. "Not while the guards were standing behind us," she responded. Wezer had a marvelous gift of accurately assessing words heard and deeds seen, even those as ugly as those we had just experienced.

Next to us were Ann Wilson and her brother Douglas, British children whose father, associated with a petroleum company, remained in Hong Kong. Like other Western families who resided in Asian countries, the Wilsons chose to place their children in a school like Brent, known for its fine academic reputation. Ahead of us, Mrs. Wilson was walking with the other women. Everyone, even children, carried loads of belongings, mostly bedding.

Very soon, it became evident to the Japanese garrison that some of the elderly simply could not manage the hike. A number of younger women also faltered badly, especially the few well along in pregnancy. When the pace slowed, the Japanese decided to truck those physically unable to continue. Guards were ordered away from the line of children to assist in loading the stragglers and their parcels onto the truck beds.

Recognizing that we were no longer under guard, Wezer motioned Rae and me to quicken our pace and catch up with Mom. Several other children followed our lead. She knew that reconnecting with Mom would relieve her of anxious moments and some of her baggage. The two Wilsons obediently stayed in line. As Wezer urged us ahead, Ann wagged her finger at us, saying "Naughty, naughty!" Mom was surprised and relieved to see us, delighted in our being together again. She took a banana from her bag and broke it into three sections. Knowing of my fondness for the inner lining of the peels, she gave me the end piece with the peel attached.

The march was only about four miles; nonetheless, it was painfully difficult for many. I noticed the many trucks and stolen cars moving in front and behind the long line of walkers. The march seemed to have been designed to humble us in front of Filipino observers. The vehicles could easily have transported all of us, but that option clearly was not on Mukaibo's agenda.

For my sisters and me, toting bags of bedding, a meager supply of clothes, and two cans of Klim was tedious, but bearable. But many parents felt overburdened and acutely anxious because of their uncertainty about the distance to be traveled and concern about the safety of their children—most of them still in line behind them. Water was not available, so thirst plagued many. Only the few who were able to pack water in their rush to gather items managed the walk without suffering from thirst.

A woman walking next to Mom, struggling under the weight of a box she was carrying, broke down, sobbing openly. Mom offered me to carry it for her. The woman refused, saying, "It's just stuff." Minutes later, she stepped out of the line and placed the box in the lap of a startled Filipina sitting on the curb. "It's yours," she pronounced. Exhausted, she squeezed the Filipina's hand and returned to the line next to Mom. As the walk continued, she told Mom that the box contained jewelry and silverware and that it "would have been confiscated by the Japs anyway."

As we approached the main gate of lush Camp John Hay, it became clear that the former American military retreat was our destination. Within minutes, we saw that "lush" was no longer an apt description for the campgrounds that many of the Americans in Baguio had come to know and love. The rolling, pine tree-lined fairways of the golf course were pockmarked with bomb craters. The roof of the stately country club revealed one large hole and downed electric lines dangling from the poles, likely cut by retreating cadets. The meticulously mowed greens and watered fairways of November were badly scorched. The clamor of Japanese vehicles moving busily about the grounds replaced the soft sounds of wind in the pine boughs.

Moments later, we were met with the threatening sight of a row of barracks surrounded by barbed wire and several standing Japanese soldiers. A guard directed us to the large porch attached to a military barracks. Mr. Herold, who had arrived earlier with the men, immediately told us that the official name of the barracks was the Igorot Scout Barracks. He was very familiar with Camp Hay and pointed out the views of the deep valleys and native villages to the south. It was a beautiful site, but my thoughts were elsewhere.

Almost immediately, Mom's marching partner who had given away her "stuff" joined us. She expressed the emotional hurt that march had caused. As the wife of a gold mine executive, her household staff had included two housekeepers, a *lavandera* (laundress), a cook, and a chauffeur/gardener. They had all been at the roadside, helplessly watching her struggle with her belongings. She was totally embarrassed and humiliated. Seeking support, she confided, "Never before have I felt so humbled. What do you suppose they thought of me?"

Mom's response was brief and comforting. "They are proud of you and love you—believe it."

That woman was not alone in her pain. Others from the Baguio region, accustomed to being chauffeured around town in private elegant automobiles, also found the ordeal of hiking and toting their heavy belongings under armed guard and the watchful eyes of Filipino servants, to be emotionally painful. For days afterward, I listened to Mom's new friends replay that painful march to Camp Hay.

*Uncle B emerged as our camp leader during the initial rough days
at Brent School and at Camp Hay. Here he stands with
Commandant Hayakawa in a rare wartime photo.*

CHAPTER 3

Camp John Hay

Dec. 1941–April 1942

. . . .

Igorot Scout Barracks

For some indefinable reason, stepping into the barracks at Camp John Hay stands out from the flood of memories during my time as a child of war. Being suddenly restricted within a barbed wire fence and living in tight quarters surrounded by hundreds of depressed men and women gave me a hollow feeling of claustrophobia.

I knew Mom was in agony after the four-mile walk on a leg still painful from surgery years earlier. Yet, she made no mention of it. As I watched her arrange our bedding on the filthy barracks floor, I could feel her quiet but deep concern for Dad and guilt for bringing her children into the hands of an angry enemy in a prison "mess hole" like the one surrounding us.

Wezer sent me to the large front porch while she, Rae, and Mom organized our things in the space we were to call home. She told me to keep an eye out for Uncle B and Ma Widdoes, essentially to get me out of the way. Joining me later, Wezer told me that many women were second-guessing their decision to surrender. They started each sentence with the "if" word: "If I had only known . . . If I had it to do over . . . If only I had done. . . ." Some women, completely exhausted and in despair at the cluttered scene of bedding and belongings strewn about, simply sat on the floor staring into space or sobbing.

There were no bunks so everyone bedded down on whatever items they had brought. Each adult was allocated an estimated fourteen square feet of living space. A number of families had managed to carry narrow, kapok (a fibrous material) mats from Brent. Mom's decision to carry mats was a good one. The lone blessing for the Widdoes was that Japanese truck drivers had delivered mattresses to the barracks for the elderly.

Sitting on the top step of the front porch, I watched Ann, the girl who had scolded my sisters and me during the march, emerge from a truck. Pleased that she had been rewarded with a ride, she smiled at me haughtily as she walked up the stairs with her mother, proud that she stayed in line during the trek from Brent School. As she strolled by, she swung a bag at the side of my head and chuckled, "Ha, ha!" Furious, I grabbed her ankle. When she fell to the floor next to me, I pounced on her, and we tussled on the porch. Mr. Herold and another adult quickly separated us, but she managed to kick me on my backside. I tried to retaliate, but the adults restrained me. Ann's mom looked amused by my frustration and seemed delighted that her daughter had had the last laugh. That encounter, I'm sure, contributed to Mom's decision twelve days later that I become Uncle B's bunkmate in the men's barracks.

As I waited to spot Uncle B and Ma Widdoes, I listened to Elmer Herold tell several of the men about his earlier visit to Hay when Japanese men were interned in the same building. He told them that our new home, the Igorot Scout Barracks, once housed between sixty to eighty Filipino soldiers. By late afternoon, four hundred American and British men, women, and children had placed their mats or blankets on the same floor.

The scene called for direction and Elmer Herold took on a leadership role. He reminded each arriving group that the Japanese had ordered the barracks to be divided by gender: women and small children next to the lavatory, and the men closer to the main entry. Mrs. Herold also helped organize the gender separation. I kept watch from the porch as latecomers arrived in trucks. On occasion, I peeked inside the barracks and saw that confusion still reigned. Finally, in the last truck, Uncle B arrived with Ma Widdoes.

The interior of our new home looked like an enclosed junk pile after all were settled. Everyone yearned for more space, but there simply was none. The early arrivals had secured the floor space next to the windows. Families coming later quickly noted the extra space afforded by a position at a windowsill, which offered a small area to hang clothing. That advantage proved a real point of contention, and several women suggested that straws should be drawn to determine who should get the places by the windows. That did not happen. Nor did the people already situated voluntarily move. The severely overcrowded conditions prompted Uncle B, Mr. Herold, and several other men to hastily create a provisional organizing committee. They immediately sought out a number of self-proclaimed puzzle-gurus in the women's section of the barracks to organize a floor plan.

By nightfall of the second day, our barracks looked like a collage of patchwork quilts. Somewhat wider aisles made passage through the barracks a bit easier. With so many other worries on their minds, the women made no serious effort to alter their space allocations. Mother and children's spaces were labeled cubicles. Those who had won cubicles adjacent to the Scout's inner periphery hammered nails into the low rafters and support poles to serve as hangers. The atmosphere seemed to improve somewhat after the adjustments were completed.

Electricity had not been restored to the barracks since the bombing of Camp Hay. As they negotiated the narrow aisles at night, children often stumbled over prone bodies. We soon learned to pick our way through the narrow aisles and strewn bedding by placing one foot directly in front of the other. The night hours brought embarrassing moments and some angry exchanges, leaving everyone with frayed nerves and anxiety about the next day.

I dreaded the arrival of nighttime. Sleep came slowly. Bodies were so close to one another that the simple act of someone turning over had a domino effect on others, thus forcing them also to shift positions. I slept on a mat between the men's and women's sections, separating my sisters from the men's area. A man whose buttocks bordered my head, nightly encroached on my mat. Waking one night after bumping into me, he muttered loudly to no one in particular but so everyone could hear, "Why the hell didn't we go up the mountain?"

Like clockwork, one young boy whined and then screamed every night. He seemed to be bothered by stomach pain. His mother tried her best to calm him, but to no avail. One evening, a Japanese guard who patrolled the quarters nightly, ambled toward the young boy, picked him up and whispered in his ear. Magically, the child quieted. His mom was terrified at first. For days afterward, however, she would beckon the guard to their cubicle to settle the boy. When that guard was not on duty, Wezer filled in. Her warm touch, soothing back rubs, and calming manner almost matched the success of the Japanese guard and made Wezer an oft sought-after sitter.

Mosquito nets over those lucky enough to have them often collapsed or became tangled at the slightest touch. Snoring, groans, other body sounds, and the stuffy atmosphere of the night hours, bothered many. So, too, did the stirring of people rising to use the toilet or going to the adjoining porch to have a midnight smoke. Some men, unable to endure the wait for their turn at the toilet, stood on the porch and peed over or under the railing.

Many parents arranged for a "pee-pee" can at bedside for their children's use during the night. I remember one night of internment at Camp Hay when a young boy's faulty aim resulted in an unwelcome shower on an unsuspecting man sleeping nearby. The incident certainly illustrates the degree of overcrowding that existed in the barracks. Only months afterward did the victim of the shower manage a chuckle, but he eventually developed a close kinship to the child and his parents.

Each morning, I found the simple task of rising to relieve myself in the dawn hours to be embarrassing. There was no privacy. For Mom, it was worse. She had to struggle out of a nightie and into a dress or pants in a room with hundreds of strange men, women, and children, all trying to start the day. Those days of gender togetherness were emotionally and physically painful for all. Still, Mom chuckled at the women who primped during those early days when the men were partners in the barracks. She often muttered, "Lipstick, curlers, eyelash goo—ugh!" An elderly woman, bedded adjacent to Mom's mat, woke one morning in a state of teary-eyed depression. I heard her plead as she spoke to Mom, "I want to die. Please help me!" Her distress in those early days was widely shared.

Mom developed a close relationship with the short, pigtailed, and straightforward Natalie Crouter soon after our hike into Camp Hay. It was quite by happenstance that they became friends: As they stared in the same mirror in the latrine one morning they both began to giggle. They then introduced themselves and a great friendship was born.

The Crouter children, Fred (Bedie) and June, were similar in age to Wezer and me. Natalie and Mom had like interests in art and writing. Their cubicles were close and both had family roots in New England. However, Mom was a missionary and Natalie was far removed from religious ties or missionary friends. Her prewar contacts were mostly with "miners," the label given to anyone not a missionary. Although friendships did not develop easily during the early months of internment, Mom and Natalie managed to put their differences aside. Rather quickly, the camaraderie between the two families led to gathering on the Tong mats each evening. There we sang and shared stories and a goodnight prayer. It was an unwritten rule that conversations begin on a positive note, such as, "Our mountain air sure beats sweating in a Manila prison."

Our group grew in numbers as the regular evening gatherings continued. Ma Widdoes and Leora Nagel joined us nightly. Only sickness, experienced by most of us at one time or another, interrupted the evening circles. Later, others formed similar alliances.

People continued to second-guess their decision to surrender at Brent School. Clearly, the adjustment from lives of comfort to life in confinement was terrible for everyone. Hunger and dysentery soon pushed patience and reason aside. We lived in a state of constant fear, extreme hunger, humiliation, and lack of privacy; our belongings were destroyed and we were commonly faced with threats of death. The only good news was that nobody had actually been beaten, raped, or killed. Certainly, those early days in Camp Hay resound in my memory as among the worst of the prison years.

Denial of Food and Water

The toilet scene worsened with each passing day. The barracks had only one wide-open bathroom, clearly built for military men. There were no privacy stalls, only a line of open toilets on one side and a long, tubular urinal on the other. An extended metal sink for brushing teeth, shaving, washing hands, and rinsing diapers extended down the middle of the lavatory. I developed the habit of rising early to be at the front of the toothbrushing lines. A goodly number skipped the process until later or altogether.

Recognizing the lack of privacy and severe congestion that resulted from both genders using one facility, Uncle B drafted some of the men to fashion an additional urinal—a ditch—under an adjacent hut at the rear of the barracks. This was for men's use only. But by straddling the ditch, some men found the urinal useful for other deliveries as well.

Surprise, consternation, and anger arose when men discovered women sharing their new ditch. To accommodate both genders fairly, the committee acted quickly to devise a half-hour interval plan for use of the new urinal.

It soon became apparent that the Japanese were making no effort to supply food or water to us. No food at all had been provided for nearly two weeks, and many feared that it was their intent to starve us to death. For an extended period of days, our captors made no response to our leaders' pleas for food and water. A formal camp committee was organized. It was made up of Uncle B, Jim Halsema, Dr. Richard Walker, and the Herolds. They immediately arranged for the pooling of the food that the internees had carried into camp. Almost everyone was supportive of the plan. There truly was no alternative. As the supply of canned food dwindled, soup, sometimes flavored with fried beetles, became our primary form of food.

Former Filipino servants tried to bring food and water to our barracks. Some toted their goods for miles in bushel baskets carried on their heads, Igorot style. On their first attempt to deliver food, a Japanese officer, Nakamura Takeshi, turned them away and ordered them back to Baguio. Nakamura told Herold that the food could have been poisoned, but no one believed that. Nakamura's steely attitude toward the Filipinos confirmed that he was our commandant and in charge. The looming prospect of starvation caused many to second-guess their choice of essentials—they wished they had brought more food and fewer pillows.

Adjusting from a life free of hunger and anxiety to one of persistent stench, constant congestion, an empty stomach, and no opportunity to be alone with my thoughts—even for a few minutes—proved extremely trying. Each night as I lay stretched out on the floor looking up at the mosquito net and unable to sleep, my mind began to wander. One night I imagined hundreds of parachutes dropping from the sky to rescue us from Camp Hay. Awakening, I felt a great despair. Despair now showed on many faces. Others seemed to show the pain of hopelessness and hunger more quickly than my Mom, my sisters, and me. Mom's long-time friend, the aging Ma Widdoes, suffered badly from dysentery and told my mother that she felt her end was soon to come. She directed Mom about what to do with her meager belongings, but then amazingly, Ma regained strength and found new spirit.

Adding to the anxieties everyone faced, complications with the water system—likely caused by the early bombing of Camp Hay—suddenly resulted in no running water at all. We could not brush our teeth, wash our hands, or rinse diapers. Worse, toilets that could not be flushed continued to be used. Impatient with waiting for a moment of privacy, a few women with children and scores of men used the outdoors. Fortunately, that alternative did not appeal to most. Nonetheless, a malodorous stink began to permeate the sleeping quarters. Something clearly had to be done.

Uncle B personally sought out Commandant Nakamura and implored him to correct the water problem swiftly. Nakamura, who always seemed to be in an obstinate mood, only responded by profanely scolding Uncle B and the camp leadership for not handling the toilet problem and other poor conditions themselves. Nakamura told him that soldiers were not available to fix toilets. In his foul mood, he continued with what Uncle B hoped was a lie. He told Uncle B that after Pearl Harbor, Americans had starved Japanese expatriates in American prisons, thereby suggesting that retaliation was in order.

The next day, Uncle B again urged Nakamura to reconsider the restoration of water and to secure food immediately. Our food supplies were nearly gone. Nakamura angrily responded, "Eat your own food and take care of the toilets yourselves." Uncle B was incensed, but not surprised. From their many interactions, he was familiar with the word *iie,* meaning "no," the regular Nakamura response to almost all requests.

Following Nakamura's hostile retort, the committee hurriedly organized a group of men and boys to dig a long, deep trench behind the barracks which would serve as a latrine for everyone since there was no running water. Miraculously, the work was done within hours. Discarded galvanized roofing was used as a temporary partition to separate the men from the women, and scrap boards gathered from the grounds were laid across the trench all along its length to provide a place for the feet as one squatted "to do one's business." Uncle B, himself, participated energetically in the entire project, employing my friends and me as wood scroungers. Even under the strain and pressures, once the trench had been completed, Uncle B added a bit of humor by announcing on a poster, "Movement has temporarily been restored."

When Dr. Dana Nance at the Notre Dame Hospital learned from Nurse Bessie Crimm that there was no water flowing at Camp Hay, he "jumped" on Nakamura. In an authoritative tone, the doctor demanded that the situation be corrected immediately. Well aware of Dr. Nance's prewar care of the Japanese community, Nakamura changed his mind the next day and agreed to allow the men, under guard, to haul in water for us. It was only a temporary solution, but a life-saving action. More importantly, he agreed to correct the problems that had caused the water to stop. Meanwhile, the medical staff at Hay, including Dr. Marshall Welles and Bessie Crimm, a professional nurse, counseled us to drink slowly and moderately and to use very limited portions for brushing teeth, washing, or flushing toilets.

Soon after Uncle B's outdoor trench became operative, the indoor taps miraculously began to flow—temporarily repaired by a magical internee who never revealed the extent of his plumbing talents. People raced to the bathroom, drank from the faucets, and mothers lined up to wash diapers. Spirits rose like a Manila thermometer. Even the rations on toilet paper increased from two sheets to three! Fern Harrington Miles wrote of the toilet paper situation in her book, *Captive Community*. She described her embarrassment when she had to admit her diarrhea problem to the gentleman internee who handed out toilet paper to receive three sheets instead of two.

When I asked Uncle B how the water suddenly ran from the faucets, he answered with his broad Eschbach smile, "It must have been heaven sent." His ever-modest manner suggested to me that he had more than a hand in bringing water back to Hay.

Dr. Nance, the son of China missionaries, was a highly respected leader in the Baguio area and was renowned in Central Luzon as a physician of great talent. Nance had earned a reputation for being straightforward with patients and brusque toward medical colleagues—or others—who challenged his judgment. Nance's base of operation had long been Notre Dame Hospital, where his surgical skills benefited those far beyond the American community. Chinese, Japanese, and Filipinos, too, knew his knife, and some had even been rescued from death through his efforts. At the time of our surrender at Brent School, Nance was noticeably absent, continuing his work at Notre Dame as if nothing had changed. He had not been ordered by Japanese officers to report to Brent, an indication that they had heard of his reputation as a caregiver to Baguio's Japanese citizens.

In Camp Hay, the number of cases of bacillary dysentery and diarrhea increased day by day. When the afflictions neared epidemic proportions, Dr. Welles and a couple of other imprisoned doctors stepped in to the rescue. Medicines approved by Dr. Nance and delivered by a Filipina nurse from the hospital brought a temporary decline in the scourge. Nevertheless, health conditions in the barracks continued to pose a serious threat to all of us—"one with the potential for calamity," as Nurse Crimm noted. For weeks, the battle to forestall catastrophe exhausted the camp's medical corps. Meanwhile, with Nance's support, Uncle B pressed Nakamura to free up the former Camp Hay Military Hospital across the sports field from the Scott barracks for our own use as a treatment center. It was sorely needed to slow the spread of sickness in the barracks.

Responding to Nance's forceful support of Uncle B's request, Nakamura okayed the use of the nearby hospital for the sick. That move separated the ailing from others in camp. With the fear of a massive epidemic on everyone's mind, access to the camp's hospital was a most welcome development. In addition, it turned out that the hospital still contained useful medical equipment and supplies. That was magnificent news. Again, we owed thanks to Nance and Uncle B for turning Nakamura's resistance to acceptance.

Soon after Nakamura authorized use of the camp hospital, Nance was ordered to confinement in Camp Hay. His imprisonment could have been payback for the demands he had made of Nakamura. After this incident, Nakamura's manner of giving and then taking away was a pattern we came to expect.

Dr. Nance took a no-nonsense approach when dealing with the Japanese commandant. He seemed unfazed by Nakamura's order of internment and brought with him vital medicines and sera from Notre Dame Hospital to help quell the cholera, dysentery, and dengue fever that threatened the internees. Immediately after his arrival he set about inoculating those at greatest risk. His presence in camp and forthright example invigorated the committee to lead more forcefully and press their demands more assertively on Nakamura. Uncle B heartily welcomed Nance's leadership.

Uncle B repeatedly counseled everyone to remain positive. Still, in those early days at Camp Hay, many varieties of human frailty showed under the stress. Instinct frequently won out over reason, and too often the "me" had a stranglehold on the "we." Amazingly, Uncle B's soft-spoken and loving manner guided many toward a more disciplined outlook that would better serve them on the morrow and beyond.

Along with Eschbach and Nance, Elmer Herold emerged as an internee leader. Prior to the war, as general manager of the Heald Lumber Company, he had employed Japanese mill workers and carpenters, including Nakamura. Since Nakamura personally knew Herold, he assigned him the title of camp liaison. Their acquaintance gained us some relief of our many needs. Herold took a lead role in organizing us in ways that would bring a modicum of comfort to our lives in the barracks.

Mrs. Herold was given the responsibility of organizing women for chores. Her sharp manner of giving directions won her the nickname "Bossy Ethel." When diets improved, she drew wider respect for her organizational acumen and ability to enlist all women in helpful roles. Resentment toward the Herolds arose, however, when the couple was granted a partitioned cubicle in the Scout barracks by Nakamura. That luxury did not escape notice. When repairs were slow in coming, spirits dipped, and the Herolds caught much of the blame, which reopened the topic of their private cubicle. However, over time, they softened the hardships of many.

Number Two Barracks

The overcrowding in the barracks was not alleviated until a few men began to move to the second barracks around January 4, and it continued to exacerbate our restlessness and strain relationships. Instances of emotional breakdowns had a domino effect on others, increasing tensions. The committee continued to hear complaints from women about embarrassing experiences that occurred because of the lack of privacy. Their concerns prompted Uncle B, once again, to challenge Nakamura. In a strategy aimed at not putting our commandant on the defensive again, Uncle B softened his tone and politely requested use of the barracks adjacent to the Scout to relieve congestion and provide greater privacy.

Nakamura resisted. He informed Uncle B that the Number Two barracks building remained in poor condition, was unfit for use, and that no help was available to repair it. Uncle B countered with an offer to enlist internees to make the necessary repairs. This made the proposition difficult for Nakamura to dodge. The next day, he capitulated and Uncle B quickly organized a repair crew. The committee decided that the move should provide gender separation. Given conditions in the Scout barracks, most of the men and women agreed to the plan. Many volunteers, including children, helped with the clean up and restoration process.

In a matter of days, the roof and floors had been repaired adequately. Toilets were cleaned and made functional, and the inside of the entire structure had been scrubbed. The Number Two barracks was, in fact, in better condition than was the Scout barracks at the time of our arrival.

After a casual inspection of our work, Nakamura declared the Number Two barracks usable, and the men moved in immediately. With a sigh of relief on moving day, Uncle B said, "I think the separation will prove a blessing." His prediction was correct. The women benefited from greater privacy in the larger cubicles and single-gender bathrooms, and the gender separation brought considerable relief to the men as well.

In Nakamura's mind, a mixed-gender move was never an option. Naturally, couples wished to stay together, but most understood that the scene in the crowded Scout barracks could hardly be defined as normal living. Only a few women expressed apprehension at the new arrangement. Their worries were for their own safety, since without a male presence, they would be more vulnerable to "lonely" Japanese soldiers during the night hours.

Interestingly, on the first night of separation there was one occasion when a soldier, tromping through the women's barracks after lights out, reached down to stretch a blanket over a sleeping young girl. His action terrified her mother, but observers of the incident reported that the soldier appeared only to be protecting the girl against the night chill.

Following the men's move, I remained with my mother and sisters for a couple of days. Then, at Uncle B's urging and with Mom's hesitant acquiescence, I moved into the men's barracks and bunked next to him. On my first night there, I stared at the ceiling above our mats on the floor and could actually see stars through holes in the roof. I thought to myself, "What if it rains?"

When Uncle B crawled in a while later, I asked him that same question. He snickered and said, "We'll get a free shower. Have you said your prayers?"

"Yup," I answered.

"Good night and God bless," said Uncle B.

Even with raindrops occasionally falling on my head, I found the night hours as his bunkmate far more enjoyable than the crowded Scout barracks. I had the liberty to visit my mom and sisters during the day and occasionally join in the evening Crouter/Tong get-togethers, but I was happy to leave behind nights spent listening to the crying of hungry babies in the women's barracks. Mom had mixed emotions about my joining Uncle B, but she could tell that my exodus from a predominantly female setting had relieved some of my stress. Nevertheless, she shared her continued worries with Uncle B about my "growing up too fast" in the company of foul-talking men. Worse, she was nervous about me possibly falling prey to some "disjointed types." Uncle B's reassurance that we were a team calmed her considerably. He also told her that efforts were underway to get school started and that classes would give me more time with my sisters.

Predictably, Nakamura accompanied his approval to open the men's barracks with a notice denying family commingling except for a one-hour period on Sunday evenings. Commingling was to occur only on the tennis court between 6:00 and 7:00 p.m. under the watchful eyes of Japanese guards. That pronouncement was very upsetting. Complaints from the Scout barracks about reduced visitation with husbands mounted. Wives were disturbed, too, by only being allowed to peek at their men through gaps in the fence. Those complaints brought wistful tears to Mom's eyes.

A mere glimpse of her husband, or even the knowledge that he was alive, would have raised her spirits to joyfulness.

Abuses of Power

In the late morning of the day after I became Uncle B's bunkmate, I noticed three civilian Japanese men stepping out of a black three-seater motorcycle in front of the barracks. Major Mukaibo followed in a handsome black automobile he had confiscated from an internee. The men quickly set up a table in the entryway to the men's barracks. Uncle B recognized one of the Japanese men as Nagatomi Akari, a local Rotarian, and greeted him at the door. Nagatomi completely snubbed Uncle B, and very quickly he could tell that Nagatomi was up to no good.

As Nakamura and Mukaibo observed from the guardhouse, Nagatomi directed his companions to order the men living in the south section of the barracks to the tennis court. The men stood on the court, not knowing what to expect. The women were told to remain in the Scout barracks. Nagatomi then ordered the men who were living in the north section of the barracks to place all their valuables and money in a large bag on the table set up at the barrack entrance. I stood next to Uncle B as we were lined up to await further interrogation. Attending guards looked under mats and other potential hiding places, occasionally gashing a mattress. It was painful to watch. The search revealed little of value, but so intimidated everyone that no one attempted to conceal any treasures.

Uncle B told me to keep my two toy cars in my pocket and stay beside him. He was one of the last called to the table and was told to hand over all his money. With his small bag of valuables in hand, Uncle B asked Nagatomi what was going on. Nagatomi did not answer, but only told him that he could keep one hundred pesos. Making no eye contact with me, Nagatomi then waved us both to the tennis court. We joined the other prisoners there. No communication was allowed among the men awaiting reentry to the barracks. They had, of course, already pieced together what was happening inside, noting the anger of the men as they emerged from the barracks. For the time being, however, they could only wait to be robbed and try to think of ways to lessen their losses.

It did not take long for the women to learn what was taking place next door. A good number of them tried to think of ways to save some of their valuables. My dear Aunt Leora swallowed her precious wedding band. Days later, she redeemed it and returned it to her finger. Some mothers placed peso bills in their children's pockets. Mom later explained to me that one mother gave peso bills to her young daughter to bury in the soil under the barracks.

Nagatomi, in an effort to quell the anger and stave off efforts to conceal precious items, assured the women that their valuables would be protected and kept for future return. Few believed him. We eventually learned that there was no record of the taken items anywhere. Naturally, from that time on Major Mukaibo and Commandant Nakamura were despised by the internees. Their complicity in allowing the raid to occur was maddening. No one doubted that the officers had enriched themselves by the thievery.

For days afterward, the lead topic of nighttime jabber in the men's barracks was the thefts of January 10. The angry men seemed incapable of softening the spiteful words they aimed at the bandits. Uncle B cautioned against loud, openly ugly expressions, which might have a boomerang effect on everyone, but his pleas quieted their remarks only slightly.

Thievery was not the only way the Japanese abused their power. One day after the morning chores, as we sat on the porch with my mom, we watched two young girls leave the women's barracks and walk toward the hospital with a guard escort. They had been boarding students at Brent, and their parents resided in Manila. Seeing them, Mom shared with me her concern for Wezer's safety. "Eloise is a pretty girl," she offered, "and I don't want to see her bothered by guards." Mom's worry for my sister's safety was real. I am certain her concern was amplified by Mrs. Herold's report of receiving a request from Major Mukaibo for several young girls to "work" for visiting Japanese officers residing at the Pines Hotel.

Don Mansell in his book *Under the Shadow of the Rising Sun* shared this account of the episode around Mukaibo's request. Mukaibo told Mrs. Herold: "They will have their food there and may stay all night—you will cooperate. We want young waitresses, and you know what I mean by young." This exchange was one of the rare occasions when Mukaibo directly contacted the internees. Ethel Herold's "reading between the lines," prompted her to ask her husband to raise the matter with the committee. Fear of sexual abuse and exploitation spread through the women's barracks and was most unsettling. Art Richardson raised the subject with Commandant Nakamura on behalf of the committee. Nakamura was unresponsive, but weeks passed and neither Mukaibo nor Nakamura brought up the request again. Nor was Mukaibo visible around Camp Hay for a long time. One could only surmise that he was involved in a moneymaking scheme to procure girls for Japanese officers visiting the city.

A January Joy

After listening to the traumatic experiences surrounding the birth of Harry Taylor's daughter on Christmas Day, I developed a friendship with him. Our morning walks together to the tennis court for roll call nurtured a closeness between us. In the barracks, he was quiet, often reading alone in the evenings. I could tell he was worried about his wife and their daughter, both still hospitalized in Notre Dame Hospital. In the Scout barracks, the very warm and loving Harriet Raymond cared for Harry's young son Don.

Nakamura refused Harry a single visit to the hospital. Only Dr. Beulah Allen received occasional permission to attend to Miriam's medical needs. On one visit, she found Miriam severely hemorrhaging and near death, but good news followed. After her next visit, Dr. Allen reported that a well-trained Danish nurse, spared from prison because of her nationality, had saved Miriam's life.

In mid-January, I watched as a very fragile Miriam, with infant Janice in her arms, arrived at Camp John Hay for internment. With Nakamura's permission, Harry met them with joy and relief. Their arrival brought the only smile I had seen on Harry's face since our first encounter at Brent. I was so excited for him. Although their reunion lasted for only minutes, the mere sight of Miriam and their baby recharged his will to survive.

Son Don was united with his mom and sister in the Scout barracks, but separated by fences, Harry and Miriam could not share in the raising of their children. Yet, the warm reception Miriam received from other mothers with infants reassured Harry immensely. That kind of support was the first she had experienced since their arrival in the Philippines. Although separation was hard for all the families, I felt particularly sorry for Mr. Taylor. The callous disregard for natural family relationships was one of the more haunting memories of prison life in Camp Hay.

Maintaining the Essentials

Water supply breakdowns continued intermittently. The system sometimes produced mere dribbles and occasionally stopped altogether. When the pipelines produced only irregular trickles and cases of dysentery and dehydration increased, Dr. Nance blew his stack. He heatedly broached the issue with Nakamura, demanding that the problem be dealt with "Now!" Uncle B, standing by Nance, also reminded Nakamura that the internee food cupboard was almost bare. Food had to be procured and, "You must do it. As you know, we have no money," said Uncle B. Confronted personally by the two camp leaders, Nakamura acquiesced and promised immediate attention to both demands.

The next morning water flowed freely from the taps, and Nakamura told Uncle B, "Mr. Hale drive truck to Baguio for food." Indeed, Ray Hale, a long-time resident of Baguio, became the regular driver, but always accompanied by a guard.

Chef Alex was occasionally allowed to go with Hale to Baguio to help buy food. Oleg Alexander ("Chef Alex") Kaluzhny was a well-known figure in the Baguio market because he had been the head of food services at the Pines Hotel. He skillfully negotiated food prices with the Filipinos. His negotiations never filled the rice sacks or vegetable baskets, but it sustained us for several months. He was also the most qualified to cook for large numbers. Without any prodding, he stepped into the role of camp chef and prepared meals for the growing number of internees. (After the war, I had occasion to dine in the splendor of the Trader Vic's restaurant on the San Francisco waterfront where Alex was the very popular head chef. He delighted in recounting the different ways he stretched the food in camp. "If I told some of those folks what I had put into their bowls to add flavor or substance, they might have strung me up," he chuckled. "That will be my lifelong secret.")

Chef Alex tried to produce the best meals possible with the food available in the kitchen. Following Nakamura's directive for only two meals a day, Alex established a plan for meals to be at 9:00 a.m. and 4:00 p.m. Hijacked pots, pans, and other cooking necessities from former Camp Hay officers' homes made Alex's tasks possible. His main cooking appliance was a large woodstove. He understood the eccentricities of woodstoves, but had little wood to burn. When he shared that problem with Nakamura, the commandant placed the responsibility for securing wood on the internees. Nakamura approved searches inside the perimeter of Camp Hay, under guard and without a truck.

Several former Camp Hay golf addicts recalled that a wagon once occupied the clubhouse garage and that large piles of wood were stacked in a number of areas around the base. Under the watchful eye of two armed guards, the newly assigned wood crew removed the wagon from the club-house, repaired it, and picked up the wood from around camp. Uncle B volunteered us to assist in carrying the stolen wood to the kitchen. Other boys and men joined the crew. Most of the stacks we found were beside or inside the deserted homes of the officers once stationed at Camp Hay. Many piles were stacked randomly along the camp's maze of pathways.

The Japanese guards accompanying the wood crew seemed unconcerned that the men also loaded the hand-pulled cart with an assortment of other finds. On trips to the far reaches of the base, the crew was rarely challenged by attending guards when items like mattresses, clocks, and books made their way onto the wagon. The guards seemed most interested in the looting forays into *bodegas* (storage sheds) and abandoned officers' residences, because of the opportunities to pocket smaller usable items like watches, cigarette lighters, and cigarette holders.

Several teenagers and I frequently accompanied the looting party on their searches. The crew called us "spies" and directed us to locate items that would be useful, especially tools and books. The guards paid far less attention to our movements than those of the men. Most books we found were in disrepair, with water damage and torn pages, but still readable. I snitched one miniature-sized hymnal, which I slipped into my shorts pocket and a like-sized book of Longfellow's poems. I read the poems often and enjoyed humming the hymns that I remembered from Davao church services. The books we found were a tonic to the spirits of many adults accustomed to a reading regimen. They passed from person to person throughout the internment years. Mom most enjoyed reading *The Keys of the Kingdom,* by A. J. Cronin.

Toward the end of January, seemingly in response to having given in to the more recent challenges by Herold, Nance, and Eschbach, Nakamura reminded us of his command powers and struck back. He posted a notice that reflected his disgust with American "living habits" and blamed us for our failure to clean the facilities. Nakamura's list included walking through the barracks in shoes, failing to bow to Japanese officers, neglecting to clean under mattresses, fussing about privacy, and failing to clean the bathrooms and floors every day. His ugly words seemed to coincide with the generalizations about Americans he had shared with Uncle B. Nakamura's sense of our habits was that we were naturally lazy and had no inkling of how to live clean lives. In traditional Japanese living quarters, cleanliness is a way of life.

Reactions to the notice were many. Mom told Uncle B during the Sunday commingling hour that the common response in the Scout barracks was that Nakamura's ridicule of American complaints was payback for his two-week internment in Camp Hay under the command of Colonel John Horan.

Comings and Goings

I was surprised one morning to see a group of Japanese schoolchildren, all uniformed and wearing white stockings, step off a bus in front of the Scout barracks. Each carried a small paper bag. Two adults, probably their teachers, accompanied them. The group seemed quite ill at ease peering through the fence surrounding our barracks, like tourists at Japan's Ueno Zoo. A Japanese photographer accompanied them. A number of us were completing our morning chores in front of the Scout barracks. Other children joined us as the guards ushered them out of the women's barracks. We looked like a bunch of scruffy waifs next to the neatly clad schoolchildren. It appeared that the timing of their arrival was planned to coincide with our "detail" time.

I could only guess at the meaning of their presence. Commandant Nakamura stood by the gate, a slight smile on his face, a hint that he was party to the Japanese children's field trip. Initially, the children on both sides of the fence stared at each other. Then Nakamura beckoned us toward the gate. I shyly balked, as did most of my friends. When he opened the gate, the Japanese children, seemingly on cue, walked cautiously toward us. Each offered a small bag of candy to whoever was within reach. Few smiled. I recall bowing politely to the girl who handed me her bag, whispering to her, "Domo," a shortened Japanese expression for thank you that I learned from a guard during morning roll call.

One father, who had been replacing loose boards on the porch steps, did not take kindly to the visitation. He yanked the paper bag from his son, slamming it against the fence, candies spilling to the ground. He explained to a peeved Uncle B later in the day that he resented the condescension of "those Japs." Uncle B reminded him that he was a prisoner of the Japanese and that angry actions, even when it seems justified, could trigger a punitive response. "Where your behavior may have made you feel better," Uncle B added, "others may suffer later because of it." That evening, the father strolled over to our bunk and apologized to Uncle B for his "lost emotions."

All regular meals in camp were prepared in the men's barracks, largely because the wood source was piled closer to our building. Daily, the men carried soup to the women's barracks in two large cauldrons. For husbands, it was a favorite chore. The women prepared meals in the Scout barracks for young children, babies, and those needing special diets. They also ladled the soup into coconut shell bowls, mess kits, or cans—each held by hungry internees waiting in line. It was common for those near the end of the line to show anger when one cauldron emptied and more than half of those waiting had not been served.

Each individual provided a container and utensils. A few had brought metal forks and knives into camp, but many, like our family, made do with utensils created out of bamboo. I usually stood in line with older boys in the men's barracks to receive my ration of soup or rice in my easily recognized white coconut shell bowl. Dad had made it for me on one of our Bagobo village excursions years prior to the war.

Hunger pangs remained a daily fact. Slowly, I began to adjust to small rations both physically and psychologically. Yet, I always felt hungry. In retrospect, it seems helpful that we were consumed with assigned chores between meals.

Uncle B's good fortune in negotiating the placement of men in a separate barracks encouraged him to try another plea to Nakamura. In a very kindly manner, Uncle B requested that the adjoining empty barracks building (Number Three) be turned over to his repair crew. The third barracks would open space to relieve the still crowded conditions in both barracks. Nakamura responded immediately with "Iie!" And with no further explanation, he walked away.

The reason for Nakamura's abrupt response became evident the next morning. As I lined up for roll call on the tennis court, I noticed a cluster of Chinese men, each carrying a tool, walking up the path bordering the golf course. Several armed Japanese guards followed them. The group, about twenty in number, worked for several days repairing holes in the roof and siding of barracks Number Three.

Three days later, hundreds of Chinese men walked up the same road we had followed on December 28, and entered the repaired barracks. In Uncle B's unpublished summation of his war experience, "The History of the Japanese Army Concentration Camp #3," he described the scene:

> They (the Chinese) walked from Baguio, carrying their personal possessions and bedding—the same as we did—and what a sorry sight they presented to our eyes as they marched over the hill and down the road into camp. It gave us an opportunity to imagine what our own arrival must have looked like as we walked from Brent School. We were allowed no contact with the Chinese during these days. Our camps were separated

by a wire fence. They had their own cooking facilities and purchasing facilities in the Baguio market. Our doctors and nurses, however, made daily visits to their barracks to help the sick people and to assist them with their sanitation and medical problems.

The Chinese settled into a routine at Hay far more quickly than we had. Our committee did notice over the course of the next few months that while the numbers of detained Chinese remained somewhat constant, many of the faces changed. One of our wood crew who walked by their barracks almost daily, humorously observed, "Theirs is an internment of Chinese roulette." Their numbers, although large for the barracks, seemed small given the huge population of Chinese men in Baguio before the war.

Daily and Nightly Routines

Early each morning we "men" marched to the tennis court for roll call and exercises. We always reported for roll call first, the women later. I tended to wake around six o'clock. Oftentimes, I thumbed through my little red hymnal or book of poems and waited for the gong that sounded from the guardhouse each morning and signaled lights out each evening. The tone of the gong reminded me of the tribal gongs in Mindanao, which had fascinated me during my younger years in Davao. The sound actually blended well with the roosters' calls that rolled up the hills from the Filipino barrios in the valleys south of Camp Hay. Rooster calls were my cue to "rise, shine, give God glory, and get in line" as Uncle B often said as he and I rose to face the new day. But for the many hungry souls on the morning march to the tennis court, our enjoyment of the roosters' serenade was preempted by wishful thoughts of eating them instead.

Normally, I walked with Harry Taylor and Don Zimmerman, who flanked me at the end of the alphabetical order. "Spread your wings, Curt," was Don's cheerful comment as we began the morning exercise routine of push-ups and sit-ups.

The women and children often gathered on the porch of the Scout barracks to wave, signal, or "throw kisses" to us as we walked to the court. Guards were usually lax in their oversight of my exchanges with my sisters. Two Formosan guards rarely paid attention to weighted notes tossed down to our group. Once, though, Rae accidentally dropped a banana intended for me over the porch railing. A guard picked it up. In dismay, I watched him eat it as he monitored our exercises. The guards, too, were hungry.

Roll call began daily with all the men and boys standing at semi-attention, facing the Japanese duty officer at center court. In unison, we bowed to him offering a hearty greeting, "Ohayō gozaimasu!" (good morning). Rich Green, who stood behind me on the court, never seemed to pronounce the greeting in quite the same way. His daily mutterings sounded like a slurred "uppo yo assu, too." When I mentioned his odd pronunciation to my mother, she said, "Don't you repeat it!"

The weeks following my change of sleeping quarters to be Uncle B's partner were happy ones for me. Although he often spent time in the evening hours discussing business with Drs. Nance, Welles, Walker, Haughwout, and Mr. Herold, Uncle B always found at least a few minutes to share thoughts and lend counsel to me before or after "lights out." He was very sensitive to people's needs, even mine. We often revisited the day's episodes before a closing prayer.

Uncle B encouraged my participation with Mom and my sisters during their evening gatherings with the Crouters. The contrast provided some respite from the men's often boisterous or venomous utterances toward the enemy. Better, it offered time for wholesome songs and positive conversations with family. Although there were no regulations regarding the time I spent with my family in the Scout barracks, after dark a guard would occasionally shoo me back to the men's barracks.

At the evening gatherings, it was very heartening for Mom to see internees who had long abstained from visiting a house of worship to find comfort in humming the melodies of popular hymns with their friends.

Gradually, a sense of order settled onto Camp Hay. Even Nakamura relaxed his usually negative bearing. In fact, one morning he posted a notice stating that within days, internees would be allowed to send one letter to a friend or relative. Mom, naturally, chose to write a letter to Dad. She wrote:

> For two months, we have lived under abnormal conditions, the strain of war, and the humility of forced submission to Japanese rule. Not hearing from you has made a terrific gap in our lives. When will we ever have a chance to talk and have a home and a normal life again? We think of you, and we wonder where you are and under what conditions you are living. We pray for your safety, for your health, and existence in a now hostile country. Rumors and radio reports are conflicting, but I gather there has been heavy fighting in Davao since the war began. Where and when will it all end?

Since December 28, we have lived in a Filipino barracks, sleeping on the floor, and eating in a common mess under Japanese guard. We had days of real hardship, hunger, and fear. We have gone on from day to day improving our [living] quarters with a mattress, water, light, and a better food supply. We have been searched for money and asked for all funds to be turned in. We have worked hard, each sharing in cleaning rice, dishwashing, keeping our barracks clean, carrying in water, wood, and supplies. Washing and scrubbing is shared by all. A library of books was established and so far, there have been five days of school. Religious services were banned, but we have had some prayer circles on individual mats. We have not failed to sing with the children and pray every night. The Crouters and Grandma Widdoes have been with us every evening, the most restful and happy time of day. My joy has been in sketching faces and sights at our concentration camp. I have written a few rhymes as they come into my head. We have made many new friends and pleasant acquaintances. We have come to know the Crouters whom we enjoy so very much. Others are added to our list. Carl has been a comfort and taken a big responsibility for Curt and our family under every situation. We are so thankful for many of the rich experiences in friendship. We have been well, a few colds, and I had a couple of boils. On the whole, we are thankful for a continued good condition. We love you and pray for you daily.

(Sadly, Dad never received this letter, but it survived among my mother's papers, poems, and sketches from that period.)

A Touch of Schooling

Uncle B spoke often of starting a school program to begin at all grade levels. The program was near the top of his list of "must" items. Nakamura seemed suspicious of schooling and thwarted all early committee efforts to establish any formal educational opportunity for the camp's children.

In late January, Nakamura finally relented and granted permission for a "trial period" for a camp school. He told the committee, however, that United States' history, democracy, and geography could not be taught. Both parents and children happily embraced the opportunity for schooling. One of my classes was held on the tennis court, others at the dining table. I had been told by some of the teenagers who had lived in the United States that students there often despised going to school. That certainly was not the feeling at Camp Hay. I looked forward to it. Classes were far more interesting than picking bugs out of rice or sweeping floors, and it took my mind off my empty stomach.

Our lessons went smoothly for almost a week. Then two passing guards noticed that our teachers were using books for the classes. Although none of those books covered subjects forbidden by Nakamura, he became suspicious about what was being taught. The next morning, unannounced, soldiers came through the dining hall and snatched the books away, and we never saw them again. That same afternoon, an angry Nakamura posted a notice that all classes were canceled because "America" had been included in a class discussion. Uncle B nearly exploded.

Following his exchange with Nakamura, Uncle B was left frustrated and fuming. He told me that evening, "I think I'm an impediment to getting school started. Nakamura doesn't trust me." Almost another month passed before Nakamura allowed classes to resume.

Not all was lost on the educational front for me, however. On the day following the school's closure, Nakamura happened by the porch of the women's barracks and chatted briefly with a guard whom Mom was sketching. The guard had peeked curiously at what she was doing, but did not approach her. Nakamura did not hesitate. He ambled toward Mom and looked over her shoulder at her pencil drawing. Later, Mom told me, "I froze, fearing a smack across my head." Instead, the occasionally volatile commandant turned, and with a smile, pointed at his own face and gestured that she draw a sketch of him. She indicated that she had no more paper. He left her, saying, "Tomorrow."

At about the same time the next day, Nakamura showed up with a short stack of paper, handed it to Mom, and moved to a spot by the railing where the other soldier had stood the day before. He set his face, and Mom commenced to sketch his likeness. When she had finished, he strolled over, looked at the sketch, and smiled—seeming to like it very much. Mom then requested that he sign it, which he did. The following day, she received notice that Nakamura had arranged for her to leave the fenced perimeter to sketch individuals and Camp Hay scenes.

This opportunity gave Mom reason to look forward to each day. It certainly took her mind away from Dad for stretches of time. When possible, I would tag along with a pencil and scrap of paper to do my own sketching in her company. The experience was not a class in history or mathematics, but I enjoyed my hours as her sidekick tremendously.

The Barracks Rumor Mill

At night, I lay on my mat and listened to the men talk as they shuffled cards between play. I usually loved listening to their chatter. It made the time fly. One evening their conversation particularly captured my attention. Their subject centered on the Japanese men, some of whom they had known prior to the war, who presently made our lives miserable.

Nakamura Takeshi was the man mentioned most often in barracks banter. He was their favorite punching bag. Nagatomi Akari, "the thief of Baguio," who had stolen everyone's money, was another target the men most enjoyed kicking around. Nakamura and Nagatomi were but two of a number of other former Japanese civilians—unknown by name—who, before the war, had joined civic clubs, clerked in Baguio shops, played golf at Camp Hay but, otherwise, drew little attention. Now, those faces were markedly visible in and around our confines.

The most surprising transformation, of course, was Nakamura's. For some time, he had been an employee of the Heald Lumber Company, but now as our commandant at Camp Hay, he was a soldier with an officer's rank. Any educated guess would suggest that Nakamura, at least, and probably other civilians, had been plants before the war. Their purpose likely was to secure the kind of information that would facilitate the Japanese takeover of the area. I remembered Dad and Mr. Matsumoto sharing their suspicions about the rapidly growing population of Japanese in Davao in the years before the war broke out. The ease with which the Japanese had identified the exact locations of American homes, businesses, and luxury cars seemed to justify the conspiracy theory.

During another evening's barracks conversation, Uncle B spoke of Japanese "civilians" who had attended his Baguio church. He pointed out that in church, the Japanese who could speak some English could easily have gathered data through "innocent" conversations with parishioners. Ma Widdoes, an active member of Uncle B's church, had regularly interacted with two Japanese newcomers after the services. During a Crouter/Tong get-together in the Scout barracks one evening, Ma identified a guard making the rounds through the barracks, whispering, "Here comes Jesus." Ma had met "Jesus" at two church services before the first bombs fell on Baguio and again the week after the first bombing. During her internment in Camp Hay, she recognized him on his nightly rotation, flashlight in hand.

I was particularly interested that those involved in the gabfests represented a diverse mix of backgrounds. Even missionaries like Uncle B entered into some conversations. In prewar Baguio, few social occasions offered the clergy and businesspeople opportunities to interact. New friendships evolved from the barracks interchanges. They helped to break down some of the stereotypes people held of each other. Respect followed. Communication became more open. Men spoke more freely, sometimes critically of one another, but not in anger. They accepted differences and conducted conversations on a first-name basis. They judged their colleagues as people, not by the jobs they had held, the level of education they had attained, or whether they were "miners" or missionaries.

While Mom was pleased at my interacting with the men, she also urged me to mix with the Crouter group in their nightly gatherings. I found the discussions in the Scout barracks very relaxed, rarely argumentative, and naturally centered on women's issues. The question "Why are we held captive, especially mothers with children?" caught my interest. Most of the group agreed that women posed no threat to the Japanese. Releasing the women would only reduce the demands on our captors to guard and feed them. Certainly, by voluntarily surrendering at Brent School, the women had displayed a spirit of compliance.

Though many women prayed for release, Aunt Leora believed that the female presence in camp actually discouraged the Japanese from using corporal punishment on the men. Mrs. Crouter thought the interned women also kept husbands from attempting escape. She said her husband would not risk endangering his family simply to satisfy his own yearning to flee. Most women agreed that if their husbands escaped, they and their children would be at great risk.

Those evening gatherings in both the men's and women's barracks helped me adjust to life as a prisoner. The open discussions encouraged me to communicate, ponder, and form lasting friendships. Mom referred to those evenings as the "high time" of each day. Yet, she cautioned my sisters and me that low times could come again. "We've also seen low times. They come with sickness and hunger. Remember that times change, and peoples' moods sometimes do, too."

The Kempeitai

On January 23 I noticed an order on the bulletin board for all missionaries to report to the tennis court at once. Almost immediately, speculation among missionaries ran the gamut from "we will be released" to "we're going to be shipped to Manila" to "we'll be lined up and shot." After everyone had assembled, the Japanese guards ordered five CLS missionaries onto a truck and told the rest of us to return to our barracks.

The men, Hugo Culpepper, Bob Dyer, Roland Flory, Rufus Gray, and Herbert Loddigs, were trucked to the Kempeitai (military police) headquarters in Baguio for interrogation. Two of them, Culpepper and Dyer, returned to Hay later that day. Flory, Gray, and Loddigs were detained.

Months afterward, we learned through outside sources that the Japanese military police in Baguio had painstakingly gone through the roster of all missionary men in camp. They had especially looked into those who had been active in China and later became students at the Chinese Language School. For several days after we gathered at the court, many additional former CLS missionaries underwent questioning by the military police in the city. Most returned to Hay the same day.

Nearly all the adults were familiar with the work of the Kempeitai. In the men's barracks, I had heard talk of the military police on numerous occasions. Dr. Nance was the most knowledgeable. In conversation with Uncle B he referred to these intelligence officers as "enforcers of torture."

When Flory, Gray, and Loddigs did not return with the rest of the CLS men, Uncle B became very upset and shared his feelings with Nakamura. The next morning, as Uncle B and I entered the men's barracks following roll call at which Flory, Gray, and Loddigs were still noticeably absent, Nakamura stood next to the signpost looking smug. That look triggered Uncle B's temper. He stepped out of line, wagged his finger at the commandant, and raised holy hell. I had never before heard Uncle B utter such heated words. He fumed about the delay in the men's return to camp and the agonizing pain their wives and families were suffering. Nakamura pleaded ignorance, and he might well have been telling the truth. Uncle B charged him to "Find out!" Coincidentally, Flory and Loddigs were brought back to Hay the following day.

That evening, Uncle B spoke in more detail of his exchange with the commandant. I listened as he told Don Zimmerman that Nakamura was afraid of the military police and made excuses as to why he could not interfere with their work. The "work" of which Nakamura spoke, as we learned later from Flory and Loddigs, had been cruel. Only in his unpublished memoir of the internment written after the war did Uncle B report, "Mr. Flory was subjected to the 'water cure,' and it is only a miracle that he is alive to speak of this experience. Mr. Loddigs was not treated in as severe a manner, but he suffered great physical injury." Mr. Gray was never returned to Camp Hay.

A Brief Taste of Freedom

On January 30, 1942, a week after the abduction of the CLS missionaries, an alarming directive appeared on the bulletin board. Within minutes, word spread through both barracks that *all* missionaries were to gather on the tennis court immediately. The suddenness of this posting startled us. Why were we being singled out again? Could it mean freedom for us? Were we to be taken to the military police headquarters for interrogation, torture, or worse? Our China missionaries, namely the Disciples of Christ denomination, feared the worst. They all remembered their horrific experience with the Japanese military on mainland China three years earlier. A number of the Disciples, sensing trouble, wished not to show up. Yet everybody did. We gathered on the court and were ordered to pack up. We would be leaving camp mid-morning. Period. No questions. No explanation.

Feeling the same anxiety as the other missionaries, I pocketed my two toy cars, picked up my toothbrush, pocket-sized hymnal, and Longfellow's book of poems. Waiting for Mom, my sisters, and Uncle B, I sat on the court scanning my hymnal. Aunt Leora sat down next to me. I had memorized the words to a number of the hymns, although I knew the melodies of only a few. Aunt Leora could read music and enjoyed acquainting me with tunes I did not know well. My favorites included, "O God, Our Help in Ages Past" and "This Is My Father's World." I liked best the last verses of both hymns. The first read:

O God, our help in ages past,
Our hope for years to come.
Be Thou our guard while troubles last,
And our eternal home.

The other read:
This is my Father's world,
Oh, let me ne'er forget
that though the wrong seems oft so strong,
God is the ruler yet.

The songs seemed appropriate, and I hummed them with Aunt Leora as we awaited being called to the truck. She was like an angel to me that morning and throughout the internment.

In the Scout barracks, Wezer joined the flurry of activity with the other missionary children. The rest of the internees watched the packing process. Some of those, Wezer noted, "were present to protect their own belongings." A few bid farewells and wished us all luck. As Wezer reached the court with Mom and Rae, she said, "The women seem more interested in our floor space than worried about what might happen to us." Mom responded simply, "Floor space means a lot right now; may they enjoy it."

From the tennis court, I watched as our belongings were thrown onto a truck. The Japanese guards ordered us aboard the same truck. Mom struggled to climb over the rails. Although it was not apparent during her daily routines, it was obvious that her injured leg continued to be painful. Wezer noticed her difficulty, too, and committed herself to watch over Mom more.

Once on board, I let myself dream that we would soon be free. No more captivity! We could eat and play again. I quickly whispered my hopes of getting "scrambo" eggs and milk to Wezer. She reminded me, "We don't even know where we are going, so don't be thinking of scrambled eggs and milk just yet." Uncle B, hearing her admonition, gave her a big smile. Others remained apprehensive.

As the truck wound down the road out of Camp Hay, Uncle B announced what Nakamura had told him moments prior to departure. We would be situated in local homes and be required to wear ID patches outside our residences. We felt relief. With few apprehensions and some unanswered questions, we were soon in the lobby of the Baguio Hotel. There, a Japanese officer, speaking quite understandable English, informed Mom that the Smiths and the Zimmermans would join us at the Eschbach home on Bokawkan Road. "You wait for transport there," the officer said. Others were ordered to return to their prewar private homes. After some wait, a hotel vehicle delivered us to Uncle B's residence. Mom and my sisters looked forward to being with Uncle B, Joe Smith, and Don Zimmerman again. They had not had occasion to talk with them for weeks.

I was excited to be free and to sit down at the Eschbach dining table for lunch prepared by Uncle B's faithful long-time servants, Maria and Marci Obilee. Very quickly, they served up heated *pan de sal*—my favorite Filipino bread—buttered heavily. That flavor, in itself, made the day a special one. (Uncle B's son, Jim, told me after the war that Maria and Marci were so loyal to Uncle B that immediately after his internment at Brent, they buried what they thought were some of his most valuable possessions—his neckties and Aunt Ruth's silverware, the latter purchased with Gold Medal flour coupons.)

Over dinner, we wondered why the Japanese had decided to free only missionaries. Mom suggested that Major Mukaibo made the decision because he, too, was a Christian, but Uncle B thought it probably came from a higher authority in Manila. He did not hold Mukaibo in high regard. "If he's a Christian, I'm Jesus," he joked. Mukaibo's Baguio office in the military police headquarters was reason enough for Uncle B to be suspicious of him.

My sisters and I were sent to bed at an early hour while the adults continued to exchange stories and make plans for the days ahead. They also talked about the confinement of the CLS men by the military police and the unknown whereabouts or fate of Rufus Gray.

Moments after midnight, Mom entered the room where my sisters and I were sleeping and whispered that Japanese soldiers were in the house and wanted to count all bodies. We gathered in the Eschbach dining room where a finger-pointing soldier, speaking mostly in "hand language," instructed us to assemble at City Hall early the next morning. It turned into a restless night. As I tossed in bed, my thoughts fixed on the idea that we would have a daily roll call each morning as we had in camp, only at City Hall.

Soon after daybreak and a hot muffin breakfast, our group walked to City Hall. Many of the other missionaries had already gathered there, and more were arriving by the minute. Others, we were told, had congregated at different hotels. By 7:00 a.m., standing in the entryway of City Hall, we listened to the voice of Major Mukaibo. He bellowed out a formal announcement in blunt, clear English, "It is the command of the Japanese Imperial Army that you shall return to the concentration camp in Camp John Hay." Everyone dutifully bowed. I was shocked and squeezed Mom's hand. Rae sobbed softly as we walked back to Bokawkan Road to pack. Mukaibo told Uncle B and Bishop Richardson that they were not to return to Camp Hay. As full-time missionaries and residents of Baguio City prior to the war, the two men were to remain in the city.

Ours was a very short taste of freedom. I had not even been afforded time for the promised breakfast of "scrambo." Maintaining her usual calm,

Wezer led Rae and me through the process of stuffing our few belongings back into a bag. In a letter never forwarded to Dad and written days later, Mom described our day of freedom: "It was a one-night nightmare. We were made to return the next day—weary and discouraged." Only after the war did I learn from Jim Halsema, son of Baguio's former mayor, that our return to camp had been ordered by Japanese Military Headquarters in Manila and that our release was the result of Mukaibo's misunderstanding of the original directive.

I sat next to Mom in the bed of the truck during the ride back to Camp Hay and tried to hold back the tears. Her hugs made me feel better, but I was still distraught—not so much about returning to internment, but about losing her and Uncle B as close companions. Mom felt bad for me and fought back tears herself as we were ordered to different barracks upon our return to Hay. In parting, she reminded me of Uncle B's promise to help our lives in any way possible from the outside.

As often as he was able, Uncle B arranged for food to be brought to others and to us, and always in the hands of a Filipina nurse from Notre Dame Hospital. Periodically, the nurse was admitted into Hay to deliver medicines to the camp hospital. Missionaries like Joe Smith, Don Zimmerman, and Harold Fildey eased my initial concerns about Uncle B's absence from barracks life. After seeing my pain during the truck ride back to camp, they took me under their wings. Gene Kneebone and others, too, assumed fatherly roles in monitoring me around the men's barracks. I came to believe that men could be angels, too.

Like our family, and all who experienced that one-day sojourn to Baguio, Marian Gray, Rufus's wife, and her young son Billy, were returned to Hay. But her day outside was unlike all the others. She had found her Baguio residence a mess, with pictures strewn throughout the house. Marian quickly realized that the Kempeitai had looked at all of the Gray family photos while they had been interned in Camp Hay. Seeing the condition of her home, Marian raced directly to Intelligence Headquarters in Baguio to demand her husband's release. The responses from officials, including Mukaibo, were mere shrugs. All feigned no knowledge of Rufus's whereabouts. Incensed and distraught, Marian returned home. After nearly a full night of going through her photo albums, she discovered that only pictures of their Chinese acquaintances were missing. Marian immediately determined that those photos were the reason behind her husband's imprisonment. She surmised that the police suspected Rufus to have been an American agent while he was in China. Nothing could have been further from the truth. But it would be more than four months before we learned of Rufus Gray's whereabouts or condition.

Recalled to Camp John Hay

Immediately upon our return to camp, we heard news of the first child born in Camp Hay. His name was Richard Hawkins Scott, son of Isabel and Churchill Scott. Because Richard's birth occurred in the Scout barracks, everyone referred to him not as Richard Hawkins Scott, but as "John Hay Scott." John Hay remained his name throughout the years in concentration.

His mother had begun experiencing labor pains shortly after our group of one hundred and fifty missionaries left Camp Hay for "freedom." Isabel's friends asked Nakamura that she be driven to Notre Dame Hospital for the birthing. Their plea was denied. Instead, John Hay was born in a temporarily partitioned area of the Scout barracks the evening before we returned to concentration. Several supportive women attended his mother, and she amazingly kept a cool demeanor throughout her labor.

We shared the excitement of John Hay's birth. Mom said the arrival came at a perfect time, diminishing any displeasure other internees might have had in relinquishing their temporarily expanded cubicles to the returning missionaries. Little did the baby know that his coming into the world at that critical time established fresh hopes for all and eased friction between "miners" and missionaries in the women's barracks. For months afterward, wider tolerance and dialogue diminished the disagreements and petty annoyances, which had been commonplace during earlier days of barracks life. One of my teachers, Phyllis Gibbons, referred to the "John Hay birth" as the "turnaround time in our lives as prisoners." Her mere mention of his name lifted spirits and focused us on what lay ahead.

My family quickly settled back into the routine of daily chores after returning to Camp Hay. Mom rejoined the vegetable cleaning crew. Each morning, Wezer helped her pick weevils out of rice. That was such tedious duty that Mrs. Herold tried to rotate the task. When not assigned onerous chores like cleaning the porch or barracks floors, I accompanied the wagon crew. We disposed of garbage and procured the ever-necessary firewood. For me, wagon chores were more interesting than barracks duties. Wezer and Rae were given additional responsibilities—washing kitchen pans or watching over infants while the mothers toiled. Each of us, though, hoped that classes would be offered again.

Our earlier attempt at formal education at Camp Hay could best be described as a "no-go" experience. But in response to mounting committee pressure, Nakamura suddenly posted a notice that classes for children would reopen in the dining room the last week of February. It could not happen fast enough for me. Our classes began with scarcely any books. Nakamura scrutinized the few that had been collected for use. Volunteer teachers were numerous. Some had taught at Brent School. They found teaching a grand escape from the oppressive kitchen details. The teachers seemed as excited as I was to be in school again. They were free to teach in a manner comfortable to them, told many stories of life in America or other Asian countries, and loved to lend humor to our classes. Formality was unknown. I knew that Uncle B would be very happy that school was in session, too.

Miss Gibbons taught my small class and held my interest without a blackboard, a book, a pen, or clean paper—all items once taken for granted. Arithmetic, which I disdained more than any other subject, came to life with her use of rhymes: "Five guards stood by our class to see—two marched on, and that left three." And "when you add a three and six—nine weevils you'll see in your hot soup mix." The ditty I thought most humorous was one she recited as a nosey Japanese guard stood over her shoulder. Slowly waving her finger, pretending to lead an orchestra so we would repeat it, she spoke loudly, "If our guard would leave us be, we could talk some history." Repeat it, we did. Then, she looked up at him with a big smile. He returned the smile and casually walked away.

The continuation of bedtime get-togethers with the Crouter family was my escape from evening loneliness. It also provided valued moments with Mom and my sisters. As was the routine before our one-day exodus from Hay, we met at the Tong cubicle, sat on Mom's mat, sang, and chatted together. Sometimes the guards edged closer to our small gathering, especially when we were singing. One of our more relaxed guards enjoyed mimicking the role of conductor as we sang. His favorite tune was "If I Had the Wings of an Angel." I am certain he had no idea what the words meant: "If I had the wings of an angel, over these prison walls I would fly, I would fly to the top of the mountains, and there I'd be willing to die." It was usually safe during relaxed moments, even with guards in the vicinity, to sing almost anything except "The Star-Spangled Banner." None of the

Japanese, and only a couple of the Formosan guards, had enough grasp of the English language to be bothered by the lyrics, but all of them, and the Tong/Crouter crew, too, knew that the national anthem was a no-no.

By late February, what we had hoped would be only a few days in prison had stretched into weeks. My inability to play vigorously each day continued to make afternoons drag. Even my short walks outside the camp fences with Mom while she sketched were now terminated. During idle hours, I gazed longingly from the barracks toward the large parade ground directly outside our enclosure. I wished all the while to be there, throwing a ball or romping about with my friends in an open space.

One afternoon, feeling a barrelful of self-pity, I planted myself in the dirt under the Scout barracks, where depressed and teary-eyed, I pushed my toy cars around on the soil. The next morning, as I began the short walk toward the tennis court for roll call and exercises, I looked upward at a fresh notice tacked on the signboard. It read simply that Singapore had fallen to Japan. Staring at that sign reminded me of the words Mom had shared with me on the day we first marched into Camp Hay: "When you feel down, look up. Someone good is watching over you." While the Singapore sign was a downer, Mom's words gave me strength and injected me with positive thoughts. (Even today, the date of Singapore's fall [February 15, 1942] reminds me to put negative thoughts aside.)

When not on a duty detail or in class, I played "cars" under the barracks. I was usually alone, but sometimes other pals or Rae joined me. She was my most regular and most adventuresome playmate. One day, while digging to make a trench-like dip on our miniature road for my two cars, I unearthed a piece of paper money. Digging further, I found more bills and some coins. Quickly, I covered up our "find" and told Rae to tell Mom. Mom said we should rebury the money more deeply. "It will be found sometime by whoever buried it," she said. We did as we were told. Many days later, again playing cars, I checked the "money spot." The cash had vanished. Mom told Rae that the owner had retrieved the money, explaining that the woman had given the bills to her young son to bury under the barracks at the time of the Nagatomi raid.

A number of the women in Camp Hay were of Irish descent. That group, recognizing that St. Patrick's Day was coming soon, decided to put together an evening of fun in the dining area. Mrs. Herold was charged with asking Nakamura to grant permission for the men to attend, and he approved her request. The dining room was packed for the event.

Without being invited, guards also attended, watching from the perimeter. The internees sat on boxes or dining hall benches. There was much light-hearted comedy in song and words that allowed us to poke a bit of fun at each other. Trademark camp happenings like tripping over others during nighttime toilet visits, trying to define the contents in our soup bowls, discovering alternatives to Kotex, and a host of other "funnies" highlighted the program. Mary Dyer's singing voice drew great applause and shouts for more. I sat with my sisters, and after the performance Wezer told me, "I've never seen you laugh so much." The evening was therapeutic for all of us and set the stage for future programs, which continued periodically until the last months of the war when energy levels plummeted toward zero.

Easter 1942

One of my more meaningful memories of prison life at Camp John Hay centers on the events of Easter Day, April 5, 1942. The rumor spread on Good Friday that a "Baguio Bunny" would make a special appearance in camp on Easter morning. When I told Mom about it, she said, "I'll bet the bunny's name starts with 'B.'" She knew Uncle B well and knew it would be "Carlesque" to pull off such a stunt.

A few missionary women had planned an Easter Sunrise service and asked Nakamura for permission to hold it on the open embankment behind the Scout barracks overlooking the ravines and mountains south of Baguio. He refused that request, but in a compromising mood sanctioned the service if it were held on the fenced-in tennis court across the drive from the two barracks. He even allowed families to sit together. Happily, for Mom, my sisters, and me, Uncle B was there—obviously with the approval of Nakamura—but not in a bunny suit.

Regrettably, Nakamura decided to hold the regular morning exercise routine for his guards on the court at the precise time of the Easter service. The Easter committee delayed the beginning of our service so that the guards' loud grunts would not be the background "music" for the service. Nakamura extended the push-up and sit-up routine for a period that seemed much longer than usual. Uncle B whispered, "He's showing off his mean side again."

After a rather long wait, the service commenced even though the guards continued their exercises. We shared chuckles when they closed their exercise routine with bows to the rising sun just as we began to sing,

"Christ the Lord is Risen Today." For a moment, it seemed as if the two groups had practiced together, since the guards' bows coincided with the extended notes of the "Alleluia."

Almost all of the able internees attended the sunrise service. A cluster of missionary men had put together a fine choral group. They drafted some good "miner" voices, too, which lent strong bass tones to the men's choir. Mary Dyer sang the solo, "I Know That My Redeemer Liveth." Even outdoors, her magnificent voice brought tears to many eyes. Our captors were also impressed with her singing. In fact, Nakamura called Mary aside afterward and with unusual warmth commended her for the solo.

Shortly after the Easter service and the guards' exercise routine, a large bunny emerged from the men's barracks and ran to the court. He waved his hands and wiggled his ears as he jogged a circuit around the court. All the adults, of course, recognized the long strides of the lanky bunny as those of Carl Eschbach. I had not realized that Uncle B was no longer sitting beside us. The children were excited by the bunny's miraculous appearance, and the guards standing around the court perimeter stared in disbelief at the large bunny's antics. Uncle B began to pass out colored Easter eggs to all the children. He later credited his loyal Filipina servants, Maria and Marci, for creating his bunny suit and coloring the eggs at his Bokawkan home.

Following the sunrise service and egg distribution, all the younger kids and a good number of the women decked themselves out in silly costumes made from items laying about the barracks. The toddlers and moms were thrilled to show off their attire and let their hair down—bringing loud laughter from their dads and husbands. All the while Nakamura stared sternly at the proceedings. He apparently saw no relationship between the early morning service and the activities that followed.

To appease Nakamura and ease tensions, Uncle B gave a colored egg to each of the guards and one to Nakamura. That gesture generated some smiles from the Japanese and left Uncle B with a good feeling as he returned to house arrest in Baguio.

Having watched the children remove the shells and devour the eggs, the soldiers did the same and became more a part of the festivities. Following the parade, in a kindly gesture and to the delight of all, the commingling hour was extended to allow the families special time together. Even our commandant's heart grew larger on that Easter Day.

From the first day of imprisonment, commingling was the lightning rod issue that most frequently created tension between Nakamura and the interned families. After most confrontations with the camp committee, Nakamura retaliated by banning commingling for a stretch of time. Following that pattern, he called a new ban two days after Easter. In my later conversations with Uncle B, Nakamura was always "Mr. Faucet" for the frequency of his turning commingling and schooling into "on again/ off again" activities.

Years after the war, Mom loved to tell the story of that first Easter in internment. She would recall, "For days after Mary's solo, the real meaning of togetherness was felt in our camp community." The early weeks at Camp Hay had certainly been strained. Turmoil, followed by sickness, hunger, and depression, defined that period of captivity. The "miners" who had roots in the Baguio community controlled camp governance. Some of them routinely spoke of missionaries as being a "bunch of Bible-toters carrying imaginary halos over their heads." With somewhat more restraint, the missionaries tossed verbal darts into the miners' hides with similarly hostile tags like "greedy gold grabbers." Most of those thoughtless labels were put aside following Easter Day. A fresh spirit emerged. The event wakened our community to laughter, hope, and wider love.

Rumors of the Broader War

Few days passed without rumors about the war around us. Posted signs proclaiming Japan's victories in the Pacific frequently reminded us where we were and what we were experiencing. Isolated from the action, the men suffered psychologically, feeling anger and disappointment because of their helplessness. Nightly I sensed their frustration, anger, and disappointment at having to squander their time in a concentration camp—not being able to disappear into the hills to join the guerilla bands and participate in fighting the war.

They all knew what the consequences of an escape would be. Except for a few young men, almost all were husbands and fathers of those in the Scout barracks. Any attempt to escape under those circumstances could have spelled extreme hardship for their families and others. Mukaibo's threats of death for an attempted escape remained fresh in everyone's mind.

Nevertheless, being holed up in Hay was a constant annoyance to the interned men. Suffering the consequences of war without any sense of its course or knowledge of what could be done to shorten it was for them hard to accept. Occasionally, a rumormonger would spread tales about

American advances in the Pacific. Early on, those rumors restored the camp's energy and refreshed our hopes that we might soon regain our freedom. Any sign, whether something uttered by a Japanese officer, a directive on the bulletin board, a note received in a food bag, or even a mere dream, could generate positive rumors. When shared, the hopeful rumors temporarily lifted spirits.

As we gathered for roll call one morning, a former mining engineer in our line of march asked Jim Halsema if there was any truth to the rumor that American forces had retaken Zamboanga and were moving northward through Mindanao. Halsema's quick response sounded like something Uncle B would say, "If it makes you feel better, believe it is true." We all came to know over time that the moments of hope generated by rumors were usually short-lived. Eventually, we learned to brace ourselves against believing what we heard.

Since arriving at Camp Hay, I had listened nightly to the barracks' "talkathons." Most of these conversations suggested that as long as our soldiers at Bataan controlled the area around Manila Bay, the tide of U.S. power would eventually reclaim the Philippines and free us. We had received periodic reports through connections at Notre Dame Hospital that our troops were holding their own on the Bataan peninsula and the island of Corregidor. Those reports buoyed our spirits immensely, and I believed them.

Early on the morning of April 10, 1942, as we returned to the barracks from our exercise routine, we passed a freshly painted sign on the bulletin board. Unlike most notices, this one covered the entire signboard. In bold print, it read simply, "Bataan fell! Finally, with unconditional surrender, on April 9 at 7:00 p.m. Now let us realize the Orient for the Orientals." Standing nearby, Nakamura smirked haughtily as we read the hard news.

The Bataan posting hit everyone in camp like a blow to the stomach and put to rest thoughts of being freed anytime soon. Many of us had connections to the American troops in Bataan under the command of General Wainwright. Our family had deep concern for the welfare of dear Dr. Brokenshire. The entire camp community immediately came to realize that the loss of Bataan, and the likely Japanese takeover of a defenseless Corregidor, meant that our liberation would be delayed for a long time, maybe months. Only weeks later did news filter into camp of the horrendous loss of American lives during the long march from Bataan to the prison camps.

For days after the Bataan posting, an invisible pall hung over Camp Hay. Those were heart-wrenching days. Hope was put on the shelf. Once again, everyone was forced to readjust their thinking to the long haul and forget the commonly voiced notions that freedom was just around the corner.

I knew that Mom, suffering from severe malnutrition brought about by vitamin deficiency, was not well and was further pained by the Bataan news and concern about Dr. Brokenshire. I very much wanted to see Mom, then a patient in the camp hospital, but Dr. Welles told me not to visit her yet. I did manage to meet up with Wezer that evening. When she said, "Mom's okay," I felt much better. She also told me that the surrender of Bataan had left everyone in the women's barracks deeply disheartened.

Gradually, the gloom of the Bataan news dissipated and led to greater discipline within our confines. When the committee put forward a plan for the assignment of tasks, acceptance of duties came with fewer challenges. There seemed to be greater understanding that our lives depended on maintaining our general welfare—not going it alone or expecting a quick liberation. For the first time, we came to accept the fact that Hay would be our home for a long time.

Strangely, just days after the Bataan posting, the unusual sight of a single four-engine plane flying low over Camp Hay startled everyone. Only a few actually saw it. I was on detail with the wood crew at the time. Most of the crew was inside a hut sorting wood to be taken to the awaiting wagon. I had exited the hut carrying an armload of firewood to the wagon. Our guard stood next to me smoking a cigarette. Suddenly, I heard the roar of a plane racing overhead. I looked up through the tree branches and saw the red circle on the underside of the wings, clearly marking it as a Japanese aircraft. The plane was larger than any I had seen during the December bombings. Apparently familiar with the sound so not bothering to look upward, the guard casually and confidently uttered, "Nihon" (Japan). The men inside the hut, hearing the loud roar, raced outside and looked in the direction of the fleeing sound. "It's American. I saw it!" shouted one of our crew. Sure enough, that evening camp gossip labeled the plane as American. Postwar pictures, however, confirm that the plane *was* a Japanese Type 97 twin-engine bomber.

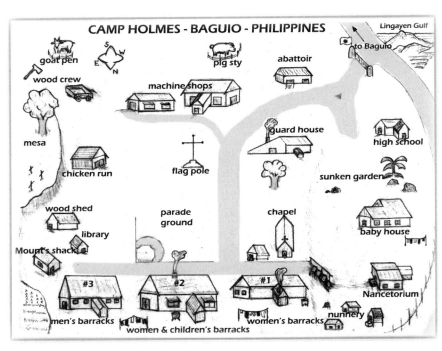

This is my adaptation of the drawing Mother sketched in 1943
of the enclosed structures and grounds of the Camp Holmes prison.

CHAPTER 4

Camp Holmes I

April 1942–Nov. 1942

. . . .

Making Camp

The next morning, in a stunning surprise to everybody, Mr. Herold announced that in two days all internees would be moved to Camp Holmes in Trinidad. Holmes was located on the Bontoc Trail, about five miles north of Baguio. Mom knew Trinidad well, but had heard nothing about a prison there.

Herold's announcement came from Nakamura, so we knew it was not a rumor. We speculated about the reason for such a move. Could the decision have some connection to the bomber flyover of Camp Hay the previous day? Optimistic men in the barracks thought the move was meant to forestall our soon-to-come liberation. I believed their claim—that an American airdrop would liberate us. Soon enough, though, thoughts of liberation would be lost in the days, weeks, months, and years of imprisonment that followed.

Herold informed us that a team of men would be bused to Camp Holmes to prepare the barracks there for occupancy. Included in the group were a number of the Chinese. After surveying the facilities for spaces best suited to the needs of our camp's various constituencies, the team cleaned out the three main buildings for living quarters.

Camp government, led by Dr. Dana Nance and several other men, first tackled the issue of where to situate the different groups. Outside of barracks assignments and the baby house, their decisions focused on particular needs and locations for schooling, storage, workshops, and a dispensary. The committee included men with the skills and understanding of the different services needed—for example, Alex Kaluzhny would look after food preparation; Dana Nance, medical needs; and Fabian Ream, construction and repair work. That crew began tackling their assignments the following day.

On April 23, 1942, the entire contingent of British and American internees were loaded onto buses and driven through Baguio to Camp Holmes. The usually busy streets were noticeably quiet during our ride through the city. Only small groups of Filipinos were in town. I recognized a few as amahs or parishioners from Uncle B's church. Most avoided waving, but dared to raise two wagging fingers in the V sign when they recognized friends and familiar faces. The Chinese men arrived days later and bunked in the Number Three barracks.

Unlike the forced march from Brent School to an undisclosed location in December, this time the transfer of the more than eight hundred internees to Holmes proceeded aboard buses that were bound for an announced destination. Prior to our arrival, the quarters had been thoroughly cleaned and necessary repairs had been made by Herold's crew. This was in sharp contrast to the Camp Hay barracks, which had not been touched, even with a broom. Our relocation to Camp Holmes occurred under more relaxed Japanese control; the guards were less acrimonious and showed little concern about our movements. Even Nakamura seemed more mellow.

Our family traveled on one of the last buses to depart Hay. As we entered the main gate of Camp Holmes and rolled up a small rise, I saw a flat open space without fences fronting a row of buildings. I felt as though a curtain had been pulled aside to expose a stage on which I could freely breathe and even run. The space was beautiful! A surge of energy told me that better days were ahead. The sight triggered a memory of our dog Army, who when unleashed used to romp excitedly around the Davao playground.

Alex Kaluzhny, sitting next to me, explained that the open space was a former parade ground and the row of three large buildings would be our new living quarters. For some reason, Wezer's attention was drawn more to the debris strewn across the grounds. It was apparent that the cleanup crew had had time to prepare only the barracks for the internees, but not the surrounding grounds.

Pointing to the middle building, Alex said, "You'll be staying in that barracks, Number Two, with your mother." Those words upset me.

I assumed that I would be again living with the men. Rae, picking up on his remarks, gave her interpretation of his words by repeating noisily, "Mommy, we're staying with The Three Bears." For weeks afterward, those barracks were "bears" to Rae. Even more exciting to both of my sisters, sections of the barracks floor had real bunks and cots. Entering barracks Number Two, we immediately noted its cleanliness. But within an hour, that cleanliness meant little as space issues became a heated topic. Family quarters were more confining than at Hay's Scout barracks, and the building was immediately dubbed the "sardine can." With very little controversy, the men were ordered to barracks Number One. Arriving a day later, the Chinese were sent to barracks Number Three. Ten days afterward, the Chinese were released to Baguio proper, which freed Number Three for the men. Single women were transferred to barracks Number One. These moves relieved the extreme congestion in the family barracks and ended a shuffle that might be called "musical dorms."

Jim Halsema told me that following the Japanese bombing raids in December, the Philippine Constabulary had fled Camp Holmes. Filipino looters had taken over the premises, leaving a trail of debris scattered over the area. It was interesting that the very needy Filipino looters found some of the items left by the constabulary to be worthless. Yet within minutes of being deposited in our new quarters, Rae and I, along with other children and some adults, scrambled over the unkempt grounds and picked up junk the looters had left behind. We reveled in looking for usable scraps and happily shared many of our finds with others.

That behavior seems an interesting commentary on our lives as prisoners. Four months in Hay had taught us that the most insignificant piece of discarded waste had a potential use. We found items like paper, shoestrings, twine, pieces of tin, and untold numbers of other things useful to our needs. Mom and Wezer, who were focused on setting our belongings out in the designated floor space, sent us outside to scavenge. My prize find was a large multicolored marble. It became my "weegie" ball in a game my friends and I created with marbles on the parade grounds. Later, under the direction of Chef Alex, I helped a team of children pick up scraps of "unusable" wooden debris for the kitchen crew to use.

We were not surprised to be greeted at our first morning roll call on the parade grounds by Major Mukaibo. Past encounters with him, though few, had always led to some trouble, and his message that morning was a reminder of his meanness. During the cleanup days, the work crew and

Mr. Herold had earmarked a small cottage at the foot of the shallow hillside and only steps away from the women's barracks to house mothers with babies. Mukaibo's morning announcement immediately rejected that decision. Because the location of the baby house offered gorgeous views of the Trinidad Valley, Mukaibo claimed it as a retreat cottage for visiting Japanese officers. The location certainly would be an idyllic one for sake parties.

A day later, following a closer inspection of the baby house that found it too small for his gatherings, Mukaibo changed his mind. It then became the residence for babies and their moms. That arrangement brought space relief to the family barracks and gave the mothers a measure of privacy for nursing. Its location also provided easy access to the hospital, the single women's quarters, toilets, showers, and dining facilities—even babysitters. Wezer was one of those. The hours spent in what she called the "baby bin" were some of her most enjoyable.

At the foot of a small hill and bordering the parade grounds, a line of nipa huts served a variety of needs. A flattened area (mesa) at the top of the slope provided space for play, adult solitude, and a resting place for the deceased.

A man named Clarence Mount lived with his wife and child in one small nipa hut close to the men's barracks. He had an eccentric personality; his wife was anti-social, and their child, mentally challenged. Mount requested private quarters for his family. The general committee, having endured his antagonistic manner with male colleagues in Hay, was happy to oblige him. With Nakamura's approval, Mount was granted his request.

The smallest nipa hut was an off-and-on library and kindergarten, and the unofficial nighttime toilet for the Mount family. The stench around that hut became such that the wood crew soon chose another path to their work sites.

The southernmost hut, initially a woodshed, served multiple purposes. On rainy days, it became a place where Ward Graham, John Ream, and I enjoyed testing our balance on the bamboo beams. Later, it was designated a classroom. For a short while, it was even home to a cow I named Deaconess Mary after Sister Mary, one of the sisters who later joined us at Camp Holmes, who often stopped on her strolls to talk with me. From Deaconess Mary I retain a small indentation on my sternum where she landed a punishing kick as I brushed flies from her tail.

The guardhouse served as quarters for the Japanese guard corps and as office for the resident commandant. Located by the parade grounds, it was a short walk from the main gate. Whenever the Japanese tortured someone, they did so by a large tree near the guardhouse and in full view of the internee barracks. Uncle B facetiously referred to the guardhouse as the "sake saloon" because of the guards' frequent drinking binges there in the evening hours. These celebrations usually coincided with Japanese holidays like the emperor's birthday or announced Japanese victories on Pacific island battlefronts.

Our hospital, the "Nancetorium," as Mom dubbed it after Dr. Nance, looked as though it had been the private quarters of the constabulary commanding officer. Conveniently located, it was a short walk from the women's barracks, the nuns' quarters, and the baby house. Sharing similarly gorgeous views with the baby house, the hospital had been Nakamura's initial choice for his residence. That plan was sidetracked tactfully and tactically when Dr. Nance promised Nakamura that a private refrigerator space in the hospital would be reserved for him to keep his sake cool.

Two structures near the entry gate to Holmes stood unbothered by other activities of camp life. They were turned into shops where Fabian Ream, Bart Rice, Willis Dunne, Ray Hale, and others—all talented artisans—created a variety of tools and utensils necessary for daily life. Mr. Rice specialized in constructing coffins. I entered their shops frequently, stopping by on my return from delivering food to the woodcutting crews in the nearby hills. Mr. Ream, my pal Reamo's father, welcomed me and seemed to enjoy his role as my instructor as much as working on camp projects.

Across the walkway from the single women's barracks were three very small structures. Initially, two were for grade school classes, but one of them later became a chapel. Off and on, the third structure served as a place for indoor play and eventually as an enclosure for the camp's dairy goats.

Camp Life

Once the various huts, shacks, and the more stable structures in Camp Holmes were identified for specific uses, it was amazing how quickly we organized ourselves into functional and productive units. It helped that the Japanese garrison granted considerable latitude for us to "loot" the vacated structures within the camp's confines. Still, moving heavy objects from one area of the camp to another proved a real challenge.

After much urging, Nakamura agreed to confiscate the wood crew's "looting wagon" from Camp Hay to help with the movement of heavy objects—but only on the condition that the wagon would be manually pushed to Camp Holmes. The most rugged members of the wood crew were selected for this task. Each man eagerly accepted, welcoming any excuse to get out of camp for a period of time. Under guard, the crew reinforced the axles and siding of the wagon at Camp Hay before pushing it back to Camp Holmes, an immensely difficult eight-mile maneuver. Along the way, the crew developed an attachment to the wagon and christened it *Carry Me Home.* As Rich Green reported, Filipinos along the trail north of Baguio surreptitiously raised fingers in the victory sign, a quiet way of telling the wagon crew "we're with you, brothers." We all greeted the exhausted men and wagon with smiles and applause on the parade ground.

Carry Me Home most often transported logs from the base of the hill to the kitchen. The mountain crew had cleared a path down a narrow ravine through which they could roll the cut logs to the waiting wagon on the campgrounds. There, another crew chopped the logs and loaded them onto the wagon for delivery to Chef Alex's kitchen. Other crews also used it to move weighty items like iron stoves to areas around the barracks and to dispose of garbage.

I found the daylight hours at Camp Holmes a huge improvement over the inactivity at Camp Hay. Standing on the parade ground, I could easily see beyond the surrounding valley of rice paddies to the far-reaching mountains, and on clear days, I even saw a small stretch of Lingayen Gulf. Regularly, I watched activity along the Bontoc Trail, which framed the north perimeter of Camp Holmes. Overlooking the trail was a huge rock formation. It featured the silhouette of a man's face, appearing much like the renowned rock face of New Hampshire.

A typical scene on the snake-like trail featured barefooted Igorots, often pulling a *carabao* (water buffalo) bearing bags of rice, sleeves of bananas, or firewood. Igorot women balancing woven baskets of food on their heads usually followed their men. They delivered their goods to the Baguio markets or roadside stands along the way.

I found observing the occasional open-bay trucks carrying Japanese troops over the pockmarked road toward Bontoc even more interesting. The wood crew observers of the mini-convoys often facetiously commented, "Who are they after today?" Following the capture of Americans in Bontoc, we learned that the area was a center for American-led Filipino guerillas from which they tracked Japanese movements north of Baguio.

Despite the early efforts by the Holmes cleanup crew to designate areas that would serve family needs best, there were dissatisfactions with barracks Number Two. It took days for the mothers and single women to settle into an acceptable cubicle arrangement. On a few occasions, a mother—protective of her children's comfort—called upon an impartial mediator to measure square footages so as not to feel cheated of space. Having carefully measured the available space in the barracks, Mrs. Herold determined that a three-by-eight foot area was sufficient to sleep one adult and one young child.

Even with the mothers with babies settled into the baby house, the family barracks remained overcrowded. Yet, once a modest amount of order was achieved, families gradually adjusted to the lack of privacy and life with limited space, noise, and discomfort.

Food of any variety was a most precious commodity, and food theft was a worry in all living quarters. During the early weeks in Holmes, settling in and developing a trusting relationship with neighbors in the family barracks was difficult. Several cubicle trades were negotiated to ease different family strains. As mothers began to adjust their lives to routines such as hanging laundry, finding ways to clean their living quarters, and ridding the sleeping areas of six-legged "critters," life in the family barracks underwent a gradual but noticeable coming together.

Innovative ideas relieved much of the tension and many of the problems in our quarters. The talented men in the workshop fashioned empty gasoline cans left by the constabulary into buckets, complete with wooden handles. Because water was scarce at the outset of internment at Camp Holmes, showers were not permitted and "bucket baths" were the rule. For the women, this could be a humiliating experience, particularly when Japanese guards chose to "protect" them during their baths. On rainy days, the buckets were left out of doors to catch "God's juice." When rationing of water became necessary, bathing rights—deemed less vital than drinking needs—might stop for days.

Kerosene and various powders, the most effective substances for exterminating bedbugs and cockroaches, were unattainable, but an English woman accidentally discovered that boiling water, trickled over the cracks in the floor, worked as well as chemical bug killers. One mother, whose children bordered my mat, chose not to use bug deterrents of any variety and appeared unaffected by the insects. Thankfully, their bugs did not interrupt my dreams, either.

The innovative restoration of "unusable" items became a way of life. Nothing was wasted. When a couple of damaged woodstoves were discovered in one of the deserted buildings, camp handymen Ream and Rice restored them to usable condition. After some mending, other stoves found on the grounds were installed behind barracks Number Two for common use.

Once we settled into a routine, with the grounds cleaned and a meal-time schedule in place, all of us, children included, attended to our assigned chores. Initially, we assumed the same tasks we held at Camp Hay.

An Escape Brings Torture

We were barely settled in Camp Holmes and feeling better about our quarters and our neighbors, when word passed around camp that one of the Chinese men, Mr. Leung Soon, had scaled the fence and escaped. The guard corps' relaxed mood quickly turned dour. Leung, apparently confused, was discovered soon after his disappearance innocently walking along the Bontoc Trail toward Baguio.

What followed was yet another reminder of the threats made during our surrender at Brent. The man who had leveled those threats, in fact, was standing by the door of the guardhouse, looking like the conductor of a symphony. But, in this instance, Mukaibo was orchestrating the torture of Mr. Leung Soon.

As news of Leung's capture and return to camp spread, groups of adult internees were ordered out of the barracks to observe his punishment. I stood next to Carroll Dickey at the far side of the parade grounds. Together we watched two guards rope Leung to a large tree facing the barracks. What followed was painful to watch. Guards took turns whacking him with sticks. One even used a nightstick. Another tossed water over him. Leung's early sounds of pain gradually slowed, and minutes later, his upper body slumped against the rope. They poured water over him again and forcefully straightened his body. The beatings did not stop. All the while, Nakamura stood by Mukaibo in the doorway. The open display of torture seemed aimed at sending a message to the Americans rather than a necessary punishment of a confused Chinese man. When Leung fell forward a second time, the guards untied him and dragged his limp body past Mukaibo and into the guardhouse.

I fought back tears, thinking him dead. Mr. Dickey thought the same. For the rest of the day, a silence settled over all the barracks. No one saw or heard anything further about Leung. Then, in the late afternoon of the next day, I noticed several Chinese men help Leung walk across the parade ground toward the Chinese barracks. It was a happy sight. A few days later, the entire contingent of Chinese prisoners at Camp Holmes was suddenly released into Baguio. Living arrangements in the three barracks were immediately altered to relieve crowded conditions.

Only days after the Chinese departure, a completely new and enlarged group of Japanese faces appeared among the guard corps. They were everywhere—the barracks, the grounds, and the guardhouse. Initially, I found them more formal and less verbal than the guards first assigned to Holmes. When a new commandant was announced a few weeks later, I wondered if the torture incident had precipitated the change of leadership.

Where to Bunk?

My reaction to placement in quarters with the women and children was an unhappy one. I had been far more comfortable in the men's barracks at Camp Hay and wished for a like arrangement in Holmes. Mom was not of the same mind and said, "No."

I found the women and children's barracks at Holmes noisy and uncomfortable. And although Mom sensed my discomfort, she explained that she was apprehensive of my living with "unpredictable men" without Uncle B as my bunkmate. (He remained under house arrest in Baguio.) Mom also reminded me that I could move freely between the family barracks and the men's quarters during the day as I had at Camp Hay.

While I knew that she was aware of the evening poker games and the frequent use of foul language in the barracks, those routine events clearly were not her main concern. I think Mom was being protective of my physical safety, even though I had not told her what happened at my bunk two nights prior to our departure from Camp Hay. However, I suspected that Don Zimmerman had informed Mom of that episode, triggering her decision to keep me under her watchful eye.

The Hay incident occurred after lights out in the men's barracks. A former missionary and professor at Silliman University, known well by my parents, and quartered in another section of the barracks, walked over to my bunk. He lifted the mosquito net and patted me on the shoulder saying, "You looked unhappy today, so I thought I'd pat your back a little to make you feel better." (Wezer had mentioned this same person as someone who had made some suggestive remarks to her. She said he was "spooky" and had told Mom about him. Uncle B had spoken cautiously of him on a number of occasions as well, but simply suggested that I not get too friendly with him.)

So, I felt very much ill at ease, particularly when his hand strayed lower than my back. I was sufficiently naïve not to fully understand his sudden and cozy advances, but old enough to know that I did not like it. The only escape that came to my mind at that moment was to say loudly, "I've got to go to the privy." I got up and quickly walked in the dark down the nearby stairway to the toilet. A Japanese guard happened to be standing by the entry to the bathroom smoking a cigarette. He must have read something on my face because after my feigned pee, he escorted me with his flashlight back to my bunk. The lingering presence of the guard in that vicinity must have discouraged a repeated visitation.

A couple of missionary men who bunked close by mentioned the incident to me in the morning. One said, "We watched your return with the guard. It was good that he accompanied you. If you are ever sick or need something at night, know that we are here." His words were reassuring. Later, Mom admitted to me that she had been alerted to the incident and that was the reason she denied my pleas to stay in the men's barracks.

While I felt lonely in the Hay barracks at times, especially after Uncle B's release in late January, quarters with the men still afforded me opportunities in the evening to play fish or wrestle on the floor with other boys my age. Even better, I enjoyed listening to the men's evening gossip about rumors, camp rules, the Japanese, lousy poker or bridge hands, anticipated deprivations, and best of all, hearing them wager on the number of days, weeks, months, or years before repatriation. When a date passed, proving someone's prediction to be wrong, the other men were inclined to share a big laugh and find fault with the loser's judgment. That kind of easy give-and-take simply did not happen in the family barracks at Holmes.

Evening encounters with girls my age or older were disconcerting, especially when they were rising or going to bed, showering, and using the toilet facilities. Mom recognized my unhappiness, but regularly insisted that she felt more secure with me in the family circle. I appreciated her concern, but I was not a happy camper. Wezer was sympathetic to my discomfort and frequently accompanied me to the toilet area behind the barracks to be my lookout. The worst time of day was bedtime when many of the young girls gathered in the lavatory to brush their teeth, shower, or primp in the mirror.

One night I got up to go to the bathroom and became disoriented in the dark as I returned to my family's cubicle. After "lights out" all the cubicles looked very similar. On that occasion, I settled down on a cot I thought was my own and fell asleep. At dawn, Mrs. Gowen tapped me on the shoulder and said, "You're on Ann's bunk." Ann was her daughter and my age. Thankfully, Ann was sound asleep and unaware of my presence on her cot. Nevertheless, I was so mortified I avoided encounters with Ann for the duration of my stay in the family barracks. In fact, I had difficulty facing her even after my move to the men's barracks months later.

Missionaries vs. Miners Baseball

The distinguishing feature of Holmes, unlike Camp Hay, was that we had space to move and could see the wider world beyond the fences. The open parade ground in front of the three barracks was unquestionably the centerpiece of the entire camp. That openness was quickly noticed by a group of men who had grown up playing baseball, mostly in American sandlots or in high school. Not long after we settled into our quarters and fell into the daily regimen of roll call, work assignments, and evening poker or bridge games, some of the more ardent baseball lovers asked who would like to play ball on Sunday afternoons. I quickly raised my hand.

Those afternoons began with "spring training"—practice throwing, batting, and fielding a ball. Almost all of us played gloveless, and our spongy, lopsided ball was more like a small softball than a hardball. I learned from Richie Green that our looting forays in one of the Camp Hay officer's quarters had produced the ball supply.

We formed teams called "Miners," "Missionaries," and "Schoolers." When the Miners showed up shorthanded, a Missionary or Schooler substituted, so the games were not taken too seriously. The Schooler team was made up mostly of high school boys. My steady presence around the playing field made me a fill-in right fielder for any team in need. The games were competitive, but unleashed more chuckles than hard sliding. I loved to play and became good enough to be asked to play regularly at assorted positions. I could catch fly balls and field grounders rather routinely, skills which earned me lots of play time. My dad first exposed me to the game as a youngster, playing catch in Davao. I wished daily that he were at Holmes to show off his skills as a catcher and slugger.

We even had a looted catcher's mask in our equipment stash. Sadly, it was mangled in a Miner-Missionary game when a Miner's hard slide demolished the flimsy wire protector. One of the shop men, using the mask's frame, constructed a new facing, which held up for the duration of our playing days. Two Japanese guards, who regularly observed our games, one day signaled that they wanted to play. A couple of weeks later, likely after some private practice sessions behind the guardhouse, the two offered to play as substitutes. They played well. All of us enjoyed their accented renditions of "Nice catch!" (naiso kacho) when a teammate did just that. The two guards became very fond of the game, and I am certain that if either of them survived the war, they likely helped introduce "besu boru" to Japanese children.

During recess from our camp school, I played on the field with my classmates and younger kids, including girls. Kim Kneebone and Rae stood out for their athletic talent, both were capable of throwing with accuracy and speed. One time, my follow-through swing of the bat made more contact with Kim's forehead than with the ball. She required a couple of stitches, but bravely returned to her infield position for our next game.

The early days in Camp Holmes removed the word fear from my life, at least for a while. When in our midst on the parade ground, a guard would occasionally retrieve a loose ball and throw it back to me. At times, the guards even smiled. Their more relaxed manner while observing our play lessened my anxieties and apprehensions about uniformed enemy soldiers.

In the long history of concentration camps, I cannot imagine one that could lay claim to a better location than Camp Holmes. Its expansive space certainly offered opportunities to run and play. The natural beauty of the area had once attracted many foreigners to the central Luzon area. Cool breezes made the climate near idyllic. Only the late summer rains and annual typhoons dampened the sunglasses of the Japanese guards and our spirits.

While our early weeks at Holmes were an improvement over what I knew at Hay, my hopes for freedom took a big tumble when we learned in May that America's forces in Corregidor had surrendered. That crushing news sent a clear message that we would be interned for a long time. There were no longer any American armed forces in the Philippines.

Angels from Sagada

Due north of Baguio sat the village of Sagada, a center of operations for a small number of missionaries led by Father Clifford Nobes. A contingent of Filipino guerillas based in the Bontoc region served as a deterrent to a Japanese attack upon the mission. Nobes was well aware that if the Japanese advanced into the area, the mission could be caught in a dangerous crossfire.

The Sagada missionary group was composed largely of Anglican missionaries, many with ties to Britain. Japanese officers had been very aware of a Western presence in Sagada since their takeover of Luzon. Armed convoys, in fact, had passed by the mission on a number of their incursions into guerilla hideouts north of Bontoc. None of the Anglican assembly had joined the Americans and British who surrendered in Baguio. Fearing the guerillas' strength in the region, the Japanese made no early attempts to intern the Sagada missionaries. Conducting a raid at that time would have been risky.

But in mid-June of 1942, Nakamura was ordered to bring all the foreign missionaries from Bontoc and Sagada to Camp Holmes. In Bontoc, a corps of Japanese soldiers led by Nakamura forcibly took Father Nobes into custody. Then, using him as a hostage, they sent notice to the scattered missionaries in Sagada—almost all of them nuns—to voluntarily and promptly report to Bontoc, or "prepare for the burial of Nobes." The Sagada contingent was given one day to report. They immediately put their belongings together and began the twelve-mile hike over a tortuous trail, assisted by a large number of Filipino *cargadores* (carriers). It was not an easy trek for the sisters. When all were gathered in Bontoc, Nakamura told them they would be trucked to Baguio immediately. Included in the group to be interned were a few nuns whose European home countries were not involved in the war with Japan.

That fact prompted a diminutive American missionary woman, brought up in Japan and named Nellie McKim, to step forward. Possessing a mildly protruding chin, her hair pulled back and covered with a small white cap, she boldly told Nakamura in fluent Japanese, "You cannot imprison those ladies." Nellie's mission board had ordered her to the Philippines at a time when Japan appeared to be moving toward a wider war. Her courageous and challenging response to Nakamura's order that *all* were to be trucked to Baguio startled him. In his home country, it was not customary for a woman to challenge a man, especially a military officer, in such a direct way. Nellie went on to explain to him that imprisoning foreigners with no ties to the war was against international law. She added that if he insisted in doing so, his superiors would probably return the sisters to Bontoc, thus causing him embarrassment, and likely, demotion.

Nakamura backed off, accepting her reasoning, but he refused her plea to reconsider the imprisonment of the American nuns. To protect himself from possible repercussions, Nakamura chose to wait for an official response from Manila relative to the internment of European nuns. For more than a week, the entire colony of Anglicans, therefore, was confined to Bontoc. Japanese officials in Manila upheld Nellie's argument, and only the American sisters were trucked to Holmes. Nellie's direct and fearless manner of speaking—sometimes even sporting a respectful smile as she spoke—worked wonders.

Prior to the war, Uncle B had driven Mom to Sagada to witness the Anglican mission program. There she had met its highly respected leader, Father Vincent Gowen. One of Mom's fondest memories of the Sagada visit was the fascinating image of a cluster of pristine nuns in a very primitive setting, going about in their dark habits and wide-brimmed headpieces.

The sisters' arrival at Holmes immediately caught my eye and everyone else's. I had never before seen people dressed in such garb. The general committee assigned the sisters to three very small tin-roofed huts at the foot of the embankment between the women's barracks and the Nancetorium. Their quarters came to be known as the Nunnery. The sisters felt humbled to be granted such privacy. The huts afforded them their accustomed lifestyle and a location where group meditation, private prayer, and liturgical music could be freely practiced without imposing upon others.

My first interaction with the sisters came a few days after their arrival, as Rae and I walked from the hospital to the parade grounds. Hearing voices, we stopped to listen to a group of them singing on the embankment north of barracks Number One. I was very taken by their rhythmic chants. When the sisters had finished singing, they walked over to us and asked our names. Obediently, we responded. One of the nuns joked, "We'll make it easy for you. You can call each of us Sister." They remembered our names and warmly visited with us throughout internment. That short encounter broke down any timidity I might have felt in their presence. In fact, I relished opportunities to chat with them.

When passing by their huts, I occasionally sat down on a nearby stump and listened to the lilting sounds of their musical chanting. The music was fascinating. Occasionally, Rae joined me on the stump, our front-row seat for the best-kept secret musical program in camp. During one of those "performances," a woman in the adjacent barracks reported to Mom that she had seen me "spying" on the nuns, but Mom knew of our occasional meanderings to the Nunnery. When walking was less painful for her, she joined Rae and me at the stump to listen to the nuns' chanting. Mom had come to know Sister Augusta Mary, who had once reminded me, "a smile will bring joy to your life," in a knitting group. Mom asked her if my presence outside her cottage was disruptive to their worship. Sister Augusta responded with a chuckle, "We include Curt and the other children in our prayers and wish more would attend."

The nuns' presence in camp offered a quiet example of calm and humility. They immediately and unselfishly pitched in to help with kitchen work. Later, they contributed food sent to them by Filipina sisters in Baguio to supplement kitchen supplies. These gifts significantly augmented our camp diet for some time. Having been spared the indignity of the well-remembered Nagatomi theft at Camp Hay, the Sagada sisters had come to Camp Holmes with some cash. From their holdings they generously and regularly contributed to purchases of milk for the camp's infants. Their monetary assistance, in fact, came at a pivotal time for many babies in need of milk, and the mothers praised their generosity. Indeed, it preserved the health, and perhaps even the lives, of some infants. One of those who benefited was Sarah Mather, the first child born in Camp Holmes. Ever after, Mom referred to the sisters as the "angels from heaven."

By late summer, the nuns had become quite active in the camp community. They taught the children, mostly girls, how to do creative things like knitting and crocheting. Katie Ream Sobeck, in her unpublished jottings titled "What Did the Children Do?" credited the sisters with having taught a group of girls to knit socks. "To this day," wrote Katie, "I can knit a sock without a pattern." Her creative dad, Fabian Ream, assisted the nuns in their efforts by fashioning knitting needles for the girls from bamboo and umbrella ribs.

Another Taste of Schooling

Once we had settled into the routine of prison life in Trinidad, approval came from Nakamura to restart school. Parents and the general committee organized a school program. All children old enough for first grade and higher began classes a week later. Volunteer teachers were plentiful, but schoolbooks remained scarce. Miraculously, more books appeared after the announcement that schooling would begin. Most were leftovers from the stash procured from vacated Camp Hay officers' homes by the wood crew that somehow found their way into the cubicles of individual internees.

Reading opportunities were limited. In a few cases, high schoolers had to pass books among themselves to complete their reading assignments. Wezer missed out on many assignments because her name was last on the alphabetical list for readings. With so many children in camp and no structure large enough to accommodate all grades, different huts on the grounds became classrooms.

Wezer particularly extolled Father Gowen's teaching skills. She claims to have heard the funniest stories and learned the most in his classes. Several of the nuns and Father Nobes—all former teachers at the Sagada mission—were also marvelous instructors.

But frequent class interruptions made teaching difficult. There were the intermittent school closures ordered by Nakamura, teacher illnesses, and intrusions by Japanese guards. All were bothersome and slowed the learning process. Still, I have enormous admiration for our intelligent and caring instructors who employed every imaginable resource, including their own life experiences, to teach us. I looked forward to every class day. Classes were small, and the gifts of learning shared with us by our treasure trove of imaginative and motivated teachers were enormous.

Cordelia Job, known as being very strict by her former students at Brent School, was one of several instructors I had in Camp Holmes. She was an exceptionally fine teacher, who without the use of a single geography book, taught me the whereabouts, shape, population, capitals, and primary resources of all forty-eight states (e.g., Iowa—corn, Florida—oranges, Mississippi—cotton, Kansas—wheat). Regrettably, I learned little mathematics beyond addition and subtraction. Math books were hard to find and figures did not appeal to me, so I showed little aptitude for the discipline.

One of my more memorable experiences with Miss Job began as I played with friends on the mesa one Sunday afternoon. Miss Job was walking down the narrow road of the parade grounds toward the women's barracks. In a showoff moment, and thinking that I would not be recognized from afar, I shouted, "Hi, Cordie!" I quickly ducked behind a dune, but my voice carried. She glanced in my direction and then continued on her way. Immediately, I was chagrined and feared that she had recognized my voice. After I returned to our cubicle, Mom greeted me with a sound scolding. She ordered me to find Miss Job and apologize. Terrified and filled with remorse, I approached her the next morning before classes. Knowing her stern reputation, I feared the worst. Near tears, I murmured my apology. Ms. Job stared down at me and listened attentively to my words. Then, much to my surprise and relief, she gathered me into a warm embrace and said, "Put that one aside young man. I know you meant no harm."

Working in tandem with Helen Angeny, also a teacher of art, Mom began drawing lessons with children ranging from elementary level through junior high school. She joked with me that art was the only "A" I received in Holmes. In fact, I do not recall ever receiving a formal report card, although some informal progress reports were passed on to parents. I certainly appreciated Mom's counsel on sketching and the importance of "filling the page" with whatever one might be drawing. The lack of paper was a serious problem in all classes. Most of the paper we used was in small sheets and came from internees who had written only on one side. In fact, sheets of paper used for any class were normally cut into halves or quarters before being handed out.

Nora Ream was one of three teens who graduated from high school in Camp Holmes. Her father, Fabian Ream, created a memorable ball-and-chain "bracelet" to go around each scrolled diploma in the camp workshop. Katie described that ornament as follows: "The ball was shaped fossil rock with a hole drilled through it to secure the chain. The chains were made from silver marksmanship medals found when we first arrived on the site. The chains were attached to silver ten-cent pieces, hammered flat and etched with the date." Masterfully crafted, these mementos far outshone the diplomas presented at my postwar high school graduation. Although formal awards were not handed out to what was the only graduating class of "Camp Holmes High School," rumor had it that Nora was the valedictorian.

Food from the Outside

Initially, after our move to Camp Holmes, the constant pangs of hunger I had known at Camp Hay were far less noticeable. A mellowing Nakamura had approved the delivery of food parcels to internees with Baguio contacts. Most of those contacts were Filipino servants. Although the increased food supply was only slight, it added nutrition to our diet and lifted our spirits.

Unlike many of our friends, my family had no local resources or alliances, other than Uncle B. Still under house arrest in Baguio, Uncle B managed to regularly send bags of food into camp, but he was allowed to send only one small bag at a time. He provided for other prewar Baguio friends, as well, so our food supplements were meager compared to families whose former servants regularly forwarded food to them alone. I certainly envied those who could eat a banana before bedtime each night. But there was some sharing of food; friends like Natalie Crouter generously gave us tidbits as treats during our evening gatherings.

As food resources dwindled with trips into Baguio becoming irregular and food availability considerably lessened, the general committee devised a plan whereby everyone became recipients of food from the outside. Nakamura had agreed to let Chef Kaluzhny and Ray Hale make trips to the Baguio market, and now, gift bags from Filipinos were to be deposited at a designated site in Baguio instead of being delivered to the camp gate. Kaluzhny and Hale picked up the marked bags and brought them to camp. They also purchased food at the market for general camp consumption. Although weight loss continued throughout internment, particularly among adults, Dr. Welles recorded that the rate of loss in Holmes was less than what we had experienced at Camp Hay.

For many adults, facing any morning without coffee was a struggle, but by midsummer 1942, coffee joined the long list of shortages in the Baguio area. Tempers grew edgy. Although coffee is not a food that sustains life, in Mom's world, coffee was a psychological crutch. She would have cheerfully traded her pair of earrings for a can of Maxwell House.

The availability of only small portions of local coffee beans forced Chef Alex and his staff to make a difficult decision. They could provide good coffee just once a week, or make it stretch by reusing the grounds a second and third day. Chef Alex decided to try the watered down plan for a week, so Saturday's coffee was the real stuff. Subsequent days were the number two or number three infusions. By Monday the coffee was widely recognized as little more than darkened hot water, yet the addicted never missed an opportunity to drink it. Alex's poll showed that the popular choice was to reuse the grounds until all the color was lost. This "submarine coffee" became a staple for the duration of our internment. One of the women, during a Saturday evening program, joked, "If I live to have another child, I'm going to name it Submarine or Submarina." When I had the opportunity after the war to ask Alex how the term "submarine" entered the coffee lexicon, he explained that the word was used to describe anything that was less than par. Alex reminded me, "For several months, even submarine goat's milk was a menu item for the infants."

Early summer days introduced a particularly topsy-turvy period in camp life. No sooner was the general committee's plan for supplementing food supplies in place than Nakamura released a few of the aged internees to their Baguio homes. Their release made sense. It afforded slightly more cubicle space in the barracks and provided more food bags for us in camp. I did miss Ma Widdoes' warm and vibrant presence at the nightly gatherings. She always called me "sweetheart," and my feelings toward her were the same. The wider living spaces soon shrank again as more prisoners from the hills were brought into camp. And for no apparent reason, Ma and Pa Widdoes and others were returned to Camp Holmes soon afterward, reducing our living space even more.

On her twelfth wedding anniversary, June 21, 1942, Mom completed her kitchen chores, sifting weevils and stones out of the rice, in the late morning. She strolled to a spot on the knoll overlooking Holmes and the faraway Lingayen Gulf. There, alone, she rested on the grass and lapsed into meditative thoughts of her beloved husband. As she often liked to do, Mom wrote a poetic note to Dad. She had no notion of his whereabouts or even if he was alive, but writing always filled her heart with hope. These notes of hers were never sent, but many of her scribbled messages survived the war. She passed them on to me during the latter days of her life—some fifty years later. The closing section of the anniversary poem to Dad read:

> To you my dear my heart goes out
> Reaching you where—I am in doubt.
> I'd like you to know the joy you've given
> Happiness that's been allied to Heaven.
> May years be added to both our lives
> And through hardships of war, we will survive
> To take up our home in a land of peace
> Where joy will abound and love will increase.

A Move to Manila?

Very few days passed following our move from Camp Hay to Camp Holmes that did not include conversations about guerillas. Mom referred to these as "guerilla talk."

In the hills overlooking Camp Holmes, periodic sightings of Filipinos by the wood crew often triggered evening card-table chatter about the guerillas. But more than any internee, it was Commandant Nakamura who talked most with the general committee about guerilla activities.

Ordered to Sagada in June to bring the entire contingent of Anglican missionaries and Maryknoll nuns to Camp Holmes, Nakamura returned with stronger fears of the guerilla threat. "They're all over the place," he told Dr. Nance and the committee. Nakamura suggested that he would look into the possibility of moving the entire camp to Manila.

Nance soon realized that Nakamura was obsessed to the point of fearing for his own life should guerillas attack Holmes. Nance tried in vain to convince Nakamura that guerillas would not attempt a raid on Holmes while Americans were interned there. He found it difficult to persuade Nakamura that a move to Manila was not in his—or anyone else's—best interest.

At Nance's urging, Nellie McKim was drawn into the guerilla talk with Nakamura. She was the lone internee whose fluent Japanese allowed detailed discussions with the camp commandant. Nellie responded in the positive to Nance and promptly arranged a meeting with Nakamura in the guardhouse.

She began by thanking him for safely delivering the Sagada missionaries to Holmes. Nakamura offered her some *sake*. He was attentive to her cordial manner and thoughts about the city of Manila, an area about which he knew little. Nellie spoke of Manila as a year-round oven and a future danger zone when the Americans regrouped to retake the Philippines. She also pointed out the ways of the guerilla groups she knew in the mountains around her former residence in Sagada. "They are more spies than fighters," she assured Nakamura. He seemed responsive. Feeling that Nakamura understood her leanings against a move to Manila, she bid him farewell.

That evening, Nellie shared the details of her conversation with Mom. Throughout our camp experience, Nellie McKim stood tall as a spokesperson for justice and was credited for having saved many POWs from hostile treatment by our Japanese captors.

Mom showed signs of advanced beriberi after less than seven months of imprisonment, and Manila was the least preferred prison option for our family. But had she known that Dad was in Manila's Santo Tomas, that of course would have been her choice. Baguio was certainly far better in terms of temperature, opportunities for exercise, and the availability of medicines as well as a highly skilled medical staff. This latter asset also benefited the Japanese garrison and was one of the key factors in slowing Nakamura's push for the move.

A real general committee concern—in addition to the unbearable heat that often blanketed southern Luzon—was the issue of living space in Camp Santo Tomas, which was severely overpopulated, having been the receiving camp for many south island missionaries and business people. Santo Tomas certainly did not need an influx of Baguio internees. Further, the additional bodies would strain the already inadequate number of physicians serving the camp. For quite some time after his talk with Nellie McKim, Nakamura did not raise the topic of guerillas or talk of a move. The subject also died away in the barracks. The committee, therefore, thought a transfer to Manila to be a dead issue.

Ray Hale was the designated truck driver from the outset of our prison life. He had been a long-term resident of Baguio and was married to a Filipina. Hale liked to brag that he "knew every pothole in the roads from Bontoc to Batangas." His first ventures in the truck, always under Japanese guard, had taken him to the Baguio markets for food. Later, he made a couple of trips to Manila to trade lumber for barbed wire.

On his most recent return to Holmes from Manila, Hale's tales of the benefits of internee life in Camp Santo Tomas excited a considerable number of married couples. He described the camp's self-governance plan, opportunities for families to live together, regular schooling for children, and the liberty to purchase food, books, and other materials outside the camp. Hale's accounts triggered a growing number of requests that the committee investigate a possible move to Manila. After several meetings, however, the committee rejected the idea and the rumors dissipated. Further discussion of the topic ceased for months.

Only when we learned that Santo Tomas—but not Holmes—had received Red Cross packages for Christmas 1942, did the topic of a move raise its ugly head again. The committee tried to quiet the dissatisfaction by reminding the camp community that any move would only come at the pleasure of General Kou Shiyoku in Manila.

Feeding the Wood Crew

The task of delivering rice or soup to the internee woodcutters on the mountain each day was the responsibility of several of us youngsters. John Ream, Fred Crouter, Ward Graham, and I were regular rice-pot porters. A number of teens, too, carried rice when their class times did not conflict with duty hours. The older boys sometimes were called upon to "pitch in" and assist in moving logs or helping in other ways.

One morning, a Japanese guard accompanying me up the path to the woodcutting site very unexpectedly ordered me to stop. Then, in sign language, he ordered me to strip down bare. He checked the pocket of my shorts and felt under the straps of my *bakyas* (wooden clogs). Recalling my bedtime encounter at Camp Hay, I initially was frightened. But, the soldier apparently was doing what he had been told to do. Within minutes—with my shorts and *bakyas* back on—we matter-of-factly continued our climb up the slope.

I guessed that he had been looking for a message to Filipinos. I had seen Filipinos often—usually young Igorot boys—walking on the path not far from the wood crew work area. Attending guards must have seen them also, although I never saw a guard try to intercept one. The boys' nonchalant manner suggested that they were not on a mission, but merely walking from one barrio to another. They never appeared to pay attention to the wood crew's activities or to the sitting guard, but their eyes could be deceiving.

I shared my stripping experience with a member of the wood crew that evening. He advised me that, if in the future I was ordered to do the same, I should simply turn my pockets inside out. The next day, the woodcutter raised the topic with committee chair, Dr. Nance. He, in turn, broached the issue with Nakamura. Nance was told that the guard had been ordered to search me, not that he expected to find a note, but to send a message to all of us who transported items up the hill not to interact with Filipinos. Nance was also told that the wood crew must not pass communications— in any way—to any Filipinos, men or children. That order spread throughout Holmes. I felt better about the incident knowing that I had not been singled out for a frisking. Yet I heard of no similar incident occurring to anyone else in camp or on the trail.

Two months passed and guerilla talk subsided. The women were granted permission to take short hikes on the hill behind the mesa. On their first walk there, Mom and Natalie Crouter came upon an Igorot boy. In her book *Forbidden Diary,* Natalie reported that they actually talked with the boy who told them "he was to see one of our men up there."

Over the course of my many treks to the woodcutting site, I noticed that guard duty on the hill was more a time for the Japanese to relax or take a snooze than to be alert to passing Igorot boys. While guards rested, I would on occasion traipse from the site to places in the vicinity where I might find a wild orchid for Mom.

The easiest and quickest path to where orchids grew was a southwestern trail to a site about a half mile away, which was occasionally frequented by young Igorots. The trail ended in a sudden drop-off. From there I could easily see downtown Baguio. Branching off the trail was a far less traveled path. It passed a huge rock formation, around the side of which I discovered a cavern. It was not deep, but sufficiently so that when I followed a slight curve in the cave, all light from the outside was obscured. There I would lean against the cool rock wall and listen to the bats signal their unhappiness with my intrusion.

As long as I was visible in the area of the woodcutting site before the day's labors ended, the relaxed guards showed little concern about my meanderings, especially when I walked in the direction of the steep drop-offs. At the designated departure time, I rejoined the crew and walked down the hill with them. Some days, I would return the empty pots to the kitchen immediately after the crew had eaten. On those occasions, I would signal my departure to the duty guard with a courteous bow and a *sayonara*.

One of the crew's guards was a Formosan—thousands of Formosans (Taiwanese) had been conscripted into the Japanese Army prior to the war. He was younger, had a more cordial countenance than any of the other guards, and enjoyed observing the wood crew's antics. He always waved with a relaxed salute and softly uttered a good-bye in Chinese, "Zai jian!" as I left with the empty pots. This guard freely used Chinese expressions if there were no Japanese in the vicinity. He never bowed to the work crews nor did he expect the same in return. One day, as I was about to take the pot back to the kitchen, he told me that his name was Wan Ju. When I told him that mine was Tong, he grinned and pointed to the empty container as if asking for its English name. Pointing to it, I responded with the word "pot." He shook his head and placed his finger inside the pot, repeating my name, "Tong." His gesture somehow prompted me to say "soup." Excitedly, he pointed his finger at me and exclaimed, "You soup!" That afternoon, I told Mr. Flory, a former CLS student, the soup story. He smiled. "Soup is "tong" in Chinese. So, you must be Mr. Soup." Regrettably, the Formosan was soon reassigned to other duty.

A Chameleon Commandant Rules

In midsummer of 1942, the Japanese command at Camp Holmes officially changed from Nakamura to Hayakawa Masago. Nakamura remained in the background at Holmes for a short period. Toward the end of his tenure as commandant, Nakamura had made gestures of goodwill toward internees and cooperated more with the general committee, a noted change from the early days of harsh words, painful decisions, denial of liberties, reduced food allowances, and refusal of outside hospital care. Occasionally, he even greeted me as I passed by the guardhouse with pots of soup for the wood crew.

Examples of Nakamura's softening manner included the resumption of schooling for children, evening entertainment (lectures, skits, dances, and plays), a relaxation of family commingling time, and permission to hold worship services. Never, though, did Nakamura allow the use of American history books in school.

In contrast to the experienced Nakamura, Hayakawa was a younger man. From all appearances, he was less than thirty years old and may have been assigned to Camp Holmes because of his modest ability to speak English. During his early days as commandant, Hayakawa made himself quite visible to the internees. Such had not been the case with Nakamura. Hayakawa was relaxed with the children, but less so with adults. I played catch with him one day as he crossed the parade ground. After that, he spoke to me warmly, even called me by name, "Cort."

With adults Hayakawa was less talkative. He particularly dodged Nellie because of her aggressive retorts to him in Japanese. Mom learned from Nellie that Hayakawa had spent many years in the Philippines. His father was a Japanese businessman. Hayakawa clearly was not an army enlistee with a *bushido* (warrior-like) manner. His more tranquil approach affected our interests both positively and negatively. Women were excited by opportunities for wider freedom of movement, including walks up the slope near the cutting site. He allowed more latitude for the general committee to manage camp discipline and administer rules. On the negative side, he did not reach out to feed us as he could have, for he feared it would upset the Japanese higher authorities.

In the autumn of 1942, Hayakawa began to allow religious services on a more regular basis. A few missionaries credited Mukaibo with the decision to allow open worship, since he continued to wear the Christian cross on his uniform lapel. But, we later learned through Nellie McKim that Mukaibo had actually opposed worship in camp.

With services now officially permitted, the general committee appointed Don Zimmerman, a Disciples missionary pastor, to be worship chairperson. As chair, Zimmerman arranged service times for the various denominations. The Protestant denominations agreed to meet as one congregation. Pastors of the Protestant groups (United Brethren, Disciples of Christ, Episcopal, Seventh-Day Adventist, Methodist, etc.) took turns leading worship. I would guess that of all the World War II concentration camps in Europe or Asia, none could boast more interned pastors than Camp Holmes. We were blessed with a collection of highly educated clergy whose intellects extended beyond their religious service.

At first, services were held at various sites. Soon, though, the small grade school across from the women's barracks served as the communal chapel. Representatives of the different faiths developed a coordinated Sunday morning changeover plan. One crucifix served all of the Christian religions. Symbolic parchments special to some groups were easily added to the altar area during holiday services. A couple of the very small faith groups (one or two families) usually held private services in the dining area or on the embankment facing Lingayen Gulf.

I found it interesting that as the length of our imprisonment stretched on over the months and years, church attendance increased markedly. What once was the non-missionary community now took an interest in attending services. Several people admitted to having never before attended a church service. The severe hardships of prison life likely sparked their wish to experience a spiritual journey. Still, for a few, attending church was simply an escape from idleness.

Although initially suspicious that services would open opportunities for arranging clandestine meetings with Filipino guerillas, Hayakawa changed his mind at the urging of McKim, Zimmerman, and Father Gowen. Hayakawa, however, did ban hymn singing and sermons.

Uncle B and Art Richardson returned to Camp Holmes in November of 1942, and they joined the others in convincing Hayakawa, that songs and sermons were not camouflaged rallies in support of the guerillas. Uncle B even invited Hayakawa to attend, but he declined.

Hayakawa made no further objections to religious gatherings, but stipulated only one service each week. "Christian is Christian," he told Nellie McKim. Again, she came to the rescue of the clergy. She explained to Hayakawa that the differences in the symbolism of Christian worship are not unlike the differing sects of Buddhism. Hayakawa accepted Nellie's explanation, and multiple services continued.

As time passed, Hayakawa became more reclusive. In particular he refused to have meetings with Nellie, feeling intimidated in her presence. Often it seemed as though we had no commandant. I saw him less frequently on the parade ground. His most noticeable failing was a lack of assertiveness in procuring food from the outside.

Notices of Japanese successes on the war front, once regularly posted by Hayakawa, had ceased. Many hoped that postings were fewer because Japan's successes were fewer. Mr. Crouter's opinion was that Hayakawa must have known that we were receiving messages in the incoming food packages, likely originating from guerilla radio transmissions. Therefore, "he could not fool us with postings of propagandized war news, and didn't try," Crouter reasoned. In fact, true knowledge of the progress of the war was scant.

Hayakawa seemed to have gradually become a "puppet" commandant, perhaps receiving his orders from military headquarters in Baguio. The guards had become the conveyors of new rules. Little attention was paid to violations of those rules; they were simply ignored. Circumventing the regulations did little to brighten the general mood of hungry prisoners. Smoking in the barracks and stealing food from the dining area—both injurious to fellow internees—became more commonplace.

The general committee addressed the bothersome issue of thefts by assigning Don Zimmerman to be the camp judge. One thief, having admitted to Judge Zimmerman that he had stolen two *camotes* (yams) from the kitchen, was ordered to a one-week confinement in a small single room attached to the men's barracks. The defendant thought it was harsh punishment, but the others applauded the penalty. Two *camotes* would feed several people for a couple of days during that period of meager food supplies. In actuality, the culprit's confinement was reduced to three days because the food delivered to his quarters from the kitchen was getting soaked in the inundating rains of a severe typhoon.

Early in his command, Hayakawa gave permission for evening programs. His approval came at a perfect time. In the tropics, the summer rainy season often means torrential rain and destructive storms. In late summer, rumors of bad news on the war front accompanied the hard daily rains. One might have thought that rain would be a welcome change from the forced labor in the mountains and in the garden patches. But it truly was not. Books were in extremely short supply, there was no radio, and the parade grounds resembled a shallow lake. Children grew restless in the barracks. Card playing interested the men for only a limited number of hours. After days of idleness, Aunt Leora comically described the situation in the single women's barracks as "death by decay." With John Ream and Ward Graham, I found wallowing in the puddles and climbing in the rafters of the "animal shack" a fun and challenging escape from crying children and a change from thumbing through my well-worn book of Longfellow's poems. Over the long rainy season, our threesome was a lonely but adventuresome presence on the parade ground.

The approved Saturday night programs offered a welcome respite to rainy day routines. At first, they featured lectures on a variety of subjects, each requiring Hayakawa's approval. I was all ears listening to Philip Whitmarsh's talk about the wild animals of Africa. It so excited me that I asked my mom if someday we could all go to Africa to see a giraffe. I dreamed of such a journey for months afterward.

Lectures followed with more frequency as persons with expertise or noteworthy stories to tell came forward to offer a presentation. Later, a group of missionary women promoted programs that would lift our spirits with laughter. Over the course of the next year, the programs expanded to include folk music, plays, and skits. Harold Fildey, a gifted pianist, enjoyed introducing internees by devising musical flourishes that fit their individual personalities. His innovative introductions always brought down the house. He was a natural comic.

One of my favorite Fildey "funnies" centered on his poetic talents and a song he composed describing a colleague's midnight "potty can call." I have forgotten the exact words of the poem, but not the roar of laughter that followed. It started with:

Tinkle, tinkle in the can
'Cause he's such a lazy man.
How I wish the guards would ban
Midnight sounds in the tinkle can.

The high school–aged young people found planning and practicing for productions a wholesome and enjoyable outlet. Wezer recalls that her introductions to popular songs like "Peg O' My Heart," "If You Knew Susie," and "Five Foot Two, Eyes of Blue" occurred during those evening shows. In prewar Davao, our family had never heard popular American music. So exposure to those tunes gave my sister great joy and naturally led to her teenage singing, and dancing. Whether as a performance or an activity, however, dancing required permission from Hayakawa. His regular approvals were a huge bonus in the teenagers' lives. Those events were the first opportunities they had to experience the healthy social interactions that naturally occur between sexes.

As a ten-year-old, I was less inclined to partake in that kind of activity, especially the dancing. Still, I was ever curious and enjoyed watching my teenaged friends. After observing one evening of music and dancing, I reported to Mom that my attractive sister, Wezer—with braids tied on top of her head—was getting her shoulder tapped more than the others were. Truly, she was a popular girl, not only among the boys her age, but with mothers also. They often sought her out to babysit when they were attending lectures or playing bridge.

Although Mom had forbidden me residence in the men's barracks during Uncle B's long absence, I wandered through there freely. I timed my visits to coincide with the men's late afternoon or evening poker games. Watching them and listening to the colorfully worded scuttlebutt about the war in progress was engaging. Rarely did any of their prognostications turn out to be true, but they did add welcome laughter to my life. Merely talking about rumors (or making them up, as Mom noted) meant not paying serious attention to such talk. Still, the tales were very entertaining.

On one of those visits to the men's barracks, however, the talk turned to trash. Most of the profane language was directed toward our enemies, not as captors, but as a culture. In today's world, such remarks would be categorized as racist. But during the hard times in prison, the men's emotional and profane comments and stereotyping of the Japanese were deemed acceptable in the barracks. Examples of their ugly commentary included, "Japanese men rarely become bald because they don't have enough brains to push their hair out," and "Japanese have buck teeth to allow for easier slurping of noodles." When I shared these bits of "knowledge" with Mom, she responded harshly, "I know you don't believe that junk, but now you know another reason why I don't want you living with that tribe."

Over our first months in Holmes, arrivals and departures of internees were commonplace. The earliest and largest group coming into camp, of course, had included the sixteen nuns, almost all Anglican missionaries from the Sagada area. Others, arriving afterward, were Americans who had taken to the hills after the Japanese landed on Luzon. They were captured during Japanese raids on hiding places in the central mountains. Following their capture and internment, we were told that their hideaways, in most cases, had been revealed by Filipino informants responding to bribes or threats of death by the Japanese. Regrettably, a number of their friends who escaped capture, lost their lives to disease or enemy fire.

People discharged from Holmes were elderly missionaries or those stricken with severe illness. They were required to have sponsors in the Baguio area that could provide shelter and funds for their living costs. Mayor Halsema was also eventually released; regrettably, he lost his life when American bombs fell on Baguio days after Christmas 1944.

By late summer of 1942, camp life followed a regular routine. Everyone knew their detail responsibilities, meal times, the best time to use the toilet facilities, the time for roll call, and the like. Except for mothers of young children, the popular plan following the late afternoon meal of rice or soup—or whatever else Chef Alex could put together—was for women to migrate to the dining hall to play bridge or other card games. These activities could be credited to Hayakawa's relaxation of the rules. Soon thereafter, with a sole guard looking on, and at the invitation of camp women, a group of men agreed to join the dining room card games. Most men were easily coaxed to play with the women. Mom was acknowledged as one of the best bridge players and could teach the game in a manner that "made it seem easy," as Joe Smith described her instruction. Later, different card games were introduced that appealed to others. Still, bridge remained the most popular evening activity throughout our internment in Camp Holmes.

Sorrell's Escape

On a damp mid-July morning, Don Zimmerman whispered to me at breakfast that someone had fled camp during the night hours. "Stick with me," he said as we departed to the parade ground for morning roll call. What Don had heard was true. Noah Sy Sorrell had escaped.

I held little affection for Mr. Sorrell. He showed no warmth toward me or my friends in the barracks. His curt manner and seedy beard intimidated younger children like my sister Rae, whom he pushed aside on a couple of occasions to "ditch" into the chow line. Although I was pleased that he was gone, I was nervous about what his escape might mean to my friends on the woodcutting crew. Their labor in the mountain areas and occasional sightings of single Filipinos made them more suspect as collaborators in Sorrell's escape.

I became frightened as we awaited the arrival of Major Mukaibo. His promised payback of death to those in any way tied to an escape kept everyone on edge. Upon Mukaibo's tardy arrival, he verbally confirmed the disappearance of Sy Sorrell, but made no immediate threats. He did command, though, a number of men to search the grounds and buildings and ordered Sorrell's bunkmates to the guardhouse. Chairman Nance also was told to report. The bunkmates were interrogated throughout the morning. Hayakawa, knowing few internees, stood by a soon-to-depart Nakamura. Watchful internee eyes focused on the "torture tree" outside the guardhouse, anticipating the worst.

We later learned that Nance tried to impress upon Mukaibo and Hayakawa that Sorrell was very much a loner with no close ties to anyone in camp. Hayakawa quietly stood by as Mukaibo interrogated the men, trying to seek out an accomplice to Sorrell's escape. Nance refuted every name mentioned to Mukaibo. Hayakawa's inability to finger anyone certainly supported Nance and perhaps saved Sorrell's bunkmates from torture. When word spread through camp that the escape was not going to penalize others, sighs of relief filtered through the men's barracks. This news was especially welcomed by the wood crew. Hayakawa may not have been a hero, but he gained considerable respect for not serving Mukaibo with names.

The saga of Sorrell did not end with his escape. About four months later, the general committee was informed that he had been captured in Pangasinan, a short distance from the Lingayen Gulf. The committee was told that Sorrell had been taken to Baguio and beheaded, leaving a mestizo son and a Filipina (Moro) wife. All were saddened at the news, but few were surprised by his fate. Aunt Leora, who had tragically lost her husband in the defense of Bataan, hoped that no one else would attempt escape because, she said, "The consequences of capture or payback to others are too great." Aunt Leora was ever caring for others.

She, like everyone else, was stunned when, in mid-January 1943, who should saunter into camp but Sy Sorrell. Uncle B, again designated chair of the committee after his return to internment, confronted Sorrell, "Don't even think about another escape. The dangers you bring to those men who would pay the penalty for your greed are too great." The arrogant Sorrell refused to promise obedience. He explained that during his interrogation he was told that the reason he was not killed was because eventually everyone in camp would be shot. Wisely, Uncle B did not pass on that bit of information to anyone, and only shared it years later with internee friends in Dayton, Ohio.

The Blessings of Medical Care

The physicians and equipment at our disposal at Camp Holmes made us more fortunate than the southern Luzon internment camps, Santo Tomas and Los Baños. Our talented group of doctors had come to us quite by happenstance. Several had been missionary doctors assigned to other Asian countries, then ordered to the Philippines by their mission boards to escape the war in China and other Southeast Asian nations.

Our accomplished surgeon, Dr. Nance, directed the Camp Holmes hospital. He was best known for performing several life-saving operations during his tenure in camp. Through Ray Hale, Nance maintained close ties to his colleagues at the Notre Dame Hospital in Baguio. His call could bring medical supplies into Holmes for whatever emergencies arose.

Another valued physician, parasitologist Frank Haughwout, was an interesting character. Small in stature and academic in his manner of speech, he was extremely attentive to anyone in camp suffering from various tropical disorders.

Many internees had suffered severe stomach maladies and felt indebted to Haughwout for guiding them through the agonizing throes of dysentery and dengue fever. Mom was particularly grateful for his expertise. During her most painful episode with a "distraught tummy," as she preferred to describe her pain to me, I conveyed her request for help to Dr. Haughwout. He handed me a note asking her to provide him with a stool sample as soon as possible.

Mom was not able to walk to the hospital, much less carry her specimen can, so she asked me to be the "stool pigeon." Not only did I take that can to the doctor, I also stayed and listened to his explanation of her condition. He led me to his microscope and invited me to look through the lens. What I saw on the slide were many wiggly nematodes. He said, "They are the bad guys who cause dysentery." A number of other specimen cans awaited his inspection, which spoke to the high incidence of dysentery in camp at the time. As I turned to leave, Haughwout said with a smile, "You fly on back. Tell your mom I'll see her tomorrow, and thanks for being a good pigeon."

Holmes was also blessed with a very creative dentist, Dr. Richard Walker. During our days at Camp Hay, his opportunities to practice professional dentistry were extremely limited, there being little dental equipment available. But in his small office in the Nancetorium, he had a chair, a kind of floss, some cleansing fluid, a minimal amount of pink substance, which hardened as a cavity filler—and lots of charm. Wezer was one of his first patients during the late summer of 1942. Unbelievably, she carried her pink filler into adulthood.

Later, Walker secured updated equipment donated to the camp by the Order of Filipina Sisters in Baguio. Oral problems were common in camp. Unfortunately, the scarcity of cavity filler limited Dr. Walker's ability to attend to all dental requests, so many went untreated. Perhaps unfairly, he was severely criticized for saving the best supplies for his friends, leaving others to manage with only temporary fillings.

Fabian Ream created an amazing treatment solution for one of Walker's patients. A woman badly needed a new set of dentures. Ream carved a set of teeth out of *carabao* bone which Walker then fitted onto a metal plate shaped to fit her mouth. This provided functional teeth and a hugely improved smile. She discovered through trial-and-one-error that drinking hot soup with her plate in scorched her gums. Her plate remained a source of general amusement for months.

Prior to Dr. Nance's internment, Dr. Marshall Welles, a missionary physician from China, organized and led early efforts to stem an outbreak of dysentery and diarrhea in camp. The mothers especially appreciated Welles's caring manner with children and depended on his counsel. He was also our highly respected dietician throughout internment. In much the same manner as Welles, Dr. Beulah Ream Allen, Fabian's sister, was an extremely capable diagnostician who gave invaluable advice to mothers. Chalmers Vinson, Brewster Mather, Augustus Skerl, and Lloyd Cunningham rounded out our cadre of very able physicians.

I experienced a number of cuts, bruises, and abrasions in camp, but was fortunate in being one of only two youngsters who escaped serious illnesses. I give much credit for my good health to the medical staff and the adults with whom I interacted. They spoke often and openly of cautionary measures that we all needed to practice to avoid coming down with dysentery. We regularly heard reminders to wash hands often, thoroughly cook whatever food we had, and carefully monitor the food coming into camp.

Contaminated water, of course, was the common cause of dysentery, one of our most debilitating maladies, especially among the adults.

Dr. Dana Nance's tenure as the chair of the general committee did not preclude his directorship of the hospital. His dual roles of leadership, understandably, placed him under constant scrutiny. Nance's medical decisions usually affected lives. Lack of bed space meant that only a few ailing internees could be kept overnight. That raised the controversial question of "who is the most sick?" Those denied a bed often felt hurt. Some chronically ill women, in particular, felt that Nance was less sympathetic to females. It did not help that Nance rudely referred to them as "whiners." Such careless comments resulted in verbal storms in the women's and family barracks. Nance, though, was thick-skinned and paid little attention to his critics. He continued his surgical duties throughout his stay in Camp Holmes.

Mom thought Nance arrogant but competent and supported his leadership of the general committee during Uncle B's absence. She appreciated his influence with the Japanese, whose respect Nance gained because of his willingness to treat their medical problems. When Mom sketched a very popular map of Camp Holmes and labeled the hospital the "Nancetorium," it was a sign of her respect for Nance and his guidance of the camp community. Despite the general impatience with his manner, most internees recognized that his Notre Dame contacts especially were invaluable to medical care at the camp.

When Nance received an abundance of cans containing ether from Notre Dame, he thought of the numerous throat-related problems plaguing children in the camp and posted a notice to parents suggesting that they schedule their children (five to fifteen years old) for tonsillectomies. Mom happily put my sisters and me on the list. A large number of other parents also enrolled their children for the outpatient procedure.

At the time scheduled for the "Tong children" to go to the Nancetorium, my sisters obediently reported, but I was a no-show. Since we were the last on his schedule that day, Nance decided to look for me. He spotted me playing on the mesa and called to me, ordering me to report to the hospital at once. I did not respond. When he tried to grab me, I bolted away from his grasp. He gave chase, but did not catch me. Postwar, I paid for my escape, going through a far more painful, costly, and complicated tonsillectomy. At a Brent School reunion in 1991, an elderly Dr. Nance reminded me of my misbehavior with a smirk and the comment, "You twerp!"

A tribute to his surgical skill came when Dr. Beulah Allen discovered she needed a caesarian to deliver her second child, Henderson, who was named after his father who died in the Cabanatuan military prison without ever meeting his son. Although Dr. Allen had crossed swords with Nance over a number of issues, she chose him to be her surgeon for the caesarian. We all came to realize how vital both Dr. Nance and Dr. Allen had been in keeping us functional. Regrettably, Beulah and her son were transferred to Santo Tomas and Nance to Los Baños in 1943.

Rufus Gray Remembered

No formal announcement about Rufus Gray's death at the hands of the military police in Baguio was ever made to the entire camp community. Internees came to suspect that he had died when he was not returned to camp with the other CLS men. Eventually Hayakawa shared the formal notice of his death with Marian, who had believed that her husband was likely dead after finding the photos missing from their home.

Several days prior to the memorial service planned for Gray, a Southern Baptist missionary, the wood crew held their own special service to honor their friend. Seated on logs, the men arranged themselves in a small circle at the cutting site. After the noontime meal I had carried up the hill, they put aside their coconut shell cups. The men bowed their heads in quietude, and I joined them. From the stump where I sat, I listened to the words shared by the men who had been close to Rufus.

Interestingly, closing thoughts included mention of a huge pine they had cut down that morning. It was not only the largest pine—it had more than eighty rings—but was also the fiftieth tree the crew had felled since their arrival at Holmes. Referring to the fallen tree and Rufus's death, one of the wood crew concluded the simple service by saying, "I think I speak for all of us when I say to these hills and to Marian and Billy, 'We're sorry.' God bless the Grays." His short message was touching. In three months' time, the crew had relieved the forest of fifty huge pine trees, each having taken decades to grow. There were some tears. Apparently sensing the somber nature of the gathering, our guard, like the others, removed his khaki cap. Moments of silence followed and then all quietly returned to their woodcutting assignments.

Days later on August 2, 1942, all of the missionaries who were able, and almost the entire camp family, attended the formal Rufus Gray memorial service held atop the mesa facing Lingayen Gulf. That occasion was my first such memorial service. It was brief, but heart wrenching. I watched Mrs. Gray intently. She stood solemnly and stoically, holding eleven-month-old Billy. Billy showed no emotion, his eyes seemed fixed on the far-off rice paddies. I asked Mom following the service why Mrs. Gray did not cry. She responded, "Marian has had many cries, I'm sure. She's just cried out."

After the service, Mom told me that Hayakawa had visited Marian a week earlier to confirm Mr. Gray's death. His gesture was unlike that of the cowardly Mukaibo, who had claimed no knowledge of Rufus's fate when Marian confronted him during our one-day release to Baguio seven months earlier. Hayakawa, perhaps feeling remorse toward Marian, her son, and the camp community, soon relaxed the rules about walks on the paths leading to the woodcutting area and the mesa. (Uncle B explained to me after the war that Hayakawa had first told Nellie about Rufus's death in private, and she told Marian Gray.)

Through her research efforts after the war, Marian Gray learned that the date of Rufus's death, March 13, 1942, was the only truth Hayakawa had shared with her. The other details of his account, perhaps given unknowingly, that Rufus had died because he refused to eat and that he had died at Baguio General Hospital, were false. Hospital records revealed that Rufus had never been admitted to Baguio General or to Notre Dame. The medical staff at both hospitals, aware that the CLS men had been incarcerated at military police headquarters, claimed his death had been the result of torture.

Moments with Mom

After the Rufus Gray memorial service, Mom began getting chills at night. Feeling better and being up and about the following week, she spotted me carrying my empty rice pot back to the kitchen one very humid afternoon. She waved to me from the front of the women's barracks and I went over to her. Mom asked if I would walk with her the next day to show her the cave I had told her about weeks before. "Sure," I responded, hoping I would be able to retrace my wanderings to the camouflaged spot.

The following morning, after my arithmetic class, I met Mom by Mr. Ream's workshop. We followed the well-worn path to the woodcutting site. Mom seemed more quiet than usual, and I asked if she was all right. She responded, "Rufus and Marian have been much on my mind." I nodded. I guessed that the revelation of Rufus Gray's death had caused her some bad dreams. Then she admitted, "I'm worried about your father."

"Dad will be okay," I said, trying to reassure her. Yet, inside I felt as she did. I too had been dreaming of Dad during those nights following the Gray memorial service.

Changing the subject and coming close to the area I remembered as the cave site, I told her to keep a lookout for a cluster of huge rocks, which would be our landmark for locating the cave. Mom spotted them first and within minutes, we were at the mouth of the cavern. At the sound of our voices, a bat flew out of the cave, prompting her to say she would take a rain check on going inside. But she did peek into the darkness. We sat on a rock ledge near the cave for some time. Again, she spoke of Dad, wondering where he might be and what he might be doing. We talked at some length about him and I noticed that she gradually became more positive about his well-being than she had been earlier.

Soon we headed back toward the woodcutting site and sat on adjacent stumps looking toward the rolling hills and the rice paddies northwest of camp. Wishing to avoid any further talk of her concern for Dad, I smilingly asked Mom if our walk could be considered "commingling." She chuckled and then suggested we play a game from our Davao days called "Rhyme Time." It was a game designed to widen our vocabularies.

In Rhyme Time, one person stated a word and another would answer with a word that rhymed. You take turns until one or the other cannot think of a rhyming word. If a person offers a word, which you doubt is real, you can challenge. If, when challenged, the word cannot be defined, that person earns an unwanted "R." The person tagged with the letter R introduces another word.

Mom started the game with the word "commingle," and I answered with "tingle." Mom followed with "jingle" and I with "single." She paused, and then came up with "dingle," which I challenged. But, when Mom correctly defined "dingle" as a wooded area, I earned my unwanted "R." She then suggested that mingle could be used another time.

The first person to acquire R-H-Y-M-E loses. It is a fun game, not unlike H-O-R-S-E in shooting baskets, but it takes a while to complete. After our first round of the game, Mom said, "I've thought of a poem, using our words. Let's title it 'Commingle'." She pondered for a few moments, and then recited this short jingle, which she memorized and recited to me again many years after the war:

As we walked through the dingle
I was touched with a tingle
'Cause with Curt I could mingle
And create this short jingle.
We are lovers, but single
And so love to commingle.

I enjoyed those rare hours on the quiet mountainside with Mom. In camp we were so close and yet so far from each other. My time alone with Mom was invigorating and reassuring. That evening, with my mini-hymnal in hand, I decided to memorize one of my favorite refrains, "There is a Balm in Gilead," so I could surprise her with a recitation during our next commingle.

A week later, Wezer caught up with me and told me that Mom had become ill following the Sunday church service. She was suffering from stomach pains, maybe diarrhea—that being the disorder of the week around barracks Number Two. Dr. Allen arranged to see Mom that evening. Wezer met me again the next morning and reported that Mom seemed a little better and hoped to be up and about in a couple of days.

Indeed, Mom did get up and out. As I walked out of the school hut, I noticed her ambling slowly toward the mesa overlooking camp and the northwestern vistas. She stopped on the grassy area atop the knoll where a small tree stood like a lonesome sentinel. It was an accessible spot and one she liked to visit on occasions when she sought solitude. Parting from my sisters, I decided to follow her. I found Mom stretched out on the grass looking skyward. I approached her. She turned her head toward me when I asked, "Are you okay, Mom?" She said nothing, only patted the ground. I lay down next to her, and she reached out for my hand. There was a long silence.

Slowly, she turned on her side, looking at me with tears in her eyes and whispered, "I'm sorry." I said nothing. She pulled my head to her chest and ran her fingers through my hair. For what she was sorry, I did not ask. Eyes closed, we remained silent for some time. Gently squeezing my hand, she pointed upward. Soaring slowly over the camp was a Philippine eagle. Eagles were common in the mountains of central Luzon, but I had not seen one since the bombs fell on Camp Hay.

Ever one to interject rhyme into her observations of beauty, Mom described the eagle over flight with a whispered: "That lovely eagle soaring there is telling us both ne'er to despair." She clearly was feeling much better, and so was I. Quietly, we walked back to camp.

As Mom gradually recovered from bouts with sickness, she sought out women to walk with her up the mountain trail in the area where much of the earlier woodcutting had taken place. Although permission for ventures up the mountain was required, it was routinely granted to women. Mom's first such outing was with Wezer and me. We enjoyed it so much that we pledged to do it again. I could tell that it was an invigorating activity for Mom. She thrilled in spotting the wildflowers growing in the more sheltered areas of the woods.

Only on rare occasions was I able to be together with both Wezer and our mother. I noticed how closely my sister watched over Mom's movements. She was a true caregiver. Sometimes it seemed, though, that Wezer's commitment to assisting Mom came at the expense of her time to be a young girl and do things with other girls her age.

On other jaunts up the hill, Mom turned into a tour guide, accompanying a few women who thought such a walk would be challenging and perhaps fun. An element of fear entered the thoughts of some women, however. They were not afraid of encounters with wild animals or sightings of an Igorot boy, but rather a possible assault by a guerilla or an enemy soldier in an isolated area. Those were understandable worries. Such thoughts never crossed Mom's mind, however. She would take short walks alone whenever her health and time away from her duties in the kitchen allowed. As rules became more rigid, though, those outings lessened and eventually ceased.

When a women's committee was organized at the urging of Dr. Allen, Mom was elected to it. The committee's primary function was to arbitrate the entanglements that developed in the two women's barracks. Mom did not warm to the role, but many of the women recognized that her manner encouraged acceptance of the decisions she often had to make. Natalie Crouter singled out Mom's role in her book *The Forbidden Diary:* "Peg stood up for the mothers . . . she has integrity and is democratic. She sifts the vexing questions, settling some quietly . . . many reach her motherly care, and her normal instinctive reaction calms some stories while they are only in the ripple stage. She has a feeling for what is right and fair, a balance which weighs the petty and important equally well."

A Cow Confrontation

One of the more vivid memories of my little sister Rae's internment experience took place in a small clearing on the downward slope of the hill leading back to camp from the woodcutting area. Rae had accompanied me one day to deliver the noontime rice pots, and on our return trip down to camp, she carried the empty pots while I whittled at a piece of wood with Uncle B's treasured knife, crafted by Fabian Ream and lent to me by Uncle B. Rae stopped suddenly, catching my attention. Only yards ahead, a wild cow stared at us from the edge of a clearing. I had seen a few wild cows on the hillside before, usually around small, open grassy areas like the one we were crossing. Previously, they had always ignored me.

This particular cow must have sensed Rae's fear or had a calf nearby. Its stare and lowered head stirred my adrenaline. I told Rae not to run, but to drop the pots and take a couple steps backward. I gave her a quick boost onto a sturdy low limb of a nearby tree. She quickly pulled herself up. I turned to see the cow, not running, but moving directly toward us, head lowered.

I accidentally dropped the knife in the high grass and scampered quickly to a much larger tree a few strides away from my sister. The cow moved directly toward her. Standing on the low branch, Rae reached up to hold a higher bough for balance. The cow picked up its pace, moving toward the branch on which Rae stood. It passed under the branch and headed toward me. I darted behind a large pine tree, only yards away from Rae. The cow drew near and butted the broad trunk behind which I had taken refuge. Peeking around the tree, I saw a second thrust coming and shifted my position slightly.

Suddenly the cow stopped, stared in my direction, and snorted loudly. For minutes she did not move, but only looked downward. I, too, stood motionless. Then Madame Cow slowly turned and ambled past the tree line into thicker foliage. Only then did we notice that there was a calf in her company.

Rae and I remained motionless for a long while, only chatting softly to one another. When all looked clear, I assisted Rae to the ground. Together, with the pots in hand, we quickly followed the path back to camp.

As we passed Mr. Ream's shop, I remembered the knife. Uncle B's knife! I had completely forgotten it. Afraid to return to the site, I decided not to go back immediately. I felt very guilty and could imagine Uncle B's hurt at losing the knife. That night, sleep only came slowly.

The next morning, I told several of the wood crew where I thought I had dropped the knife. Miraculously, one of them spotted it on the way up the mountain and handed it to me that afternoon. I felt extremely relieved. I placed it in Mom's care for eventual return to Uncle B who was still under house arrest in Baguio.

Fabian Ream, the grand creator of metal objects and the artisan of Uncle B's knife, heard of the incident. He knew well of my fascination with woodcarving from my frequent visits to his shop, so he lent me a small knife that would not be missed if it were lost. To this day, I hold many fond memories of Mr. Ream's kindness.

From Prison to House Arrest

As I was returning to the barracks from the Nancetorium on a September evening, I passed Sister Marcella who stopped to greet me. "Oh, Curt, how happy I am for you. We will miss you, but you will be free," she said with a big smile. I must have looked perplexed because she continued, "You probably have not heard. Do talk with your mother." I did. Indeed, we were to be freed. My sisters were excitedly putting their belongings together for our exodus to Baguio the next morning. I, too, grew excited. My first thoughts went straight to my stomach and Maria and Marci's home cooking. I hoped we would be sharing time with Uncle B at his Bokawkan Road home.

Before noon the following day, we boarded a canvas-covered truck. I asked Mom why we were leaving without Reamo, Ward, or Bedie. "They are only releasing missionaries with ties to Baguio; I think Uncle B will be our host," she answered. We were driven out the front gate to freedom with a number of other families. I felt a sense of remorse at leaving my pals in Holmes to continue prison life.

Winnie and Joe Smith, their son Fred, and Ma and Pa Widdoes joined us at Uncle B's home. He had been residing in Baguio for nearly seven months. It was a treat to be with him again, and I was very happy to put Uncle B's treasured knife into his hands. Maria and Marci had prepared real vegetable soup and cheese sandwiches. It was not America, but that food went a long way to fulfilling past dreams.

That evening, we sat rapt listening to Uncle B's tales about his months on the outside. He told us, too, of the morning plan to report to Military Police Headquarters for orders from a Japanese bigwig. My sisters and I were sent to bed early because we would be rising very early. I found it strange sleeping on a bed with a mattress. I tossed about until nearly midnight, replaying the sudden developments of the past twenty-four hours.

In the morning, after a breakfast of scrumptious scrambled eggs, our family walked with Uncle B to the Japanese headquarters in downtown Baguio. Badges were pinned on each of us. We were instructed to wear them at all times whenever we were out of the house and not to leave the city center. An officer handed us a list of other rules and restrictions. On our walk back to his house, Uncle B told us he had seen little of the Japanese, but knew he was under observation. He described his days as being not much different from at Camp Hay—a kind of house arrest, but with a more comfortable bed and good cooking.

That afternoon, Uncle B arranged for the Smiths to move into a friend's vacant house across the street. Their move freed up sleeping space in the Bokawkan house.

While we were sitting in lawn chairs behind Uncle B's house the next afternoon, he asked me many questions, most of them about the mood in the men's quarters. He had worried about challenges the men might make toward Japanese rule. Of most concern to him was the possibility of an escape from camp, which he suggested could bring dire consequences for many. Uncle B told us that he would have felt more useful and productive inside camp. I sensed his concern that he—living on the outside—would be a suspect in the eyes of the Kempeitai should anyone escape from Holmes. He had heard of Sorrell's escape and was relieved that no one had paid the price for his folly.

We had not been in Baguio many days before I began to miss my friends in camp, the treks up the hillsides carrying soup to the woodcutters, listening to their talk, and my classes with Miss Job. On Sundays, I walked with Uncle B and my sisters to his Baguio church. A Filipino pastor led worship. During the service, my thoughts drifted from the sermon to the missionary-miner baseball games at Holmes on Sunday afternoons. Days seemed to drag. I felt more restricted in some ways than I had felt under Japanese guard at Camp Holmes. My sisters felt the same. Nonetheless, Wezer enjoyed her busy hours as a babysitter for the few released missionary families. Rae frequently accompanied her on those details while the adults shopped or played bridge.

For the first couple weeks, my days were spent alone in Uncle B's yard. There were no others boys in the vicinity. My occasional walks with Mom to the Baguio market helped fill time for me and relieved Maria and Marci of shopping tasks. With more people occupying Uncle B's home, they had more cleaning, cooking, and other chores to do. We found that downtown Baguio lacked the bustle of prewar days. Food varieties were limited. Burnham Park retained a mere spark of its former vitality. We saw only a couple of children on the swings, slides, and paths that ran through the park. The traditional G-string clad Igorot men and cigar-smoking women were very rare sights in town. My days mostly centered on Mom's home schooling efforts and our cleaning chores. She was a fine teacher and diligently tried to make math easier by showing me simple shortcuts in practicing multiplication and division.

Only a short walk downhill from Uncle B's residence was an open field with a steep embankment at one end. I remembered the field well. On a brief holiday a year before the war, Bob Eschbach and I had played with Filipino boys there. It was our playground, but without parallel bars, slides, or swings. Mom remembered it as a safe place for me to play cars, throw balls or boomerangs. But now the embankment was dotted with paper targets attached to wooden frames.

Early each morning, Japanese soldiers practiced war games there, sometimes with pistols, other times with rifles. They occasionally sat, but usually stood or lay down to shoot at the targets. Unbeknownst to Mom, I wandered that way on occasion, obediently wearing the required badge on my shirt. I was mesmerized by the shooting practice. After the soldiers completed their drills and drove away, I wandered onto the field, picked up spent shells, and commenced to play cars on the embankment. I took some empty shells back to the house, where I kept them on the windowsill next to my bed. I often used them to decorate the paths in the dirt under the house where I played cars.

On what turned out to be my last visit to the practice range, a large shiny black car with a Japanese flag attached to a pole on the front bumper pulled up. The car stopped next to me and I recognized the officer inside as Major Mukaibo, the same Mukaibo who had scared the dickens out of me whenever I saw him in camp. I felt numb as I watched him get out of that shiny black car. He walked directly up to me and said harshly, "What do you want?"

"I want to go home." I replied.

"You go home now!"

I turned and headed home, and then he ordered me back. Poking his finger at my identification badge, he angrily repeated his order that I return to "your Mr. Eschbach!" I did just that, but said nothing to Mom or Uncle B about the encounter for fear that both would curtail my future wanderings.

At breakfast the following morning, Mom announced to my sisters and me, "After class this morning, no one goes anywhere without first checking with me, and there will be no more visits to the rifle range." I wondered how she knew of my encounter with Major Mukaibo. Thereafter, our morning routine continued as usual. Lessons changed from arithmetic to spelling to geography.

We had always attended Uncle B's church on Sunday before internment, but services were now much different to conform to Japanese regulations. In the old days, Uncle B often involved uniformed Filipino cadets from Camp Hay as ushers and collectors of the morning offering. Their snappy right and left turns as they marched down the aisles had always intrigued me and held my attention more so than other aspects of worship. Now, of course, those cadets were missing, as were American civilians. The pews were nearly empty.

Guerilla Executions

On a mid-morning in October 1942, I walked into town with Mom to do some shopping at the food market. There seemed far more commotion than usual in the downtown area. As Mom and I approached the plaza, we found mobs of Filipinos gathered there. All eyes seemed focused on five handcuffed Filipino men standing in the street facing the crowd. Two of them were shirtless and wore khaki military trousers. Two others wore shirts with khaki pants. The one in the middle wore only a G-string and had his hands bound on top of his head. Three Japanese soldiers wearing swords stood in front of the handcuffed Filipinos. I asked Mom why they were handcuffed. "I have no idea, but we don't want to stay to find out," she answered.

We had not taken a step away from the ring of observers before a Japanese soldier with a loud shout thrust his bayonet into the abdomen of the nearly naked man. There were groans from those watching, and then another soldier thrust his bayonet into the same man, whose blood spurted out. They seemed to be taking turns. I heard many "oohs," and saw women retreat to the rear of the crowd. I was completely shaken.

Mom grabbed my hand and quietly led me back toward the house. Her only words were tearful ones, "This makes no sense." She went silent until we had reached the house, then she explained that the Filipinos were probably guerillas being made examples of, so others would show more respect to Japanese authority.

"Keep this under your hat," she whispered. No mention was made of the scene at the lunch table, but while washing my hands for supper that evening, I overheard Maria and Marci in the kitchen talking about deaths in the plaza and further learned that "one was beheaded." The image of that morning's event haunted me for many restless nights.

Uncle B made passing mention of the executions at suppertime, stating only that "Everyone in Baguio is on edge right now because of guerilla activity in the hills. It would be a good idea for all of us to just stay put for a while and say little." I followed his admonition and played "clam" for days afterward. Mom reminded us the next morning to be certain to wear our badges outside the house, to let her know when we were going outside, and to stay together in close proximity to the house.

Reports of guerilla activity in the hills around the city became a daily item. Uncle B's usual, fun-loving manner with my sisters and me also seemed tempered by the recent events in the plaza and/or perhaps other matters on his mind. Mom felt his tenseness, as did others, but he said nothing to suggest that anything was bothering him.

Near mid-October, we began to hear radiocast rumors of American mistreatment of Japanese civilians held and tortured in a number of concentration camps in America. The same information was passed on to Filipinos in paper pamphlets. Filipino friends passed a couple of the pamphlets to Uncle B. Naturally, worries about retaliation of some variety—whether the rumors were true or not—would be felt locally. Uncle B's take on rumors like those was to disregard them.

Another item of news, mostly learned secondhand from Maria and Marci, was that Japanese troops had freed Japanese nationals in America soon after taking over Seattle, Vancouver, and other cities on the West Coast. At such moments, my dreams of returning to America vanished.

Mom was not persuaded by such stories. She remembered Nellie McKim's counsel about unsubstantiated gossip, "Unless you hear it on Armed Forces Radio, bag it."

At supper on October 15, Uncle B shared news from Ray Hale that there had been guerilla activity during the pre-dawn hours in the hills overlooking Camp Holmes. Several shots had been fired, but at what, no one could tell. He also learned that no one at Holmes had been hurt, nor had anyone been targeted. Given what we had witnessed days earlier on the Baguio plaza, Mom said, "I hope nobody has to pay for that outburst."

Halloween Abduction

I was playing cars on the narrow dusty path beside Uncle B's house when a Japanese truck pulled into the drive. It was October 31, 1942. I had set up a small wooden bridge on the path that spanned a miniature two-inch-wide imaginary river. Embedded in the dirt, six of my shell casings from the rifle range lined the car path as make-believe light poles. I heard the truck door slam. It startled me and I turned to see four black-booted legs standing behind me. Two Japanese soldiers had stepped over to where I was squatting on the ground. One stared down at my rifle casings. He reached down with the tip of his bayonet and with one swipe of the blade, sent the casings flying. "Dame!" (bad!) he shouted sharply.

Those two then joined other soldiers inside the house. The foursome almost immediately came back outside. They had Uncle B with them. He was not carrying anything, and winked at me as he passed on his walk to the parked truck. Since he had no bag, I thought he would be back soon. As he climbed into the back of the truck, I noticed several other men seated in the dark interior of the covered bed. The soldiers lowered the canvas flap and drove away.

Rae was shopping with Marci at the time, but Mom and Wezer were inside. I joined them immediately. Mom was fighting off tears as she reached out to hold me tightly.

"Where is Uncle B going?" I asked.

"I don't know," she answered tearfully, "but he should be back soon." Soon turned out not to be that evening or the next or the next.

Mom called the Smiths minutes after Uncle B's abduction. Quickly, Winnie, Joe, and Fred hustled over to Uncle B's, where they stayed with us for several nights. Mom felt better in their company, especially having a man's presence in the house. We prayed each day for Uncle B's return. The adults learned that on the morning he had been taken away, so too had Art Richardson and Marshall Welles. Like Uncle B, they had been picked up by Japanese soldiers. We hoped they were with Uncle B at a nearby location.

Each night afterward, I replayed the scene of the soldier's swipe at my shell casings and worried that that might have triggered their taking Uncle B away. When I shared my fears with Mom, she said, "No, they did not come by to see your shells. They had other thoughts on their minds. Don't even think about it." Yet, I felt guilty. More days passed with no word from or about Uncle B and the others. Mom had wanted to go to the Kempeitai office the day after his abduction but reluctantly decided to wait, thinking that pressing the Japanese might anger them so that they would round up others like Joe Smith.

Days later, Mom's patience ran out. Alone, she walked directly to Kempeitai headquarters. She intended to ask where the men were and why they had not been returned. The first person she encountered inside the front door was Major Mukaibo, our "favorite pastor," as Uncle B facetiously referred to him. A couple of hours later, Mom reported to the Smiths, my sisters, and me that Mukaibo was surprisingly cordial, telling her only that the men's whereabouts, and the reasons for their having been taken away, were subjects about which he "knew nothing." Also, Mukaibo claimed that he had no authority to intercede in such matters. Although he did not speak directly of the imprisoned men, their condition, or their location, Mom felt confident upon leaving the headquarters that they were alive and confined in that building. She came to that conclusion by reading between the lines of Mukaibo's "sweet-talking lies." Still, thoughts of Rufus Gray's long imprisonment, the rumors of his torture, and his ultimate death were on everyone's mind. They certainly weighed heavily on my mind as I continued to worry about the shell-casings episode. Nonetheless, Mom insisted that Mukaibo's tone had given her a shred of hope.

More days passed and still we received no word. But we did learn through the Baguio grapevine that four other men had been imprisoned. We were also informed that—in an attempt to establish guerilla ties—a number of the Baguio homes from which the men had been taken were ransacked. The Eschbach residence, however, was untouched.

Return to Holmes

On November 11, 1942, eleven days after Uncle B's disappearance and almost seven weeks since our family's departure from Camp Holmes to "house internment" in Baguio, a Japanese officer came to the house and ordered us to pack. Matter-of-factly and in broken English, he told us we were to be re-interned at Holmes. We heard that Ma and Pa Widdoes were allowed to remain in Baguio. Their frailty and advanced years must have made them seem nonthreatening to the Japanese authorities.

The Smiths and others were picked up first and returned directly to Camp Holmes. Our family followed shortly afterward. As we prepared to board a truck to camp, Uncle B was foremost in our minds. We all worried about him and the other men about whom we had still heard nothing. Returning to prison ourselves was not our primary concern. As we stepped into the dark canvas-covered truck bed, Mom asked the officer if Mr. Eschbach was going to Holmes also. He did not respond. Being the first to climb in, I found a seat on a side bench near the truck cab. I noticed a cluster of unkempt, bearded men seated in the darkness, staring outward from against the back of the cab. I recognized none of them. They sat like mummies in the shade of the canvas cover. My first thought was that they were dead people.

Uncle B made the first sound. Hearing his voice, Mom became teary-eyed and leaped from her seat to embrace him. Recognizing Art next to him, she gave him a hug, too. She heard Marshall Welles's voice and reached over to him, but was ordered to sit down and be still. Her sobs of joy echoed around the truck. My sisters and I had to wait until we arrived at Camp Holmes to share our affection with Uncle B because a Japanese soldier signaled for us to remain seated.

Internees who had heard through Nellie McKim of our imminent arrival were in front of the barracks to greet the truck. Some did not immediately recognize the men who had been held in the chambers of the Kempeitai. That evening, I visited Uncle B in the men's barracks as he was resting on his bunk. Bearded and smiling, he lightheartedly apologized to me for leaving us suddenly without notice. "On Halloween Day, the spooks came and got me," he said. This was Uncle B's way of passing off his experience with the military police. In addition, he told me that he had not eaten for several days, but only drank water, and that he was not hungry. He said that some of the men had taken more water than he did, but unwillingly. Beyond that, Uncle B mentioned nothing of his days in confinement, nor did I ask.

Uncle B and Art were seeing Camp Holmes for the first time. They were placed in bunks in the men's barracks, which would be home for the duration of their internment in Baguio. For days, Uncle B moved about gingerly. Indeed, it took some time for him to regain strength and settle in at barracks Number Three.

On Thanksgiving Day, with Uncle B's encouragement, Mom approved my joining him as his bunkmate in the men's barracks. I was greatly relieved to be out of the women and children's barracks and away from the many girls. Indeed, I was in high spirits to be with Uncle B again. The more relaxed commingling rules instituted after our departure in September gave families longer and more frequent opportunities to be together. That meant I was allowed time with Mom while again bunking with the men.

The return to Holmes's chow lines was far less satisfying than dining on Maria's fine cooking. Socially, though, I was much happier. In many ways, living outside the fences had been more confining than life inside. I actually felt more restricted at Uncle B's Bokawkan residence and missed the hours spent with my pals in camp.

Uncle B frequently brightened my hungry bedtime moments by placing a few peanuts, a piece of bread, or part of a banana in my hand. At such times, with his grand smile, he would share one of his little rhymes: "Good night, young man, enjoy your Tuesday simple sample," or "Have a taste of this honey, it is better than money." His favorite, but not mine, was "Try one of God's pods" (a piece of bamboo shoot). His renewed casual humor was a sign that he was recovering from his ordeal with the Kempeitai.

Still, it took some time for Uncle B and the other men to fit into the routine of camp life. It was understandable that friends had questions about life on the outside and their torture by the military police, but Uncle B and his comrades tended to deflect those questions, probably to insure that their responses did not find their way to enemy ears. "Payback for idle chatter, we don't need," responded Art Richardson to curious internees. For several days Dr. Skerl met with the "seven from heaven," as he called them, to keep tabs on their health.

Uncle B never referred to the treatment the other imprisoned men received, nor did he ever whisper the word "maltreatment" in describing his own Baguio confinement. Yet, it was obvious to me from the bruises on his hands and shoulders that he had been mistreated. I surmised from his gaunt appearance and markings that he had experienced some measure of torture and obviously was denied food. I had never before seen such a physical change in a person in such a short time.

Uncle B talked freely with me about Mukaibo watching him being interrogated. The import of that fact did not register with me until Mom reminded me of Mukaibo's "know nothing" conversation with her when she had sought out information about Uncle B's whereabouts and well-being. Mukaibo had lied to her.

I did not tell Uncle B about my frightening encounter with the soldier the day he was taken away. What Uncle B shared with me, however, went a long way toward relieving my guilt about the rifle shell incident being the cause of his imprisonment. He told me that when news broke of guerilla activity in the nearby hills, he knew that someone in Baguio would be suspected of collaboration. It did not surprise him that he was one of those picked up for interrogation. Uncle B knew that the Japanese were terrified of the guerilla movement. In fact, that was the main subject of questioning by the Kempeitai during the long captivity of the seven men. Uncle B concluded that his captors believed they had knowledge of guerilla activities, and those suspicions had brought about their incarceration. I felt so relieved that the discovery of my shell casings was not an issue.

Camp Leadership Defined

The general committee was the primary internee leadership group in camp. Initially, Dr. Richard Walker served as chair. Internees recognized him as fair and Nakamura respected him. Dr. Nance followed Dr. Walker as chair around the time of Hayakawa's assignment as commandant. A women's committee formed soon after the move to Holmes. At first, the men of the general committee handled women's issues that required commandant action. This procedure seemed bothersome to Dr. Beulah Allen and a large number of the other women. They felt that the men could not fully appreciate their needs, especially with regard to the inadequacy of the lavatory and cramped conditions in the barracks. I shared the women's unhappiness with the toilet scene for the reason that boys in the women's barracks had little or no privacy.

Fortunately, Nellie McKim's strong influence in all decisions made her the natural spokesperson to carry women's issues forward. She commanded the full trust of both committees. A month following Uncle B's arrival at Holmes, he became chair of the general committee. His patient, less abrasive manner in working with the women seemed to quiet most of their aggravations.

Most everyone welcomed Uncle B's leadership. Very much a "people person," he was delighted to be among friends again and serving their interests. He found his camp responsibilities more rewarding than life under the watchful eyes of the military police in Baguio during his months-long house arrest. After the many confrontations Uncle B had with Nakamura in Camp Hay and time for reflection away from camp, he now had a better understanding of how to interact with Japanese leadership.

Uncle B and Art Richardson established a rapport with Commandant Hayakawa that resulted in a number of improvements to prison life. Richardson had sorted through educational materials at Brent while in Baguio for those he felt would be acceptable to Hayakawa. Even with his credible English skills, it took Hayakawa considerable time to review the Brent books. Eventually, though, he approved most of the texts for camp use, and they improved the quality of our classes immensely.

A milk shortage was one of the first challenges Uncle B faced after resuming the role of committee chair. Mothers pleaded for him to address that acute need with Hayakawa. The difficulty of procuring milk threatened the lives of many of the camp's infants. In response, the men's group negotiated a plan with Hayakawa to purchase dairy goats and to construct a pen for them in the small meadow behind the woodshop. On our return walks from the hills, Ward Graham and I made the goat pen a regular stop. It was great fun to visit the goats and pet them when they came to the fence.

Although the quantity of milk they produced was not as much as hoped, the purchase of the goats had averted a crisis. They also were fun for the young children to watch and pet. I told Wezer one evening that she should visit the goats to which Reamo and I had given names. Since they were all nannies, we named them after some of the nuns in camp: Brigita, Juliana, Ursula. . . . Wezer giggled and suggested that those names be kept secret. Mom added, "Let's hope we can't blame the Maryknoll sisters for the goats not giving much milk."

Soon afterward, the committee procured chickens and then pigs. Eggs produced would be a regular source of protein to supplement children's diets. Pigs were fed the remnants of garbage. They were also possible food sources should supplies of meat not be purchasable. Regrettably, only two pigs and a small number of the chickens lived up to expectations.

Another problem soon confronted the general committee. They had to deal with the repulsive Clarence Mount, an internee with a most self-serving approach to life. Mount and his mestizo wife and child lived in a small shack adjacent to the men's barracks. His frequent transgressions with alcohol and periodically exiting the camp perimeter in darkness to obtain whiskey colored his reputation and put us all at risk. A number of the men knew Mount conducted a whiskey business with Filipinos—selling some in camp, consuming more. An alcoholic, he became belligerent on numerous occasions. In almost every encounter I had with him, he reeked of whiskey. Others shunned him and did their best to avoid standing beside him in line at mealtime. He socialized with no one outside his shack.

In his unpublished writings about the war years, Joe Smith tells about one time Mount entered the dining area after it had closed. The kitchen staff, including Joe, sat at a table eating soup. Mount wanted something to eat and sat down across the table from the staff expecting to be served. Accustomed to Mount's tardy arrivals, Joe asked, "Why can't you get here on time like other people?" Mount's response to that query was a monster punch to Joe's eye, leaving him with a shiner that lasted several weeks.

Only a few men knew the source of Mount's alcohol supply. Most presumed he was not manufacturing alcohol, but was getting it from the outside. Japanese guards knew that liquor was getting into camp. Initially, they suspected it was coming in food bags from Baguio. When their inspections revealed nothing, Hawakawa placed guards on night watch to overlook suspected hiding areas across the fence from the barracks. Their nighttime observations discovered Mount conspiring with a Filipino family living beside the Bontoc Trail. The guards also found liquor hidden in a disguised underground compartment outside the perimeter fence. After darkness, Mount sneaked the goods into camp. One night in early December 1942, the guards caught him outside the fence and arranged for his public punishment the next morning.

Many of the men in camp were ordered to view Mount's beating. It began with a drubbing with what looked like a baseball bat. His screams affected me far more than had those of Mr. Leung Soon, the Chinaman caught wandering outside Holmes eight months earlier. While the beating was not as long as what Leung had gone through, it was as violent and ended with Mount crumpled on the ground, motionless, appearing dead. I was surprised that Mrs. Mount stood by their shack showing no emotion. A number of men were ordered to carry his limp body to the Nancetorium. There, Dr. Nance worked to save him by stopping the bleeding. Miraculously, Nance restored him to consciousness, but Mount was rarely visible around camp thereafter. The message of the Japanese was clear—not only to Mount, but also to a number of men at Holmes who had bought liquor from him. Uncle B quietly informed those men that the committee would not support future violators. Those men kept a low and nervous profile for months after Mount's flogging. Luckily, the Japanese never knew of their transgressions.

Food shortages had been a problem for some time leading up to Mount's punishment, and that did not change. Hayakawa, responding to all committee pleas, insisted that food was not easily attainable. The Japanese, he claimed, faced scarcities also. He openly insisted that Mount's violations were not the reason for our hunger, and Uncle B believed him because the food bags sent into camp by Marci and Maria were also meager.

Kid Details

After reuniting with Uncle B in the men's barracks, I became a part-time draftee to the garbage detail. The *Carry Me Home* wagon, initially used to carry firewood and pilfered items into Camp Hay, now served broader needs. The wagon continued to haul logs to the camp kitchen, but it also brought *carabao* manure scavenged off the Bontoc Trail to enrich the soil in the gardens. For days, the men quartered at the east end of the men's barracks inhaled the stench without complaint. Hayakawa encouraged gardening as a means to supplement the meager food supplies trucked into camp. Joe Smith oversaw the garden, a responsibility that became more complex after he discovered that some surreptitious sampling of the maturing *camotes* (yams) was taking place. Garden duty became an added chore for children and some mothers.

Another of *Carry Me Home*'s primary functions was to haul garbage to a waste dump off the Bontoc Trail leading to Baguio. Several teenagers regularly joined the men assigned this detail in pulling and pushing the wagon full of garbage out of camp. Periodically, I assisted them. It was one of my favorite duties because it allowed me to leave the camp boundaries. Our crew members always looked forward to those occasions when a compassionate Filipina onlooker might hand one of them a banana or a bouquet. Such lucky days occurred only when a relaxed guard accompanied us. The younger members of the crew, like me, did most of the pulling, pushing, and attending to *Carry Me Home*. We, therefore, rarely received any handouts. Instead, we got to savor the smell emanating from the wagon.

During one of our garbage excursions, a young Filipina about my age ran around the side of the moving wagon to hand me a long-stemmed gardenia—Mom's favorite of all flowers. I was excited because that day was Mom's birthday, and I now had a lovely present for her. I slipped the flower to Mom at suppertime. The gift caught her by surprise, and tears came to her eyes as she gave me a huge hug.

On yet another outing with the wagoneers, I spotted Marci Obilee, Uncle B's housekeeper, standing by the dumping chute off the trail. She held something in her hand that she wanted to pass to me, but the attending soldier shooed her away. He was in no mood to allow any interaction with Filipinos. I shared my encounter with Uncle B and apologized for not delivering the item to him. With his big smile, Uncle B brushed the incident aside. "She probably thought I needed a pair of socks," he said.

Our garbage crew always hoped for a short stop at a roadside stand where you could purchase bananas or some other goodies. Most guards disallowed that small luxury. I had no money, so those rare stops meant little to my stomach. Occasionally, though, a crew member would share a goody with me. Whether or not I received anything, the buyers' broad smiles made me beam, too.

Though all of the children big enough to work had specific chores to do, we also had time for play. After my return to Holmes from confinement at Uncle B's home, I discovered that the harmless but imaginative guerilla games of earlier days had taken a new course. Previously, the games had featured attacks with mud balls. The summer rains had made the shaping of mud balls very easy. Games played after our return to a dry camp, however, required buckets of water, and we frequently added small stones to the mud balls, making hits painful and sometimes bloody. I must admit I was a partner in that crime and took part in the practice of placing stones in our missiles. The rules of the game were similar to those we had followed back in the summer. One team began at the bottom of the slope, the other on the ridge atop the mesa bordering the parade ground.

The team declared winner had to be in control of the ridge top when the supper bell rang. The losing team had the consolation of being closer to the supper line.

If adult referees had been involved and stricter rules applied, our form of play could have been labeled "educational *and* enjoyable." Under the new rules, the games were educational in a way—but not always fun. Our style of play not only included loaded mud balls but the occasional "pantsing" of a defeated and obnoxious opponent. The pantsing victim was usually a boy held to the ground while his captors removed his shorts. To avoid such humiliation, it was imperative for potential victims to beat a fast retreat toward the chow line after defeat. On only a couple of occasions was a girl the pantsing victim, and the girls from the opposing team performed the task. It took a truly detestable act or comment by a girl to draw such harsh retaliation.

Rae was a frequent participant in the guerilla wars, always my teammate, and an adept player. She ran fast, could scale the slope with ease, and was amazingly accurate at throwing mud balls. Parents of the combatants were generally too preoccupied to notice our games. A few informed parents, alerted to the reputed dangers, forbade their children from participating. Indeed, the games led to a few visits to the dispensary for a stitch or a dab of mercurochrome. Amazingly, no child suffered serious injury.

For the most part, the teams remained constant because penalties imposed on traitors were severe. During play emotions occasionally became heated, as one might expect, but rarely was there boasting or retaliation in classes, in the food lines, or in our cubicles. When combat was over, it was over. In retrospect, I think our violent play was in part a carryover from our closeness to the war, a kind of outlet that substituted for commonly accepted school games, since we lacked the equipment to play those.

Bad war news sometimes caused tempers to flare, too. I was not above periodic displays of emotion directed toward another child—most commonly Derek Whitmarsh. He was a Brit like Ann Wilson, with whom I had experienced earlier tussles. Derek frequently caused my blood to boil. One late afternoon, as I returned from the hills with the woodcutters and was about to enter the men's barracks, I encountered Derek standing in the doorway. In his British accent, he greeted me, "Here comes Chinky . . . looking stinky." Now, others had called me Chinky before and I normally did not mind it since our family name, Tong, certainly sounds Chinese. But they hadn't ever rhymed it with stinky.

"Are you going to take that?" one of the wood crew asked me. I responded by charging Derek. I delivered the first punch and Derek answered in kind. In moments, our swinging had turned to grappling; first one of us rolling on top then the other. The ground below us was pebbled and hard. The wood crew and a rather large number of men gathered to watch us fight. None attempted to intercede, so our struggle must have been good entertainment, something to take their minds off woes. When "Judge" Don Zimmerman finally stepped in to bring order to the show, Derek and I were out of breath and staring at each other's bloody faces. After looking over my abrasions and a couple of Derek's scratches, Don walked us both to the infirmary where Nurse Bessie Crimm applied mercurochrome to our wounds. We must have looked like a pair of leopards walking peacefully back to the barracks with Don.

Family Talks

Upon our return to Holmes from Baguio, we learned that Hayakawa had sanctioned strolls on the parade grounds following supper. Our family joined the routine. We walked slowly for Mom's benefit, always following the barbed-wire fence perimeter, which circled the camp proper. Mom liked to stop periodically for short conversations with different couples or single women. Folks always had gnawing, burdensome thoughts on their minds which, when shared, seemed to lessen their heavy loads. Mom's chats often ended with hugs and loving whispers—each one thankful for the exchange of goodwill.

Our family conversations on those strolls inevitably turned to Dad. Mom fought back tears when Rae blurted unanswerable questions like, "Where is Dad now? What is he doing?" Questions crossed my mind, too, but I rarely asked them because I did not want to see Mom's emotional response. Not a day of prison life passed without thoughts or recollections of my father. As a way of reacquainting us with Dad's features and habits, Mom would often describe "that handsome face," which drew the attention of the women of Davao. She also spoke of the "Walter chuckle," which Uncle B referred to as Dad's signature sound. I would reflect, too, on the occasions when I had witnessed Dad's flashes of temper. Little angered him more than when the advantaged citizenry increased their riches at the expense of others like the uneducated poor of Davao or the defenseless aborigines of central Mindanao.

My most vivid recollection of Dad's impatient side was a confrontation he had with a Bible salesclerk in Davao. The salesclerk, wearing a white suit, marched into a ward at Mission Hospital, walked down an aisle of ailing patients, and stopped at each cot to hawk crucifixes and expensive, white Bibles. Upon sighting the hawker, a nurse alerted Dad to what was happening, and he immediately set out for the sick bay. His angry, fast-paced entry into the ward startled the peddler, who stashed the bag of Bibles under his arm, jumped up from his stool, and tried to run by him. Dad reached out, grabbed him by the nape of his neck, shoved him to the front door of the hospital, and kicked him down the front steps. Dad was livid!

Although it pained Mom to talk about Dad, she wanted to remind us of his work and values. She also spoke of his deep love for the indigenous tribes of Mindanao—the Bagobos, the Moros, and the Ata. He loved the soil, which sustained life for those people, and the artifacts, which he enjoyed excavating and piecing together for museum curators. Dad held only respect for the island dwellers, be they the naked tribespeople, Japanese plantation owners, or barong-clad Filipino executives. Mom also shared with us her many anxious days during his extended forays in the mountains.

Our walks with Mom provided the only real opportunities for family talk. The topics usually centered on the circumstances, which constantly surrounded us. Mom cautioned us not to become impatient or overly judgmental of fellow internees. "They too are under stress and will, at times, succumb to selfish, sometimes hostile, or derogatory remarks toward others. People tend to act out of character when they are hungry or their children's space is threatened. Be patient with them," she advised. "The rainy season is soon upon us and they get grouchy."

Trapped in an environment in which many ugly words of hatred toward the enemy were voiced, Mom also worried about our receptivity to such influences. On one of our evening strolls, she spoke seriously to us about the use of demeaning words such as Japs, Nips, yellow-bellies, slope eyes—all easily recognized by our guards. "Those terms only open the door to trouble," Mom said. "Please don't use them." She shared her own guilt for having uttered "Japs" in an angry response to watching the guards torture the Chinese internee in the days following our arrival at Holmes. "You and I must remember," she said, "that because we see cultures and colors as different, that does not make them evil. We must learn to understand and respect."

As a follow-up to our conversation that night, Mom led us by singing softly: "Jesus loves the little children, all the children of the world; brown and yellow, black and white, all are precious in his sight; Jesus loves the little children of the world." Reflecting on Mom's counsel as I walked away from the girls toward the men's barracks, the word "yellow" had a new meaning.

Betting in the Freedom Pool

Hope for liberation sagged as our life in concentration neared its first-year anniversary. A considerable number of the "no cash" bettors in the men's barracks had thought that the war would be over by Christmas 1942. I never saw anybody actually anteing coins into a pot. Nonetheless, they seemed to enjoy betting on the closure date of our life in prison.

The most commonly picked date in the betting battles was either a Fourth of July or a Christmas Day. "Will we be free or still holed up on Christmas Day?" was the common question. The hands raised were about even. Clearly, those who had wagered on repatriation by Christmas Day 1942 looked to be losers. As the months moved on, additional losers saw July 4 and then Christmas 1943 slip past.

On the bright side, wagering helped time fly, creating a few laughs and opportunities to chide betting pals about their dumbness. Aunt Leora enjoyed listening to my accounts of the freedom predictions in the men's barracks. She would frequently remind me to share her unchanged prediction with them. And I did. Hers was always the same—Easter 1945. "They just aren't reading my horoscope!" she giggled. Although not a resident of the "betting barracks," Aunt Leora became barracks Number Three's best bettor with each passing holiday.

Through Jim Halsema's secret source of information—a radio embedded in a wall of the Nancetorium—news leaks of battles in the Pacific revealed a few American advances. Severe setbacks were also reported. Mom told Uncle B that depression stemming from the news reports seemed more prevalent in the women's barracks, especially among the elderly. Certainly, dejection could be read in the faces and words of my teachers through periodic asides aimed at Commandant Hayakawa, the guards, and the Japanese generally. After depressing reports about battles in the Pacific, the level of profanity and anger toward one another over poker games increased in the men's barracks.

Although feeling quite upbeat himself, Uncle B could feel the negative mood. On Christmas Eve, one loudmouth aiming uncouth language at the enemy received this cordial admonition from Uncle B: "Let's not blame God on his birthday. He's the best friend we have." Uncle B's manner with people was respectful as a rule, and his messages were straightforward. He was held in high regard throughout the camp community for his frank but soft-spoken manner. To many of the men, his spiritual example was most important. Like others in Holmes, he recognized the futility in fighting what he could not change. Even so, Uncle B maintained a positive countenance, which was contagious. For one who had very recently undergone torture and starvation, he was a meaningful role model.

Before Christmas but several weeks after our family hiatus at Uncle B's residence in Baguio and our subsequent return to Camp Holmes, trucks bearing more American missionaries arrived at camp. Included in the group were Catholic priests and nuns. Following the bombings in Baguio in December 1941, the missionary group continued their work in a number of central Luzon barrios. They did not report to Baguio to surrender, but neither did they try to evade capture. For nearly a year, they were left alone, apparently seen as harmless by the Japanese. Enemy troops were preoccupied for most of the year with fighting guerillas and securing port villages on the western and northern shores of Luzon.

Soon after the Japanese deposited the Catholic missionaries at Holmes, another group—all non-missionaries—arrived by truck. A few of the new internees had undergone long stretches of confinement, starvation, and in some cases, torture by Japanese soldiers in scattered mountain hideouts. Several of the men bore fresh wounds. Our numbers had swelled to more than five hundred.

Charles O'Dowd, the most renowned of the new contingent, was a wealthy American known by many internees prior to the war. He stepped out of a truck looking like warmed-over death and carrying nothing. During the next few days, O'Dowd related a story to the committee that Uncle B described as having "made my hair curl." O'Dowd, hidden in a mountain shack, had been betrayed by Filipino stoolies for ransom money. Somehow his family had escaped capture. Others of the group had many sordid tales as well. All had experienced maltreatment and worse while confined. They looked disheveled and spoke with sharp hostility toward the Japanese. O'Dowd was by far the most vocal of our new neighbors. His ire was aimed mostly at General Douglas MacArthur. He accused the general of "conducting a war in the Pacific with the Philippines at the bottom of the priority list."

I had heard similar accusations and complaints about General MacArthur from my bunkmates many times, even prior to the arrival of those who had been in hiding. When like minds came together, the volume of anger directed toward MacArthur increased. They loudly scolded him for not attempting to repatriate all civilians.

General Jonathan Wainwright, in contrast, was practically revered for being the stalwart leader in the army's efforts to hold off a larger and stronger Japanese force at Bataan and Corregidor. We learned later that MacArthur had fled to Australia and did not have the necessary force to muster a retaliation. Following MacArthur's exodus from Bataan, thousands of American soldiers and sailors were killed or died of starvation. Only a small fraction survived the war.

While I listened to the men's war commentary, their complaints were not mine, preoccupied as I was with what was going on directly around me. Being a child in confinement was perhaps a blessing. I was not sufficiently schooled in life's expectations to draw informed comparisons between what should have been and how we were living. I certainly could not make a knowledgeable judgment about military strategy. I generally followed Uncle B's advice, "Put aside yesterday and tomorrow, focus on today."

Our Davao friend, Mr. Matsumoto, took this photo of Mother, my sisters,
and me during his surprise visit to Camp Holmes in April 1943.
Dad carried it in his wallet for the duration of his life.

CHAPTER 5

Camp Holmes II

Dec. 1942–Dec. 1944

Christmas 1942

Toward the end of our first full year of imprisonment, with Christmas approaching, life in Holmes reversed course. In response to the sudden influx of new internees, Hayakawa became stricter. Commingling rules were tightened, evening activities occurred less frequently, and food was sparse. Quite suddenly, in fact, severe food shortages had become commonplace. Hayakawa was apologetic but made no effort to improve the situation. He informed Uncle B that staples like rice and yams were scarce throughout Luzon. Our meager rations, he insisted, were not meant as punishment as the committee had suggested. There likely was some truth in Hayakawa's explanations. Unquestionably, the rounding up of internees from the central Luzon hills swelled camp numbers and led to shorter rations and stricter rules. Quite naturally, grousing increased.

In December, as thoughts of Christmas entered our minds, Hayakawa graciously granted us permission to hold Christmas services. He also allowed use of one of the nipa huts adjacent to the parade grounds for choir practices. I often played with my friends on the hillside behind the hut—a natural incline on which to slide or roll down. The embankment also offered the perfect slope on which to cut out winding paths for my toy cars, which I patterned after the zigzag trail to Baguio. The music from the nipa hut frequently caused me to stop playing and listen to the choir, especially when they sang carols like "We Three Kings of Orient Are" or

"Away in a Manger." My favorite, though not a Christmas song, was also scheduled for the Christmas service: "There Is a Green Hill Far Away Without a Prison Wall."

On Christmas Day the choir performed masterfully, lifting our spirits. Santa Claus surprised young children and parents, especially since he was first spotted stepping out of the guardhouse door. For Hayakawa and his immediate subordinates, the event provided a fascinating glimpse at a special segment of Western culture. Although he had grown up in the Philippines, Hayakawa had never witnessed a Christmas celebration before. The entire guard corps observed the festivities with keen interest. At Uncle B's request, Hayakawa agreed not to display rifles during the festivities. The soldiers appeared more interested in watching our varied activities than being guardians of our flock.

On Christmas afternoon, the guards opened the main gate to Camp Holmes to Filipino visitors with prewar ties to the internees. Maria and Marci of course were present. A few elderly missionaries released earlier from camp, like Ma and Pa Widdoes, joined a group of Filipino amahs, housekeepers, and gardeners in attending. (Sadly, soon after Christmas, the Widdoes were transferred to the Los Baños camp in southern Luzon.) Gifts for the internees had to be inspected. Hayakawa had arranged for special foods to be brought into camp for dinner—yams, sugar, coffee, and pork—and candy for the children. A piece of pork was the first morsel of meat I had eaten in several weeks. The events and foods of the day heartened all of us. "Few have thought about the morrow, and that is healthy," commented Father Gowen as he and his followers met for prayer that evening.

It truly was a time to think positively. I am sure that many assumed the end of internment was near and that a year hence we would be looking back on the Christmas of 1942 from a historical perspective. The best present I received that Christmas Day was the news that Major Mukaibo had gone. (Commandant Hayakawa later told Nellie McKim that Mukaibo and Nagatomi had been ordered to Manila where they were reportedly charged as accessories to theft and inhumane treatment of civilians. Mukaibo was temporarily jailed, then dishonorably discharged and sent back to Japan.) Mukaibo's threats of death at Brent School had weighed heavily on my mind every time I encountered him. His departure from Holmes and the Baguio scene gave me hope that we might live to know freedom someday. My bad dreams of dying under machine-gun fire faded.

Those haunting memories of Mukaibo were reawakened when, as an adult, I discovered more about his life before and after the war. I was stunned to learn that Mukaibo Nagahide had earned a Ph.D. in theology from Boston University Divinity School in 1938. Postwar, he was certified as a pastor in 1949, became a professor, and served as president of Aoyama Gakuin Women's Junior College for over a decade, beginning in 1950. Months after his death in 1981, he was awarded the Emperor's prestigious Order of the Sacred Treasure. Mukaibo's effect on my life and the lives of other internees can best be described as paradoxical.

Women of Strength

Throughout the internment years at Camp Holmes, Mom proved a trusted counsel to scores of women. While I was aware of her sit-down conversations with women suffering from the emotional pressures of imprisonment, Wezer alerted me to the growing frequency of those get-togethers as we entered the second year of internment.

Although Mom was a member of the women's committee, her impact was greatest when she helped others persist despite their frailties, hurts, and moments of depression. She sincerely cared about her companions. Natalie Crouter once asked Mom how it was that she could identify the moods of others. Mom responded that she recognized down times because she experienced them in her own life and understood their insidious ways of debilitating a person for long painful periods if not addressed. "Besides," Mom said, "I enjoy visiting with people because it keeps me up." And up she was through most of those years.

But melancholy could surface when her thoughts turned to Dad or when she was bedridden and in pain. "For me it is therapeutic to keep my mind focused on other things and on the people around me," she told Natalie. Keeping busy, whether she was removing weevils from vegetables for camp soup, teaching art, sketching faces, assisting in arranging worship services, or "trying to keep track of [her] sometimes naughty son," distracted her from worrying about Dad and the war. Conversations with Natalie, Leora Nagel, Winnie Smith, and a host of other women were a tonic for her, as well as for the others. By nature, she enjoyed company. Conversations often served as reminders of the need to "keep the faith."

Mom found the "miners'" perspectives on life extremely interesting. Her relationships, indeed deep friendships, with those folks were as close and dear as those she had with missionary women, and they continued to be so after the war.

Mom took her role as a mother seriously. She gave my sisters leeway to reach out and explore whatever form of wholesome growth a prison community could offer. Wezer and Rae openly talked with Mom before bedtime about their daily duties, classes, and encounters with other young people. During Uncle B's absence from prison, when I was not sleeping in the men's barracks, I too participated in these bedside conversations. At our evening get-togethers with the Crouters, Robinsons, Ma Widdoes, Leora, and others, I noticed how Mom brightened spirits by gently kidding around with whoever might be in the throes of self-pity.

For example, I recall Mom's response to the women's woes when toilet paper was unavailable. With a straight face, she told her friends, "I'm sure it would never have occurred to me during my graduation ceremony at Drexel that on some future day I would be exploring with dear friends how to deal with wiping our fannies. Let's brainstorm!" And they did. Their temporary solution was to each find a rag, mark it as one's own, then wash it after each use and dry it over a tree branch for the next lavatory visit. The decorated tree branches set an example for others to follow.

Mother's routine of cleaning rice and vegetables began in Camp Hay and carried over at Camp Holmes. It was a time-consuming chore, which started early in the morning and ended before noon. That schedule allowed her time to sketch, teach, and visit with troubled friends in the afternoon. Picking weevils and other critters out of our meals-to-be was not fun, but necessary. It also offered time for more conversation. Months after our arrival in Holmes, men in the workshop created sieves from looted pieces of old screening that permitted the separation of weevils from rice in half the time. In one of her occasional, imaginary notes to Dad, Mom scribbled these lines in rhyme about her kitchen duties:

> Please try not to believe
> That my labors are evil
> I sift rice through a sieve
> So not to eat weevil.

Mom was not the only active and strong woman in camp. Winnie Smith also recognized the need for constructive mind-cleansing activity. Like Mom, she felt strongly that involvement in creative ventures could fend off anger, self-pity, and even depression. Mom referred to Winnie as the "angel of optimism." When it came to brightening spirits in the camp community, Winnie knew what to do.

Her graduate study in religious drama at the Chicago Theological Seminary made Winnie a sought-after director for theatrical productions at Holmes. A group of teenage girls and their teachers were the first to ask Winnie to help organize a performance, and she happily complied. After discussing their options, the group decided on the legend of Pocahontas as a doable and entertaining program.

All hands immediately began to gather the necessary supplies—borrowing or crafting props like axes, arrows, feathers, and headdresses. The show featured Captain John Smith and Pocahontas. I still remember the dramatic climax when Pocahontas saved Captain Smith from having his head chopped off by Chief Powhatan's followers.

The success of the Pocahontas performance prompted requests for more productions. Parents, particularly, were eager for their children to have the opportunity to develop their imagination under Winnie's spirited and knowledgeable direction. Soon she had developed a program for boys and girls, and later programs for adults.

The Stone Man of the Mountain

By our second year of internment at Camp Holmes, the woodcutting crew had developed an organized regimen. Each morning they hiked up the mountainside to the day's cutting site, packing their tools and empty lunch cans or coconut shells, and accompanied by one of the Japanese guards. The crew's detail was to cut down selected pine trees and section them into three-foot lengths. This was tedious and painstaking labor since it all had to be done with two-man handsaws. Over time the men learned to conserve energy by regulating their cutting pace and rotating chores. However, there was no shortcut to the task of carrying logs to the delivery chute. The chute resembled a deep narrow riverbed; it was free of large rocks and other obstructions and banked high enough on both sides to contain the rolling logs. Even in camp, we could hear the men's yells of "Timber!" as the logs began their downward tumble. At the low end of the chute, other men stood by *Carry Me Home* until the day's supply of logs had rolled down. Occasionally, a log got jammed in the chute, requiring one of the crew from above to crawl into the rollway and release the jam.

The guard usually sat on a stump near the cutting area to observe the crew's work and make certain that nobody drifted far from the site. He would occasionally stroll over to the ridge trail, likely to keep an eye on the Igorots or Filipino boys passing through the vicinity. While seated, the guard would smoke or catnap. My usual routine was to accompany another guard to the worksite shortly before noon. If doing solo duty, I carried two pails of soup up the hill, but only one if I had a buddy with me. After the crew had eaten, the guard who had accompanied me remained at the site, and the one who had ushered the crew up the hill in the morning returned to camp with me.

Sometimes the routine changed, probably due to a shortage of available guards. One soldier would escort the crew up the mountain. Then, unguarded, I would tote the buckets of rice or soup to the cutting site for lunch. On those occasions, I would usually remain on the mountain with the crew until the duty guard escorted all of us back to camp at the end of the workday.

On one such day, I wandered toward the nearby ridge trail while the crew ate their lunch and the guard, seated on the ground with his back against a tree, snoozed. The trail would take me either northeasterly toward the rocky projection known as the "Man of the Mountain" or southwesterly toward the overlook of Baguio. I had often thought about trying to get a closer look at the stone man, but had never attempted to follow that trail because it was off limits. As I stood on the trail, gazing in the direction of the stone face, I glanced back to see if the guard was awake and had noticed my absence. He appeared to be dozing, just as I had left him.

From the campground, the "Old Man" appeared to be only a short distance from the tree cutting area. Impulsively, I began to walk toward the rock face. Time passed. Noting that the guard was not behind me, I continued walking. I still saw no sign of the Old Man when I peered around each bend in the path. Soon the trail forked, and I was not sure which led in the direction of the Old Man. For some reason, I assumed I would not be missed until it was time for us to go back to camp, so seeing no sign of the guard, I went on. At each turn in the trail, I expected the stone-faced man to appear. "Just one more turn," I told myself again and again and again.

As more time passed without a sighting of the Old Man, I paused and then grew alarmed. The trail back to the woodcutters looked like it headed in the wrong direction. After replaying the route in my mind, common sense returned. Doing an about-face, I started to run back toward the work site. I had taken but a few strides when I suddenly heard movement on the trail coming toward me. Not knowing whether I was about to encounter a cow, a Filipino, or the Japanese guard, I slid into an area of thick brush on the downward slope of the trail, hoping to be passed unnoticed. As the follower approached my hiding area, I peeked upward through the brush and recognized the guard! The thought struck me that he had only been faking a snooze and had followed me soon after I left.

The guard stopped abruptly at the very spot where I had slid down into the thicket. He stood on the trail for a moment looking in my direction. Then, he said something in Japanese. What he said, I do not know. But his tone was not friendly, and I knew it was directed toward me. When I peered through the brush again, I saw the guard attach a bayonet to his rifle. At the sound of "click, click," I called out, "I'm coming!" Quickly, I stood to reveal myself and crawled up the embankment toward him. He was not smiling. "Ikimasho!" (Let's go!) he growled. I knew that expression well, since guards used it most days to start the crew back down the mountain. He nudged my fanny with the blunt edge of the bayonet. Terrified I led him back to the cutting site.

It was nearly time for the crew to return to camp when we entered the clearing. Mysteriously, another guard was at the woodcutting site. I could only guess that he had somehow been paged to oversee the crew while his partner followed me. It was a quiet and embarrassing walk down the mountain. I followed the crew carrying my two pots, the guard behind me. I am certain the woodcutters were curious as to what I had done or where I had gone, but no one said a word. As we walked quietly past the machine shop, the guard pointed me toward the guardhouse. The crew, as was their custom, continued on their way to the barracks unguarded.

We entered the guardhouse. I saw Nellie McKim first. Commandant Hayakawa was standing behind her. Maintaining a stern face, Nellie winked at me. That gesture erased a fleeting thought I had about Mr. Mount's beating. Then she took charge of the interrogation. First, she asked me about my walk with a leading question that prompted a safe answer, saying, "You've been exploring out-of-bounds?"

"Yes," I answered.

"Am I correct that you didn't see any Filipinos?" Again, I answered in the affirmative. Nellie knew I was harmless, but dutifully asked questions and responded in Japanese to Hayakawa and to the guard. Hayakawa understood some English but said nothing. I remained frightened until I noticed Hayakawa's relaxed smirk. Then I felt relieved. Nellie also asked my guard a question in Japanese, which he answered briefly and shrugged his shoulders.

Informed by one of the crew of my whereabouts, Mom showed up at the guardhouse. Hayakawa courteously ushered her into the interrogation room. I knew I had let her down, and my eyes grew moist. Nellie sternly informed her of the afternoon's events. Hayakawa appeared calm, but warned both Mom and me that more severe consequences would follow such behavior in the future.

Nellie remained in the guardhouse as Mom and I finally were ushered out the door. I anticipated a severe scolding from her, which did come, but only after she placed a loving arm around my shoulders. I felt spoiled. My sentence, as I learned from Nellie at suppertime, was to forego bucket-carrying duty for a week and return to assisting the garbage crew. I felt great relief and thanked her. She was ever an angel.

I prepared for lights out that evening and Uncle B followed me to our bunk. He spoke to me in soft tones. "There is a war going on young man, and it is not a smart idea to test the patience of the Japanese." He reminded me how lucky I was to be protected by guards whose cultural instincts showed respect for children. "But," he added, "they do carry weapons. Don't ever test their instincts like you did. Promise me!"

As I put down my pocket hymnal at lights out, a guard appeared in the darkened bunk aisle. He looked toward my bunk and strolled over to it. It was the same guard who had followed me on the trail and escorted me to the guardhouse. I did not quite know what to expect. Then, reaching down, he patted me on the side of the head and left a piece of hard candy on my pillow.

Commandant Fukuhara

One morning I reported to roll call at the parade ground with Uncle B and awaited the usual formality of bowing to Commandant Hayakawa, followed by the "hai hai" (yes, yes) ritual indicating one's presence. On that day, Hayakawa walked toward us with another Japanese man by his side. Strangely, and with no introduction, the man stepped forward and introduced himself as Commandant Fukuhara. He followed this by loudly announcing his plans to improve life in Camp Holmes—in quite fluent English. With his broad smile, upbeat manner, and promises of improved rations, Fukuhara struck me as someone I would like. Along with many of the others, I left the grounds with hopeful feelings.

Coinciding with Fukuhara's arrival, a bacillary dysentery epidemic was causing great suffering for many internees. The beds of the Nancetorium were full. Other patients, mostly women, had been bedded down in the barracks. Their neighbors gave Lysol baths to anything suspected of carrying the infection. Handmade posters were placed around camp warning against contact with flies. Mr. Ream's crew diligently created flyswatters out of bamboo sticks attached to screening. Fukuhara gave our doctors permission to secure additional Lysol from Notre Dame Hospital. It was a welcomed gesture.

Interestingly, Hayakawa showed neither remorse nor happiness at the change in leadership. We noticed that he continued to appear at roll call and was more visible around camp, but he still dodged conversations with adults. He remained at Holmes, apparently with no authority, sort of an adjutant to Fukuhara.

Sitting on my bunk one evening with a relaxed but pensive Uncle B, I shared my thoughts with him. I told him that I thought Fukuhara seemed nice and eager to be helpful. Uncle B, not one to make judgments, quickly said, "I hope you're right." Mom's reaction to Fukuhara's promises was similar to that of Uncle B. "We'll see what is on his mind—something surely is," she said.

In the following weeks, Uncle B observed Fukuhara's frequent visits with internees, but noted that the new commandant had not approached him. He asked those involved in conversations with Fukuhara about what topics he was exploring. Initially, Uncle B seemed reassured that the discussions focused on food and other camp needs. As the days passed, however, more of Fukuhara's questions centered on internees who had been longtime residents of the Baguio area. Almost daily, Uncle B heard reports that Fukuhara's questions were growing more pointed. He was primarily interested in talking to internees whose prewar friends had not surrendered at Brent School. Accounts of all those interactions with Fukuhara made their way to Uncle B.

The reports eventually prompted him to meet with the general committee. They agreed that adults should be advised not to share details of Americans on the outside with Fukuhara. The committee also cautioned internees not to mention any news getting into camp. Thereafter, the internees played dumb when Fukuhara approached them.

Six weeks later, the mysterious Fukuhara was gone. Hayakawa was again our commandant and would remain so until the year's end. We could only surmise about the rationale for Fukuhara being sent in as our leader, especially since he wore only partial military attire during his tenure at Holmes. Uncle B labeled the whole episode "guerilla roulette."

Playing bridge with Mom one evening, Uncle B admitted that Fukuhara had been one of the men he had seen almost daily during his November incarceration at Military Police headquarters in Baguio. "Those recollections prompted my suspicions about his presence in camp," he told her. Subsequent to Fukuhara's departure, we were to welcome to camp one American family that had tried to evade the Japanese by taking to the hills.

On April Fools' Day of 1943, the Moule family—Bill, Marge, and their three young children—were trucked into Camp Holmes. For months, they had been undergoing hardships hiding in the hills south of Baguio. Sickness, betrayal, and starvation accompanied their flight from Japanese soldiers. Bill was hospitalized almost immediately upon his arrival at camp with a serious case of malaria and a painful leg.

The Moules' decision, only days before Christmas 1941, to dodge surrender at Brent School hinged on their belief that Japan had no plan for long-term occupancy of the Philippines. Bill thought that invasion was only an attempt to send a message to America that the Pacific Islands belonged to Orientals. Bill, too, had read of the German concentration camps. The very thought of an experience like that for his family haunted him.

Unfortunately for the Moules, the defeat at Bataan opened the door for wider Japanese attention to guerilla movements throughout Luzon. Enemy intrusions into those hills placed great pressure on American civilians who, like the Moules, had retreated to the rough mountain country. Nearly all such families were eventually captured or murdered.

We were happy to have the Moules alive and a part of our camp family. Mom and Marge quickly developed a friendship as they worked side by side in the camp kitchen. Mom enjoyed her stories of life in the hills, and Marge appreciated Mom's counsel relative to "making do" in Camp Holmes life. Walking with me to the Nancetorium one day, Mrs. Moule expressed her fond feelings for Mom. She told me that Mom's "parting with her halo" had opened the door for their close relationship.

News of Dad

On a handmade calendar she pinned on a wooden beam by her cot, Mom had kept a record of each passing day since she had last heard from my dad, her dear Walter. His phone call to Baguio after disembarking the inter-island ferry at Cagayan de Oro in mid-December 1941 had been our last contact with him. That date stood out with a circle around it.

On the evening of April 15, 1943, Mom made a second circle on her calendar following a stunning surprise. Shortly after noon that day, she was ordered to report immediately to the guardhouse. Apprehensive and hoping that I had not again misbehaved, she crossed the grounds and opened the guardhouse door. There standing beside Hayakawa was our close Davao friend, Mr. Matsumoto.

Matsumoto stared at her with no hint of a smile or an inkling of warmth. Tears welled in Mom's eyes, yet her instinct to rush to him with a big hug was checked by his emotionless expression. Matsumoto's coldness prompted Hayakawa to allow him a short visit with Mom.

Both walked slowly across the grounds, accompanied by a Japanese guard. Matsumoto quietly apologized to her for his "rude greeting," explaining that only because of that cold look would he be granted time with her. "Your commander appeared suspicious," he added. Stopping briefly in front of the family barracks and appearing to take in the western hills, Matsumoto told the accompanying guard to locate the Tong children and bring them to where he and Mom were standing, so he could take a picture.

That request provided a few private minutes for Mom and Matsumoto to talk about Dad. Her immediate fear was that Matsumoto's message might be a devastating one. But he informed Mom that he had seen my father two weeks previous but dared not risk carrying a note from him. Her moist eyes reflected her joy. Matsumoto described the conditions of the Davao POWs. He told her that Dad and Frank Cary, a prewar missionary in Japan and close friend of Dad's, were presently building a runway designed to land Japanese Zero planes a few miles outside Davao. "The Japanese fear U.S. carriers operating around the Celebes Sea and Moro Gulf," he said. (In September 1944, an American bomber devastated the Sasa Airdrome runway near Davao that Dad and other internees had spent months constructing prior to their transfer to Santo Tomas on Christmas Day 1943.)

Although Dad's internment camp had no running water or toilet facilities, there had been little sickness among the prisoners. Matsumoto told Mom that the camp had no doctor and that Dad was filling that role as best he could. "In serious cases of illness," he went on, "internees are taken to Davao Hospital where Doctora Sexon cares for them, but only for short periods."

Mom also learned that the Davao internees were all Americans, most of them had been affiliated with scattered plantations during the prewar years. Many internees were associated with the huge fruit-growing Del Monte plantation in the area, and a few with Matsumoto's own Ohta spread. "You know many," he said. Some gold miners, too, were a part of the group. There were few missionaries in the Davao camp. Those few were brought in from neighboring Mindanao provinces. When Mom asked about internee treatment, Matsumoto admitted, "The early treatment was cruel. It was in retaliation for the severe actions of Filipino guerillas against Japanese civilians before the invasion."

He apologized again for not having brought a written note, but emphasized that there would be great danger to him and to her if he was discovered to have done so. Still, he asked Mom to scribble a short message on the back of a picture he carried of his own family, a risk he felt he could take. After my sisters and I had been gathered, we walked to the guardhouse as a group. With Hayakawa's approval, Matsumoto arranged to have a picture taken of our family. He would pass it on to Dad following his arrival in Davao. Dad carried that picture with him for the remainder of the war and thereafter.

Only a month before Matsumoto's surprise visit, Natalie Crouter wrote in her diary that Mom was experiencing low moments almost daily when "she stands on the edge looking deep down and wondering how she can go on." But Matsumoto's nearly one-hour visit confirming that Dad was alive and in good health, renewed Mom's spirit to continue the fight to survive.

As we departed the guardhouse, Mom was in a state of elation that I had not seen for a long, long time. It was as if a *carabao* had been removed from her shoulders, just to learn that her dear Walter was alive. The change in her outlook was dramatic. She was like a new person. Mom had never reached the point of giving up on life, but much of her movement and interaction with others was possible only because of her disciplined mindset. Her natural self tended to reach out to others, and after Matsumoto's visit her fervor for assisting others soared. Her big smile returned. It certainly buoyed my own spirits. I was thrilled to be able to talk about Dad again without upsetting her.

Easter 1943

For weeks in the spring of 1943, I noted a rather large number of men, almost all of them missionaries, allowing their hair and beards to grow.

I did not have the nerve to ask anyone why they were beginning to look like an enclave of Wise Men. I had never seen them looking so unkempt. When my curiosity got the better of me, I asked Uncle B, who had retained his usual clean-cut appearance. "I think they are planning to surprise their wives at Easter," he said. With Easter drawing near, I expected the men to clean up.

Meanwhile, Uncle B, anticipating Hayakawa's possible rejection of an Easter Passion Play, decided not to request permission, but rather to inform the commandant that there was going to be a play. Further, he told Hayakawa that the general committee would like to invite him and the guards to the performance as special guests. His diplomatic approach followed Nellie McKim's suggested pattern of "informing not asking," and it paved the way for a memorable April 22 performance. When the news was broken to all the internees that a passion play would take place on Maundy Thursday, beard sightings sent clues as to who the actors would be. As plans progressed, Hayakawa, too, got caught up in the excitement and offered to allow Filipinos with ties to the internees to attend.

Behind the scenes, considerable planning had quietly been taking place under the leadership of Aunt Winnie Smith. She had volunteered to undertake the huge responsibility of preparing and directing a performance that would buoy spirits in Camp Holmes. Her first order of business was to select a person to portray the lead role of Jesus. It turned out to be her easiest decision. She chose her husband, Joe. Because of his natural humility, it took considerable persuasion for her to convince him to play that role. He did not wish to come under criticism because he was Winnie's husband. In truth, he was a natural for the role. His whole being radiated goodness. Joe's performance so influenced me that, to this day, my visual image of Jesus is Joe Smith. Mom jokingly suggested to Winnie that she draft Sorrell and Mount to play the roles of the robbers who flanked Jesus on the crosses.

Winnie initially had difficulty securing male volunteers for other roles—crowd, disciples, etc.—but once a few had agreed, others thought it might be fun and quickly volunteered, even agreeing to grow beards if necessary. Suddenly she had nearly two dozen possible disciples—more than there were parts in the play. So, she simply increased the numbers in the crowd scenes. The Smiths put the script together, beginning with the scene of the Last Supper and closing with the Crucifixion of Christ. A large group of women worked diligently for weeks to create costumes, decided who was to do what, and assisted in writing the dialogue. Although

Winnie remained in the background, everybody knew that she was the Easter maestro behind all the planning.

Curiosity brought a contingent of Japanese guards and Filipinos from Baguio to witness the traditional Western celebration of Easter. Interestingly, one of the Japanese was recognized as one of the military police who had participated in the November interrogations of the tortured men. Afterward, Uncle B facetiously told Mom that he hoped the MP "did not get any ideas from the cross-hanging scene."

The passion play was a remarkable success. The entire camp attended and many, like me, were moved to tears. It would have been difficult for a professional troupe to top the performance set in such a striking location. Large boulders and shrubs stood out on the natural sunken garden stage. The scene helped me imagine what Gethsemane must have looked like. Views of the eastern mountains and the stately pines west of the garden framed Mother Nature's stage perfectly. The embankment extending northward from the guardhouse provided ideal seating for the audience. Magically, our prison became a theater.

A great deal of cooperative preparation went into the creation of gowns, robes, helmets, shields, etc. The production was the first all-camp project and amplified our spirit of friendship and respect for one another—clearly the finest feeling that we had experienced up to that time. "The whole shebang," Mom later recalled, "pulled many hearts toward a Christ that some never before had known." She was particularly excited to note that missionaries did not dominate the cast. The "miners" had joined in and taken on a goodly number of the roles.

Two days later, a sunrise service on Easter morning capped Easter week. As we stood to sing, "Christ the Lord is Risen Today, Alleluia," what had started as a misty morning seemed like it was touched by God's hand as the sun's rays cleared the skies over the eastern mountains. I shall always recall that week as the most poignant of my internment years, indeed, of my life. The hymn also brought back memories of Easter a year earlier when the guards' bowings toward the sun had added spice to our closing alleluia.

Testing Rumors

In the spring of 1943 rumors about the war in the Pacific bloomed everywhere. Rumors had been a part of our lives since Ray Hale first drove a truck into the Baguio marketplace in January 1942. Given his questionable sources of information, Mom and others ignored most of what trickled into camp through Hale. A few of the men around the card tables found the recent rumors, true or false, to be only therapeutic chatter-fodder.

But the current rumors leaking into camp seemed to have more substance. For the first time, different sources shared the same intelligence, making the information we were receiving more credible. Almost every adult in camp was aware that radiocasts were being received within our confines. However, only a select few knew that a shortwave radio was hidden behind wall panels in the backroom bowels of the Nancetorium. Jim Halsema, the lone operator, was Uncle B's source of confidential information. The radio did not always function, but Halsema seemed able to find the solutions to the technical problems. He was a mechanical genius.

During the early days of the radio's existence, Halsema never shared what news he heard. Japanese suspicions about a hidden radio, therefore, were eventually allayed. For more than a year, much of the news coming across Jim's radio proved inaccurate anyway. Most was propaganda broadcasted by a woman known as Tokyo Rose. Jim Halsema labeled her constant patter "so much hot air."

At one point, Halsema found that reports from Tokyo were almost identical to those coming out of San Francisco. The news painted a picture of American setbacks in the Pacific. After following the reports very closely for a week, Halsema realized that all the broadcasts had to be emanating from Tokyo. He believed that Tokyo radio falsely credited the news as coming from San Francisco. The San Francisco voice, seemingly a plant, was very American. Halsema surmised that the word from "Frisco" really came from an American voice in Japan. "Likely a POW," he told Uncle B.

Had the Japanese somehow intercepted San Francisco broadcasts, or were the reports truly sad accounts of America's losses in the Pacific war? Halsema could not be sure. Gradually, his hopes for American progress waned.

Suddenly though, his spirits took a U-turn after radiocasts began to mention American plane losses of eight to twelve for every Japanese plane lost. That tidbit totally contradicted reports he had picked up weeks earlier, reports he trusted as coming from the U.S. sources. It seemed nearly impossible that such disparity could occur so rapidly. Halsema realized that the losses claimed were simply too much of an exaggeration to be true. That single report helped dispel the fears of a major American defeat in the Pacific and restored hope at Camp Holmes.

The Art of Necessity

On Saturday mornings, Fabian Ream regularly worked alone in the workshop. He was highly respected in camp for the magical way he could turn almost anything into something useful. He performed miracles with leather, metal, tin cans, wire, and wood. His shop contained a variety of junk procured from looting raids, the garbage dump, or discarded items given to him by internees to use in any way he saw fit.

Mr. Ream always welcomed me when I strolled into his shop. I loved watching his fingers move. As I observed his motions, he would hum to himself or launch into commentary, "Now we put a drop of solder here," etc. Mom admired his ability to answer personal or camp needs without fanfare, and she raved about his handsome beard. Women, particularly, lauded Ream's skill at crafting items like cooking utensils, rings made of Filipino coins, and other jewelry. Mr. Ream was a patient teacher, as well. He showed me how to grip a knife to carve wood safely toward my body. He also taught me to follow the grain of the wood, and where to place my fingers when "edge cutting."

An artist herself, Mom valued artistic talent. At her postwar speaking engagements, she often mentioned the "Ream Team," which included Fabian's sister, Beulah, and several other men, most notably Bart Rice and Ray Hale. "If ever I were to be isolated on a Pacific island," Mom said, "I would want to be accompanied by that team."

Fabian Ream was our camp's Benjamin Franklin with his innovative discoveries. His products included a wicker rice shaker, which separated inedible particles from rice, saving hours of onerous labor for the women charged with that duty.

Ream's most renowned creation was the legendary Banana Machine. That amazing gadget took up the duties of those charged with handing out a banana to each person passing through the food lines. Prior to his invention, if a blemished or small banana were handed to the next-in-line internee it was frequently received with a dirty look or the charge, "Why do I always get the small one?" The Banana Machine laid out only one banana in a groove to the next person in line. It may have been the biggest, softest, or most green banana, but it was the only one that person could take. Rejecting it meant returning to the end of the line and hoping for better luck the next time. Of course, by doing that one took the risk that the day's supply was short and there would be no bananas left. Ream also invented a peanut-shelling machine. It was made of two wooden slats that moved back and forth, crushing the shells and allowing the nuts to fall into a basket.

In addition, with the application of solder or tar, Ream extended the life of pots and pans made from plant containers. The dentures he carved out of *carabao* bone drew many chuckles, but they were a masterful and useful piece of art.

With the help of his shop comrades, Bart Rice constructed a petite coffin with wooden slabs obtained from loose boards found around the camp barracks. The coffin became the resting place for toddler Woody Bartges, Jr., whose premature birth meant he would not survive due to the lack of necessary medicines.

Changing Camp Fashions

By the summer of our second year of captivity, most of our clothes and footwear had passed the point of usefulness. For me, only a single pair of khaki shorts remained wearable, largely because they were rarely washed. That fact bothered Wezer. "Washing them on the rough washboard," I told her, "only causes the shorts to wear thin faster." So, I continued to resist her efforts to launder them.

"But they stink," she chided me. Thankfully, she never attempted to remove them forcibly. My Keds had long since gone to the dump with the garbage detail, so barefoot was my *modus vivendi* around the grounds of the camp, and I was not the only shoeless child.

Recalling those barefooted days, I remember only a few stubbed toes and no lacerations. It is amazing how quickly shoeless feet can become calloused. I felt no pain running over stones, hot concrete, or on wooded paths. All the Igorot children I had seen went shoeless. They often walked long distances along hot tarmac roads carrying heavy loads with no apparent discomfort.

A few of my pals and many adults had taken to wearing *bakyas* for footwear, with only a strap holding the wooden clogs in place. I found them a hindrance, particularly when trying to run. The talented men of the shop manufactured clogs from wood or sandals from discarded auto tires. I wore a pair during my climbs up the mountainside, not for comfort, but only because of my fear of stepping on a snake. Rarely did a week pass on the path to the woodcutting site that I did not see one. The crew assured me that snakes were more startling than dangerous. Yet, my recollections of the boa swallowing a baby in a Mindanao barrio caused me to be cautious and to wear the *bakyas*.

It always intrigued me to see the unique creations people put together to serve their many needs. Not only Mr. Ream and his colleagues in the shop used their imaginations to fashion good things with few resources. Headbands and berets, for example, made of coconut or bamboo palms, all crafted in camp, were commonplace. Some wives devised clever G-string creations, so many of the wood crew could strip down to that garb for their long hours of sawing timber on extremely hot days. On more than one occasion, a woodsman or two went the way of wearing "skin-tights" (no clothing). Two of the crew, thanks to the sewing skills of their wives, had Japanese soldier-style hats with bands of cloth hanging from the back of the cap to protect their necks from the afternoon sun.

Jim Halsema was not only a skilled radio "fixer-upper," but a gifted wood sculptor as well. Always in need of oil to give his woods a lustrous finish, Jim realized that teenagers like Wezer had an oily substance on their faces. He harvested those oils by rubbing his thumb and forefinger down the sides of the nose toward the cheekbone. Applying this to his piece of wood gave it a finished tone. One mother complained that this was abusive behavior, but Mom thought it was creative. Regardless, Halsema passed up my face, branding my moisture as "just sweat."

A number of people enjoyed whittling decorative earrings made of white, brown, or black coconut shells. Some even sold their handmade earrings during the early years of concentration when modest forms of dressing up were still in vogue and some money was available.

Most women's clothing was completely worn out by the last year or so of internment. But by that time, everyone paid more attention to survival than appearances. The attire women made to replace worn clothing came from a variety of sources, including old curtains and pillowcases—oftentimes put together in a patchwork fashion. Their distinctive coverings made individual women easily identifiable from across the parade ground. Mom kiddingly called Aunt Harriet's checkerboard skirt, "Harriet's Passion." My sisters and I found much of what the women devised to be eye-catching.

Of greater concern than shoddy apparel was the lack of staples during the summer of 1943. A couple of the Japanese guards capitalized on the shortages by surreptitiously trading certain hard-to-procure food items for watches or money. A small number of internees had managed to hide money for their own future security.

Cigarettes, sugar, and fruit of any variety were the most sought-after items. I felt sorry for the addicted smokers for whom a cigarette meant more than a meal. They paid handsomely, even for a Japanese brand called Cherry. Toward the end of internment, more than a few heavy smokers would give away almost anything to secure a pack of Cherrys from a Japanese guard.

The guards were particularly fond of foreign watches and enjoyed dickering with the few wood crew members who wore them. During a lunch break on the hill, one of my woodcutting friends was prepared to trade his Swiss watch with a guard for two packs of cigarettes and a banana. I told him moments before he sealed the deal that I had seen two bananas in the guard's small satchel. Thus, he proceeded to bargain with the guard for two bananas, not one. After the trade, my friend gave me one of his bananas. That was my first introduction to the world of negotiation. Both men seemed happy with the deal. Only rarely did guards dicker in the camp confines, simply because such interactions with internees were not permissible.

Hiawatha

Aunt Winnie decided upon *The Song of Hiawatha*, by Henry Wadsworth Longfellow, for her second student theatrical production. Her chosen site for the play was a stretch of level ground, once a tennis court, at the base of the slope leading to the sunken garden. The production featured a teepee and council ring constructed by our cast of children and parents. We hand-crafted bows and arrows and decorated our faces with "war paint." A volunteer mother was our Nokomis. Winnie created the other girls' parts also.

Aunt Winnie told me to play the role of Hiawatha in the all-children production. I am not sure whether she selected me to play this part because she knew that I had read the poem or because I had the darkest tanned body of the boys in camp. Indeed, after many readings of my favorite lines with a nice rhythm, I had memorized bits and pieces of the poem in my little book. Winnie adapted the production to fit the lines I had memorized instead of following the order of Longfellow's lengthy story.

I neither possessed then, nor do I now, any acting skill and was quite nervous throughout the performance. The speaking lines of the play were almost entirely mine. When I needed help, Winnie would whisper a cue to me from behind a small partition. In one segment of my recitation, I spoke the lines, "Many things Nokomis taught him of the stars that shine in heaven, showed him. . . ." There was a pause and Winnie whispered, "Ishkoodah, the comet." I had no difficulty with my favorite lines like "by the shores of Gitche Gumee, by the shining big sea water, stood the wigwam of Nokomis, daughter of the moon, Nokomis." I shall always remember that day as my first and only attempt at launching an acting career. Only Mom and Wezer celebrated my debut and Rae's background performance.

Most of Aunt Winnie's productions were single-evening events in the dining hall. They were well attended and brought a touch of hilarity to lives in need of laughter. One comedy sketch, which she arranged on a rainy evening, featured children displaying their individual talents—all in their soaked clothing. Jim Halsema, in a very professional manner, added a touch of color by introducing each child with a concocted, humor-laced resume. Rae, who had written a poem with four verses about life in internment camp, was one of the performers. Halsema introduced her as "the child with a God-given smile and the feet of a rabbit." The last line in each of Rae's verses was identical, exclaiming, "Oh, how I want to go home!" In her diary, Natalie Crouter noted the children's feature song, written by Marvin Dirks, titled "Have You Tried Rice?" I have long since forgotten the words, but the song was such a huge success that it became a staple of camp life, often sung at audience request as the encore to other performances.

Following Winnie's lead, others later produced programs. Most of the performances poked fun at one another or at members of the Japanese guard corps, usually through song or characterizations of their habits. Those brought huge laughs. A guard or two always stood at the back of the hall and watched the proceedings. Although unable to understand the dialogue maligning their behavior, they laughed with the audience. The guards seemed to like the musical programs most and were often seen tapping their toes or swaying a little with the tunes, even when the words mocked their mannerisms.

Rumors, Sickness, and Scandal

In midsummer 1943, a new and interesting set of rumors found their way into Holmes. Since Nellie McKim had a 100 percent batting average when it came to sorting truth from fiction, her positive response to those rumors lent them credibility. She told the general committee that groups of Americans from each internment camp in the Philippines were to be freed. Those selected would gather in Manila and be put aboard a ship to sail to America. In return, America was to send a like number of interned Japanese to the Philippines where they would be sent on to Japan. The committee posted the information, and naturally, many in Holmes began to imagine gaining their freedom.

We heard later the same day, again from Hayakawa via McKim, that *all* families would be repatriated. But Nellie attached a caution to that announcement. "All will not be repatriated. You can bet on that," she said. Despite her words of caution, the pronouncement aroused so much excitement that a few of my poker-playing pals, who had consistently wagered on a Christmas 1943 release, began to get a little tipsy.

That same evening, Nellie told Mom that, according to Hayakawa, the number to be released was actually a mere handful. And each day afterward, the likely number dwindled. "If it comes down to one, dear Nellie, I hope that Carl will be the only domino standing," suggested Mom. She and Nellie shared that wish. Uncle B, whose family had left for the States before the war in an attempt to salvage the eyesight of son Bob, most deserved the opportunity to go home.

Given that my dad's location was still unknown, Mom was not at all anxious to board an evacuation ship unless her Walter, too, were a passenger. When the final decisions were made in Manila, we discovered that only one name from Camp Holmes made it onto the evacuation list. The numbers of internees released from Santo Tomas and Los Baños were far greater.

Our selected representative was Bill Portrude. He turned out to be an excellent choice. Following his selection, he was told he could not take anything in writing from camp. For weeks after the announcement, he took great pains to memorize every family's name in alphabetical order and as many United States addresses as he could. That feat was an amazing accomplishment. He then promised to contact families in America with some news of their kin. Indeed, once stateside, Portrude managed to track down every single family. His achievement was nothing short of heroic.

As our third wartime Christmas neared, I became dreadfully worried about the state of Uncle B's health. First, he suffered a serious bout of dysentery. He looked exhausted, and the huge smile, ever reassuring me that all was well, had vanished. Dr. Skerl ordered him to the Nancetorium. Carrying his small bag, I walked a wobbly Uncle B to the hospital. Dr. Skerl told me to avoid further contact with known dysentery cases. "I'll keep you posted on Carl," he said. Uncle B was hospitalized for more than a week.

In all the barracks, many suffered from fevers and nausea. Charles O'Dowd, one of those struck down with dysentery, suffered an accompanying heart attack. Amazingly, he was back in the barracks within two days and seemed as ornery as usual. He never fully recovered, however, and died on September 13, 1944, from torture-related complications.

Days after entering the hospital, Uncle B felt a little better. That was encouraging news to everyone in camp. While visiting him on a day approved by Dr. Skerl, I noticed several Igorots also being treated. The sight of them startled me, since I had not seen Igorots there or anywhere else on the grounds before. I wondered whether the Japanese had approved their care, or whether they had entered the hospital through the backdoor facing Bontoc Trail. In many ways, their lives on the outside were more tenuous than ours. The Igorots certainly had no immediate access to medical centers or medicines, and it seemed a good gesture to care for them. The doctors had heard of the food scarcities in the Igorot hamlets. Most of their plantings had been lost to the severe flooding that had followed the heavy rains in the fall months.

The flooding, according to Hayakawa, was the major reason for the food shortages in camp. Most believed him. Facetiously, a few cynics in the men's barracks spoke loudly that there was no lack of hearty meals consumed by the camp kitchen crew. Those cynics, in fact, claimed to have witnessed a meat orgy following a supper during which no meat had been served to others. Those kinds of assertions surfaced periodically, and since one could never be certain of the truth, they routinely evoked scorn and anger. For a while, the atmosphere in the men's quarters was poisonous. I felt very unsettled in such tense moments. It was at these times that I most missed Uncle B's presence as a bunkmate and his way of calming anger with a sharp, "Enough of that!" Uncle B's return to his cot brought relief to me and order to barracks Number Three.

Word of another so-called scandal circulated widely during the bridge games in the dining hall. It centered on Ray Hale, the camp truck driver. It so happened that his wife, a Filipina living in Baguio, had a baby while her American husband Ray was interned in Camp Holmes. When I asked Mom how that worked, she responded only that the Filipina's little girl "was a gift of God." I came to understand the story more clearly after reading some of Mom's postwar notes about the Filipina wife who had surreptitiously visited her interned American husband on occasion.

Natalie Crouter's account in *Forbidden Diary* describes the incident well. She writes that Ray, the proud father, had boasted, "Wouldn't you like to know how we managed it? I told you we could make anything at the shop, and now I've proved it." (At a Holmes reunion in St. Augustine in 2007, I spent time with the interesting and humorous Emma Hale. With a broad smile and a hearty laugh, Emma described to me sneaking into camp at night and her periodic rendezvous with Ray behind the tool shop.)

Soon after Uncle B's bout with dysentery, Mom's almost constant battle with swelling in her legs got to the point where walking had become near impossible. Wezer, ever motherly in her dealings with Rae and me, spent many hours with Mom at that critical time. Dr. Skerl readily identified Mom's condition as "advanced beriberi and gradual emaciation." He handed Mom a small sleeve of bananas with the admonition, "Eat these, don't share them." She thanked him with a smile and whispered, "I haven't seen one of these in a long while."

Very slowly Mom regained strength. Friends stopped by to see her in her barracks cubicle. Aunt Leora was a regular. She had a keen knowledge of biblical passages and shared one with Mom from the book of Matthew that related to her struggle with starvation. Leora read, "Behold the fowls of the air: for they sow not, neither do they reap. Yet, your heavenly Father feedeth them. . . . Are ye not much better than they?" Mom's condition improved gradually, and several days later she was walking slowly. I spent my short visit with her in hugs, a few tears, and a shared prayer.

A further December distraction for bedridden Uncle B was Commandant Hayakawa's sudden order to close the camp high school. That pronouncement followed Hayakawa's decision that, henceforth, the school building was to be his private dwelling place. Hayakawa explained his move to Nellie McKim, saying that he did not trust his own guards and therefore did not want to remain in quarters with them. Luckily, Uncle B and the committee did not have to tackle that issue, since a day later, one of the committee members visited Uncle B to inform him that Hayakawa was to be relieved of his post. A new commandant would be reporting shortly. That notice lent hope that high school classes might soon resume.

Tomibe Rokuro

In December 1943, we were introduced to our third official commandant. His name was Tomibe Rokuro. Tomibe's first contact had been with Nellie McKim. Unlike Nakamura, an émigré, and Hayakawa, a long-term resident of the Philippines, Tomibe was a bona fide Japanese soldier with years of prior military service in China.

On the parade ground, Commandant Hayakawa stood by Tomibe. Although Hayakawa stayed on for a short while as Tomibe's underling, it was clear from the outset that Tomibe was in charge. He made that point clear by announcing that the high school program would restart in January.

Uncle B was happy that Tomibe offered no prohibition against teaching history in the school and granted approval for foreign language classes. That pronouncement offered teaching opportunities to a number of internees with foreign language skills. Initially, Spanish, French, Greek, Chinese, and Tagalog were taught to teenagers. Other classes were aimed at adults. Nellie McKim, for example, taught *Nihongo*. Additional adult subjects included art, ikebana, Bible study, biology, and bridge. The mere endeavor of learning something new or unique—testing minds—lifted spirits immensely.

Soon afterward, Tomibe found opportunities to ease the pains of prison life for all of us in ways that would not draw the ire of his superiors. Within weeks, parents in particular, recognized his benevolence. Tomibe treated the children with affection. His efforts to improve camp life were genuine, unlike earlier commandants whose shallow promises rarely materialized.

Within a month, Tomibe's humanitarian manner had won him the respect of almost everyone. Naturally, there were those who retained the "Jap is a Jap" attitude. However, Mom often referred to Tomibe as being a "non-Christian Christian." She pointed out that his innate sense of goodness led to decisions that preserved lives and restored hopes for our knowing freedom someday.

At Tomibe's first meeting with the general committee he revealed his earlier administrative role in Manila. He had surveyed internee life in Camp Santo Tomas and found that the camp was organized under civilian leadership, a form of governance known as self-rule. That meant all activity in camp—including classes, entertainment, workshops, family living arrangements, etc.—fell under the control of the internee leadership. The security of internees and the provision of food and other essentials procurable only on the outside was the responsibility of the Japanese Army.

While working in Manila, Tomibe was informed of his forthcoming assignment to Camp Holmes and learned that the Red Cross packages designated for Holmes in December 1942 had never been delivered. He guessed that the packages earmarked for Baguio went instead to Santo Tomas or were stolen by Japanese officers who sold their contents to Filipinos.

Tomibe told the general committee that his primary goals upon arriving at Camp Holmes were twofold. The first was to ensure correct delivery of the next shipment of Red Cross supplies designated for Holmes. Second, he would introduce the concept of self-rule as he had witnessed it at Santo Tomas.

He discovered that the topic of self-rule was already under consideration by the committee. Since Uncle B found Tomibe willing to consider self-rule for Holmes, the committee moved ahead with its discussions and put forward a tentative plan. At first, there were a few objections. A group of women resisted because they were to be granted only the right to vote on the administration of self-rule—not on self-rule as a form of governance. Their strong reluctance led a recovering Uncle B to point out several aspects of self-rule that bothered him as well. For the time being, further consideration of self-rule was suspended.

Uncle B's resistance centered on Holmes's vulnerability to guerilla activity. Guerillas were not a concern in Santo Tomas. He pointed out that an escape from Camp Holmes would be far easier than climbing over the steel fences surrounding Santo Tomas. Having experienced days of hell in the cells of the military police, bedridden Uncle B knew that if an escape occurred, as chair of the committee he could easily be singled out for another round of torture or worse. However, he made no mention of that personal concern to the committee.

After regaining his energy, Uncle B joined the committee on a regular basis. Their discussions put forward a compromise plan for self-rule to Tomibe. They also addressed concerns vis-à-vis leaders' responsibilities in camp oversight. Tomibe readily approved the committee's recommendations. In reality, approval was a token gesture. Everybody understood that the Japanese command could veto any questionable recommendation at any time.

But not only did Tomibe endorse self-rule—and what later became known as the family unit arrangement—he complied with the internee vote to eliminate morning roll calls. Uncle B was nervous about Tomibe's roll-call cessation and reminded the committee that, "If someone turns up missing some morning, guess who has to explain the absence?"

Somewhat surprisingly, when self-rule was put before the internees for discussion, the topic triggered a sudden outburst in the men's barracks. The minority opponents to self-rule became vehemently vocal in their opposition. This group was largely composed of the evening card players. Their raised voices were quite unlike the more mellow sounds I heard when they reacted to poor card hands. One of the men brought a game to a halt by throwing his cards on the table and loudly pronouncing, "Who the hell do we think we're kidding? Self-rule ... Jap-rule ... what the f— is it going to change? If the f——g Japs decide to shoot us, do you think they are going to pass it by a self-rule committee before they fire? Good night!" I did not share my evening eavesdropping with Uncle B until long after such issues of concern had become non-issues—and then not verbatim!

With Christmas Comes Hope

Returning from a routine truck trip to Manila in late December, Ray Hale shared the most recent news from Santo Tomas with Mom and Natalie. All the concentration camps on Mindanao and other islands in the southern archipelago were being moved to Manila. Those words raised my family's hopes immensely that a very special package, my dad, might soon be forwarded to Baguio. Mom suggested that Dad could be exchanged for former Holmes high school students who had put in requests to join family in Manila. It would not have been the first prisoner exchange between camps.

In fact, six months earlier Brent boarding students who had been interned in Baguio and whose Manila-based parents were imprisoned in Santo Tomas were trucked to Manila from Camp Holmes to be with their families. The return trip brought a couple of young girls to Holmes to be reunited with their parents. That small exchange supported our hope that Dad, too, might be sent to Holmes. Nightly I prayed for his arrival. It was also encouraging that on several occasions the general committee and Commandant Tomibe held discussions regarding the possibility of negotiating exchanges in Manila while securing the Red Cross packages there.

Accompanied by Dr. Walker and two soldiers, Ray Hale drove Tomibe to Manila for the primary purpose of securing the Red Cross packages designated for Camp Holmes. Wielding his officer rank, Tomibe boldly cut through the red tape and arranged for the Baguio-labeled cartons to be immediately removed from Manila and transported by train to a storage shed in Bauang, only sixty kilometers from Baguio. At Tomibe's request, his long-time friend, the general manager of the Makayan Copper Mine, Mr. Nagano, agreed to provide trucks to transport the Red Cross shipment from Bauang to Camp Holmes.

With the Red Cross cartons secured, Tomibe addressed the matter of a prisoner exchange with the Japanese commandant in Santo Tomas. Amazingly, on the following morning, seven Santo Tomas internees rode back to Camp Holmes with Tomibe and Walker—Hale at the wheel. The truck pulled up on the Holmes parade grounds late in the afternoon of December 22. Internees streamed toward the vehicle, eager to see if Red Cross supplies were onboard. A few, like Norman Whitfield, stood by on the off chance that his wife Evelyn might happen to be on board. (Prior to the war, Norman was a logging engineer in northern Luzon and was interned in Baguio without his wife, who had remained in Manila.) I ran out to the baseball diamond to watch the truck unload. Mom, hoping and praying that Dad might be on board, watched from the barracks window with my "aunts," Leora, Winnie, and Natalie. The curious and the skeptics gathered to see who or what might emerge from the bed of the parked truck.

Disappointment showed on many hungry faces when the guard started handing down only personal belongings from the deep bed of the truck. Nothing was marked with a bright red cross. Clearly the Red Cross packages were not on board. The sight of a suitcase, however, prompted hopes that perhaps some people were. Dr. Walker stepped down from the dark cab first, a young girl behind him. A father suddenly waved his arms in joy at the sight of his daughter, as did her mother. Barely noted because no one knew him, Maryknoll Father Robert Sheridan also stepped down from the truck bed.

Norman Whitfield suddenly let out a whoop, overjoyed at recognizing his diminutive wife Evelyn. I was excited for Norman, who had befriended me and spoke often in the men's barracks of his dear Evelyn.

Mom searched the crowd for a sighting of Dad. Noting that my sisters and I had not reacted excitedly and all passengers seemed to have disembarked the truck, Mom broke down, sobbing openly, supported by her friends.

Mr. Hale, who had driven the truck from Manila, approached my sisters and me. He told us that the Mindanao internees were not yet in Manila but were on their way by sea. We were encouraged when he said that Dad, therefore, stood a chance to come up with the Red Cross boxes—if he arrived in time.

I raced upstairs to tell Mom that news. At that moment, all hope seemed to have drained from her body and she was visibly shaking. Word that the Mindanao POWs were on a ship en route to Manila eased her pain somewhat.

A day or so after Evelyn Whitfield arrived at Holmes, she stopped by Mom's cot, introduced herself, and told her that the Mindanao prisoners were not yet in Santo Tomas. Evelyn's warm support brightened Mom's spirits. The two unrelated Whitfield women, Margaret (Peg) Whitfield Tong and Evelyn Whitfield, became dear friends. Mom often referred to Evelyn as her "sustaining sweetheart"; their friendship developed into an intimate one that lasted throughout the war years and after.

As Christmas approached, mothers hoped to make it a meaningful holiday for their children. All truly wanted to believe that Christmas Day 1943, would be our last in confinement. In our starving state, we looked forward to the arrival of the Red Cross packages—assured by Uncle B and Tomibe that they would come—with great anticipation; that was at the top of everyone's Christmas list.

Well after darkness on December 22, eight trucks marked "Red Cross" in bold letters passed through the entry gate and stopped in front of the guardhouse. The folks who spotted them first shouted with joy. All at once the barracks emptied, hands waved, joyful screams filled the air, and tears flowed down happy faces. Fresh hope had indeed arrived. Nagano's drivers, who had earlier cleared the storage sheds of the crates marked for Baguio, emerged from the trucks and Tomibe greeted them. Bedlam reigned. The general committee notified everybody that there was a plan in place for distributing the cartons on Christmas Day. Only that announcement prevented total chaos.

Only a brigade of American soldiers marching through the gate at Camp Holmes would have evoked stronger feelings of joy than those we felt at that moment. The amazing Christmas gift from the Red Cross rekindled the spirits and vigor of even those most skeptical about surviving. Everyone patiently awaited the distribution on Christmas Day. Even the bedridden peeked out at the excitement. Knowledge that a bona fide eleven-pound carton of Red Cross food for each person would soon supplement our very meager rations was the miracle of that year's Christmas celebration. More than anything else, the "gifts of God," as the boxes of tinned meats and other nourishing foods were referred to at the Christmas service, let us know that America was indeed aware of our plight and had a plan to free us. We felt hope again.

A sidelight to the arrival of the Red Cross shipment was the kindly gift of ten packs of Chesterfield cigarettes forwarded to Tomibe's friend, Mr. Nagano, in appreciation for his support in providing trucks for the transfer of the packages from Bauang to Holmes. Those Chesterfields were nothing compared to the cartons of gifts from the American Red Cross.

Although the excitement over our packages overshadowed the Christmas pageant, Winnie directed a very professional performance. The scenes featured Joseph's search for a place where Mary could bear her child. As with the Easter pageant, the scene was set in the sunken garden. A choir hid behind a large, shop-crafted screen, but their spirited voices rang out clearly and powerfully. Spectators packed the embankment overlooking the garden. When Tomibe walked from the guardhouse to sit on the hillside for the pageant, nearby onlookers spontaneously applauded him. Together we watched colorfully clothed Wise Men addressing Herod, groups of children and goats in the shepherd scene, and Ruth Zimmerman as Mary singing "Away in a Manger" to the newborn Christ child. Indeed, the pageant was like frosting on a most memorable Christmas Day cake.

Tomibe's sincere commitment to getting those Red Cross packages to each of us, overriding the system that had stolen the Red Cross shipments the previous year, increased our deep respect for him. None of the former commandants received such admiration. Yet one cynic, spreading his usual venom, suggested that Tomibe was "setting us up for something." But we all knew that the arrival of those Red Cross food packages saved lives at a critical time. The contents included raisins, coffee, Spam, sugar, powdered milk, cheese, chocolate bars, soap, and cigarettes.

The day after Christmas, Halsema's hidden radio brought news of President Roosevelt's Christmas address. That raised spirits even higher. People passed slips of paper around camp with Roosevelt's inspiring words written on them. The slips read, "A human typhoon is gathering in the Pacific . . . be ready." To all of us craving the end of our confinement, Roosevelt's words were like a dessert from a Red Cross can, and they proved a forerunner to freedom.

Commingling . . . the Family Hour

The commingling hour had been a regular feature of camp life since the second week of internment at Camp Hay. Next to the word "hungry," "commingling" was the most commonly used word of the war years.

Camp rules kept married couples—and there were many in camp—from having natural lives together. Commingling rules generally provided for a one-hour opportunity to visit from 6:00 to 7:00 p.m. most evenings. Rules governing commingling changed from commandant to commandant and even from week to week. Sometimes, meetings between couples were suspended, but at other times they could enjoy relaxed hour-long strolls on the parade ground. If the commandant sensed abuse of the regulations or an untoward happening in camp, canceling or shortening the commingling hour was a slap-on-the-hand reminder to obey the commandant's wishes.

At Camp Hay, the fence around the tennis court had separated husbands from wives, and brothers from sisters. Couples were required to "walk and talk," to reduce the opportunities to exchange notes or other items. Later, a double-fence arrangement denied passage of anything back and forth. A duty guard could easily spot any attempt to toss a weighted note or a banana over the fences.

At Camp Holmes, a short straight stretch of fence separating the men's barracks from the women and children's quarters precluded much of a walk. Only occasional private conversation was possible, and then only if the fence line was not too crowded. During the waning weeks of Nakamura's tenure as commandant, commingling rules were softened. Passing messages through the fence, even at hours other than the prescribed visitation periods, occurred with greater frequency, and with far less intervention by the guards.

Following Tomibe's assignment as commandant in December of 1943, guards tolerated handholding by couples walking in a circuitous route and even quick kisses or hugs. Long embraces, however, remained taboo.

Couples developed verbal calls or whistles when they wished to get their mate's attention and call him or her to the commingling fence for an exchange of words or small items. "Over time," Wezer remembered, "I could tell by the whistle, birdcall, or loud cough who was being paged. If a woman was doing her wash or was in the bathroom, I would race down and tell her that her husband was paging her." My favorite call was Dr. Augustus Skerl's melodic rendition of a goose call common to Great Britain. It was not a pretty tone like that of a whip-poor-will or an oriole, but it had a deep resonance that easily caught Mrs. Skerl's attention— and Wezer's.

A Heaven-Sent Gift

For long stretches in February and March 1944, we suffered from unseasonably hot weather. Our clothes hung on us like dead chickens prepared for an Igorot fiesta. Ordinarily during that time of year in Baguio, powerful westerly winds spiraled up the ravines from the Lingayen Gulf toward Trinidad.

On March 13, 1944, the ferocious gales finally arrived, blowing clothes off the lines behind the women's barracks, and extending the "rising sun" Japanese flag such that it pointed toward the eastern hills. On the heels of those winds came a surprise that gave Mom occasion to circle another date on her special calendar.

It was not uncommon to see a Japanese troop truck drive through the main gate of Camp Holmes and stop at the guardhouse flagpole to drop off supplies or a few newly assigned soldiers for guard duty. But on that wind-swept March day, the truck stopped only momentarily by the flagpole. Commandant Tomibe stepped out of the guardhouse and with a brief wave directed the driver to enter the camp proper. The truck eased its way across the parade ground to the barracks area. Trucks rarely advanced beyond the guardhouse. My last recollection of one unloading in front of our barracks had been the arrival of Father Sheridan and Evelyn Whitfield from Santo Tomas three months earlier.

On this March day, we had had no advance notice of the cargo coming in. Curious internees gathered around the truck on the off chance they might know someone getting out of the truck bed. Mom had observed the incoming vehicle from the second floor of barracks Number Two and my sisters stood on the outer ring of a growing number of spectators around the truck. I stood alone behind Mount's shack where I had been throwing stones at imagined targets on the embankment below the cemetery. I knew a truck had arrived because I'd heard a child yelling excitedly, "The brown truck, the brown truck!" Everyone else hushed, waiting for someone to disembark or something to be tossed over the side.

The first item to emerge was a roll of barbed wire that was flung to the ground. Then, I heard Rae scream, "Daddy, Daddy!" Mom disappeared from the window, suddenly finding the strength to run. She and Wezer struggled to squeeze through the gathering of people. When she finally saw him, Mom shouted, "Walter, Walter!" and raced into the waiting arms of her tanned but gaunt husband.

The suddenness of their screams shook me. I felt like I had been smacked across the side of my head by a bag of sand. I sprinted away toward the goat pens behind the workshop, tears rolling down my cheeks. Dad must have seen me racing away. Within what seemed short minutes, I heard footsteps approaching the large bush behind which I lay on matted cogon grass, sobbing.

I did not look up. Dad laid down next to me, put his arms tightly around me, and placed my head on his chest. We both broke down, tears flowing freely, with nary a word exchanged. I had never felt Dad's tears before. That moment we shared was like no other before or since.

I had always looked upon my father with ardent affection. In my eyes, he could do no wrong. My favorite moments as a child in Davao were spent with Dad. When alone with him, I learned much. When apart from him, I looked forward to his return. My favorite recollections were of we two together. On reflection, my instinctive race away from the mob scene on the parade ground as Dad climbed out of the truck was really a dash toward a time and place of private togetherness.

When reality began to settle in, he whispered, "I love you, young man . . . let's join the girls." I had no answer, only a sob. As we began to walk back toward the parade ground, arms around each other, Mom and my sisters spotted us. Wezer and Rae ran toward us. Dad embraced us and we embraced him in a teary-eyed five-person hug. Breaking the heavy emotion of the moment, Dad said softly, "Now you'll have to teach me how to commingle." We certainly had violated all the rules of commingling with our public display of affection.

Somehow during those precious moments the wind had completely stopped. It was as though it had blown in a gift from heaven and then gone on its way leaving us that peaceful time together. As we walked toward Dad's bag on the parade ground, Commandant Tomibe, standing alone by the flagpole, bowed slightly and offered a kindly wave.

Dad's arrival in camp brought something like an adrenaline rush to our spirits. I had never seen Mom so happy. She would not let go of him, even knowing that he would be living in the barracks next door. I felt lucky that Dad would be with me in the men's barracks. Uncle B graciously gave up his bunk, allowing Dad to share the double-decker with me. I slept on top. As we settled in before lights out on that memorable first night together in Holmes, Dad patted my back softly as he had at bedtime in Davao years before. It was a joy to feel his touch and to hear his voice. That moment was like living a dream.

Dad had never been one to talk openly of his dangerous escapades in Mindanao before the war, so I did not expect him to tell me stories of the hardships he endured as a prisoner in Davao. He spoke mostly of his supportive internee friends and some of the general happenings in the Davao camps and Santo Tomas. He had special praise for Mr. Matsumoto. His efforts in Davao to influence Japanese officers toward fair treatment of the POWs came at considerable risk to his own well-being. Matsumoto also leaned on the Japanese military to improve food rations and pressured them to allow prisoner treatment at the Davao hospital when medical needs exceeded what Dad could administer, since no trained physicians were interned in the Davao camps.

A good deal of time passed before we learned all that Dad and the other Davao POWs had experienced aboard a Filipino freighter that had been renamed *Shinsei Maru*. Dad's postwar account of the voyage conveys the full horror of that trip. "The miracle," he said, "was that only one of our group died on the way to Manila." Everyone had been stuffed into the cargo hold below the surface of the sea. Dried seaweed floating in hot salty water with an added dab of rice was their sole form of food. Ample servings of hot "tea" bearing an obvious seawater flavor were available. There were hundreds of very hungry rats on board, and nearly everyone in the hold suffered bites. Cecily Mattocks, a child at the time and a passenger on the freighter, notes in her book, *Happy Life Blues*, "The hold was alive with screams, children crying, and wailing babies." After Dad's arrival at Camp Santo Tomas, he was bedridden and in considerable pain for a long time, his rat bites taking weeks to heal. Dad eventually told me of his bout with dengue fever while interned at Santo Tomas. He lost considerable weight and energy, but recovered under the care of Dr. Beulah Ream Allen, the same doctor who had been Mom's supportive friend in Camp Holmes prior to her transfer to Santo Tomas.

During the days that followed, Dad also told Uncle B and me of his supportive friend, Frank Cary. Cary's fluent Japanese and deep understanding of Japanese culture had been a powerful force in sustaining American lives in the Davao camp. Frank Cary was Davao's Nellie McKim. Indeed, Dad and Cary were a team.

Wedding Bells

It did not take many days for my father to become an active member of the Holmes community. His arrival coincided perfectly with the excitement generated by the preparations for the first wedding in Camp Holmes, that of Wilma Park and Carroll Dickey. Fern Harrington and Cleo Morrison spent many days putting together a checklist of jobs, items to procure, and persons with specific talents to create accessories needed for the forthcoming wedding. Excitement mounted daily. Commandant Tomibe granted formal approval of the wedding, and the date was set for March 23, 1944.

In some small way, almost everyone helped prepare for the Park-Dickey nuptials. Skinny as he was, Dad's broad shoulders must have led Cleo to select him to head up the "piano gang." He led a group of men carrying the heavy piano from the dining hall across the parade ground and down the steep outdoor stairway to the sunken garden, where the wedding would be held. Wilma chose Uncle B to serve as the celebrant. Don Zimmerman was his assistant and one of the men in the shop forged matching wedding bands from prewar Philippine coins.

The exciting lead-up to the ceremony was therapeutic. The women's barracks was abuzz as they gathered materials and completed their assigned tasks for the wedding. With Tomibe's permission, bridesmaids dresses and a fashionable Saks Fifth Avenue wedding gown were procured for the ceremony from an internee woman's Baguio home. Graciously, the woman gave Wilma her gown as a wedding gift. Understandably, such a treasure from the past meant far more to Wilma than to the very generous donor.

Weeks before the "I dos," my curious Mom queried Wilma about what had prompted her decision to marry Carroll in Camp Holmes as opposed to waiting until after the war when their respective families could attend. After giving Mom's question some thought, Wilma's witty response said it all, "I have always dreamed of a large wedding and where else will I ever round up five hundred people?"

So perched on the embankment, I witnessed my very first wedding. Captain Tomibe, Nellie McKim, and a group of Japanese guards sat a few yards away. For me, the highlight of the ceremony was listening to Mary Dyer's gorgeous voice ring out over the garden as she sang "Because." I even had to move from my seat because the reverberations of her song seemed to bring red ants out of the earth. Tomibe and his guards appeared entranced by the proceedings. Their participation reminded us that our enemies, consumed as they were in watching every detail of the wedding, were not so different from us.

Before the wedding, Tomibe had asked Nellie McKim what an appropriate gift might be. He followed her suggestion, and without fanfare, presented Wilma a bouquet of calla lilies and two bottles of champagne. Further, he granted a delay of lights out for the entire camp so we could attend the joyous reception in the dining hall. Earlier, Tomibe had given the groom permission to revamp the small woodshed next to the hospital as their newlywed home, and Fern and Cleo offered their hospital cubicle to serve as the honeymoon suite for several nights. One of the most meaningful moments, Wilma told Mom days later, was opening the handmade guest book and seeing Tomibe's signature. That gesture had to be a "first-time happening" in the history of Japanese commandants.

4/4/44

As a resident child in a barracks that housed adult men and a few high-school-aged youths, I was only an observer of the evening activities and talk. But daytime work details offered me closer interaction with the men. I learned that two young men on our garbage detail had been soldiers prior to the war. A considerable number of men in camp knew about their military past, but it was never openly discussed. The two single men, Gregory Herbert (Herb) Swick and Richard (Rich) Green, were exceptions to the clusters of married men, be they missionaries, "miners," or executives, and they were the only former soldiers. Herb Swick was in his late twenties, tall, swarthy, and soft-spoken. He and I rarely talked, but often exchanged smiles in the small mirror hanging over the washbasin where we brushed our teeth each morning. Swick's closest friend in camp was Rich Green.

On garbage detail runs, along with Swick, Green, and others, I pushed and pulled *Carry Me Home* to the riverbed on the mountain trail outside camp. Among the men on the junk jaunts, Swick got the most attention from admiring Filipinas. Young girls along the route and at the dumping site were attracted to his handsome features and kind smile. They greeted his friendly words with giggles and affectionate responses. I held him in high regard mostly because of his very physical, manly appearance, but also for the respect he showed others on the crew—even kids like me. Therefore, when Dad woke me before roll call and told me that Mr. Swick and Mr. Green had escaped from camp during the night, I was shocked!

The two single men fled camp soon after midnight on April 4, 1944, three weeks after Dad's surprise arrival in Camp Holmes. While his presence had inspired positive feelings about our family's future, the news of the escape reawakened my fears. I worried that Dad and Uncle B might suffer retribution for the Swick and Green escape.

Uncle B, with trusted interpreter Nellie McKim, met that morning with Commandant Tomibe before roll call to inform him of the escape. Initially, Tomibe was shocked, then enraged. Uncle B had never seen Tomibe in that state. He told Uncle B and Nellie that the chosen escape date (4/4/44) was no coincidence. Nellie fully understood the significance of the number four. In Japanese, the word for four—*shi*—is a homonym with the word "death." (In some ways, the number four in Japan parallels the number thirteen in America; both signify bad luck.)

Whether the date of Swick and Green's escape was actually planned to send a message to the Japanese or a matter of happenstance, we may never know. But I do know that the coincidence unsettled Commandant Tomibe tremendously. Days afterward, he reiterated to Uncle B that the chosen date for escape was intended to hurt him personally. Yet he showed no animosity toward the others in camp. Tomibe said, "I think some like me and I like too."

Tomibe knew that his military superiors in Baguio and Manila would blame him for the escape and that he would be subjected, at the very least, to a reduction in rank and dismissal as commandant. He feared harsh interrogation or even falling victim to physical harm at the hands of the military police. Tomibe was aware, too, that the Kempeitai would make every effort not only to locate Swick and Green and make an example of them, but also to punish severely those in camp who may have abetted their escape. The only man who knew of their escape plan and aided their departure was Douglas Strachan. Luckily, neither Tomibe nor the other internees suspected Strachan, therefore, he evaded torture.

Whenever an escape occurred the policy of Baguio officials was to kill two people, possibly even one woman, in retribution. For days after the getaway, Tomibe lived in trepidation that the Kempeitai might pursue this plan of human sacrifice. He knew his superiors wanted to send a serious message to the entire camp about the consequences of escape, and especially for the slap-in-the-face choice of the 4/4/44 date. At the very least, Tomibe knew that new prohibitions would be imposed on all internees.

My own take on the date issue—after visiting with Tomibe in Japan in 1981 and Swick at a Baguio reunion in 1991—is that Swick was unaware of the significance of the date. However, Swick's guerilla leader, Lieutenant Colonel Russell Volkmann, who had arranged the escape, may have known its meaning. Volkmann was a high-ranking officer who had participated in the battle of Bataan and who presumably had some knowledge of Japanese customs.

Very soon after Swick and Green made their getaway, the military police took into custody four men suspected of being accomplices or having some knowledge of the planned escape. The four included Bill Moule, who had known Swick from their encounters in the northern mountains before being interned in Camp Holmes; Jim Halsema, son of Baguio mayor E. J. Halsema and former editor of the *Baguio Bulletin;* Gene Kneebone, a prewar affiliate of the Atok Mining Company, and Anders Lofstedt, Kneebone's camp bunkmate and a close friend of Swick.

Only Lofstedt avoided torture and was returned to camp the same day. The other three did not return for more than a week. Gene Kneebone endured the "third degree" to draw confessions. Moule was hung by the thumbs and beaten severely. Halsema had the same treatment as Moule but for a shorter period. Still, Halsema sustained more severe physical damage. The three received scant food, little water, and slept with frequent interruptions in very unsanitary cells.

The absence of the three men caused considerable anxiety in camp and extreme emotional distress to their wives. The general feeling in the women's barracks was that the escape had been a selfish act. Green, who had been interned since the mass surrender at Brent School and had heard Mukaibo's promise of death to others as punishment for any escape attempts, knew the potential consequences to fellow internees. The Sorrell escape in July of 1942 had caused far less anxiety because the military police knew of his ties to a Filipina wife and his likely whereabouts. Sorrell was easily tracked down.

In the men's barracks, there was dismay that Swick and Green would take such a risk at the expense of fellow internees. But there was some applause, too, for their bravery. One man said that young single men like them could help America to shorten the war through guerilla activity. After their return to camp, Halsema, Kneebone, and Moule—all having undergone severe torture—remained relatively quiet about the escape and the punitive events that followed.

In 1989 my respected friend John Ream interviewed Swick at a reunion in Los Angeles and learned some interesting facts about Swick's guerilla activities in northern Luzon during the months after his escape. Having been a conscripted officer in the U.S. Army prior to his internment at Holmes Swick felt justified in his decision to escape. He pointed out that Sorrell's earlier breakout caused no hardship to anybody. Swick learned of the weeklong beatings administered to the three men only after the war had ended, and he told Ream that he "saw each one of them after the war and they said that they did not carry a grudge."

Swick was correct, to a point. Following the war Halsema told me, "I understood." Kneebone said simply, "They were forgiven." Immediately following Moule's torture experience and return to camp, he angrily announced to anyone within earshot, "I will kill with my own hands anyone who dares another escape." By war's end, however, his reaction had softened. Moule, like the others, graciously said he understood their actions.

The price of the Swick and Green escape was costly for all of us, but we were relieved that no one had been shot as we had been promised so loudly at Brent School. Certainly, we were happy that Swick and Green were not captured. Most would agree, however, that the torture of three men in retaliation made any future escape untenable.

After consistently behaving as a humanitarian in his relationships with POWs, Tomibe felt the Swick-Green escape was like thrusting a dagger into the heart of one's father. Although he showed outward calm, he was inwardly livid. Throughout his remaining days as commandant, Tomibe felt betrayed. He shared these feelings with the general committee and informed Uncle B that he remained undecided whether to defend those who must have known of Swick and Green's plan. He was clearly in an awkward position.

Bunking Battles

Tomibe managed to disguise his lingering anger about the Swick-Green escape and worked closely with the committee to improve conditions in camp. His major effort centered on creating an arrangement in which families could live together. He believed the practice of family separation poisoned the atmosphere and shared these thoughts with the committee. Dr. Walker and Tomibe had seen a family unit plan in operation during their stopover at Santo Tomas to secure the Red Cross packages. Walker also saw merit in replicating that living arrangement at Holmes.

The general committee spent long hours working out a cubicle arrangement that would be practical and acceptable to most families. They worried about cramped quarters and the shortage of private spaces. Still, the committee believed the families would voice a unanimous "hurrah" for the idea. Instead, the plan gave rise to many heated arguments.

At our bunk, a frustrated Uncle B shared his surprise with Dad and me after a committee meeting in the dining hall one evening. The committee had discovered that a considerable number of very vocal husbands and wives vehemently opposed the plan. "Wow . . . were we ever misinformed!" Uncle B shook his head in disbelief. He understood how single people might be opposed; worried that family living would likely "increase the number of babies in camp at a time when severe shortages of milk, food, and medications were already a serious problem." A possible baby boom was a reasonable concern. But after all was said and done, the committee went ahead and passed the family unit plan anyway. Interestingly, only three babies joined our camp family following implementation of the new living arrangements—and then only during the final weeks of imprisonment.

Talking with Dad and me one evening, Uncle B lamented the anger created by family living. He blamed himself for not taking time to review the issue with more members of the camp before finalizing the proposal. "I goofed," he said. He then turned to me and asked, "Would you like to live with your mom, dad, and sisters in a private cubicle?"

"Sure," I answered. "Would you be with us?"

Uncle B only chuckled, and we shared a goodnight prayer together.

This farewell photo of Commandant Tomibe (front row center) includes his guard corps and respected internee leaders: Uncle B (second from right, back row) and Nellie (left of Tomibe), 1944.

Tomibe recommended the construction of small, private cubicles beneath the single women's barracks and the refurbishing of some huts in the compound for family living. Internees opposed to the plan disagreed. They expressed concern about the extensive labor needed to remove soil from beneath the barracks, the lack of materials available for construction, and the lack of physical energy. Access to toilet facilities also posed a challenge. The general committee found themselves caught in a quagmire over the issue.

Finally, with Tomibe's blessing and encouragement, the committee decided to allow families who wished to develop a unit to do so. Those who did not want to move could remain where they were. It seemed the only recourse. The final decision pleased Tomibe. A day later, he bade farewell to the general committee.

As the man in charge of our detention at the time of the Swick-Green escape, Commandant Tomibe lost his command. Japanese authorities in Manila demoted him to the rank of second lieutenant and reassigned him to demeaning tasks in Manila, a city afloat in a sea of turmoil in mid-July 1944. It was only after we had been released from our third confinement at Bilibid Prison that we would learn of the hardships Tomibe faced as the war in the Philippines continued.

Our Goat House Unit

As the family unit plan moved ahead slowly, a few ambitious men constructed isolated cubicles beneath the women's barracks. Additional units crudely formed out of scrap materials took shape behind the barracks. Seeing the others' progress, early objectors to the plan also began to put units together, too. They partitioned a few spaces in vacated areas in the women and children's barracks, and even a couple in the Baby House. The tide had turned. Families did not want to appear opposed to living together.

Dad and Mom chose the togetherness option in mid-October, weeks after Tomibe's departure from Camp Holmes. Our family found space in one of the tin-roofed huts on the west side of the parade ground. The Whitfields occupied a smaller cubicle in the same hut.

At different times, our hut had served as an elementary school classroom, a makeshift chapel, and for a short while, a goat pen. For Mom, especially, our move was a good one because there were no stairs to negotiate. That eased her pain considerably. My favorite feature of our new residence was the sound of rain on the tin roof. The pitter-patter reminded me of the

Davao rains that put me to sleep during my happy childhood years. Never one to admire structures with dull names like "Library" or "Hospital," Mom cheerfully created a small sign to go over our entry door—it bore a painting of a horned goat and the words "Goat House."

On occasion, I strayed from our Goat House to visit Uncle B in the men's barracks where he was recovering from another bout with dysentery. As we sat on his bunk one warm December evening, we overheard loud exchanges among some of the single men and the boasts of one about how he was going to even the score with the "f——g Nips" after our liberation. I rather expected Uncle B to intercede as he sometimes did when hearing such language, but he sat quietly and said, "They need that. But please don't get overly excited about such gutter talk. Just help your mom and dad in every way you can in the upcoming weeks. We are nearing the end."

Shifts in the War and Camp Leadership

Three months after the Swick/Green escape, we were introduced to Tomibe's replacement, Lieutenant Oura. Standing erect, he immediately declared in a loud voice that he was in charge. His arrogant manner made us realize how much we missed the straightforward, caring, and honest Tomibe. Prior to his departure, he had forewarned Uncle B that hard times would follow. Tomibe could not have been more accurate.

The subsequent months under Oura—a somewhat nasty individual—brought only misery, pain, and severe depression to the camp. The committee attributed our hardships to Oura, even though his actions may have been ordered by the military police, still angry about the escape. Oura became enemy number one from his first decree, which called for a double fence around the camp's boundary. He instituted roll call twice a day, at 8:00 a.m. and 7:00 p.m. and set up machine guns on the south hill facing the barracks and parade ground. Foxholes—extending to the north and south—flanked the machine guns. It was clear to everyone that these severe restrictions and threats were undoubtedly ordered by the Kempeitai.

Oura immediately prohibited all freedom of movement and ordered a cutback of food supplies. High strung and never hiding his feelings, Oura's every announcement and posted notice expressed his anger toward the committee. Although Oura often shared worries about his future, his family in Japan, and the loyalty of his soldiers with Uncle B, he showed no concern for us or our needs. We were simply not on his agenda, and camp morale fell to new lows.

Soon after Oura took charge of Holmes, a gnome-like character named Yamato became Oura's English interpreter. After talking with him, Uncle B immediately became wary of Yamato's purpose in camp, and alerted the committee to be cautious in their interactions with him. Uncle B surmised that Yamato might well be trying to ferret out information about anyone involved with the Swick/Green escape. Word quietly passed through camp not to engage in deep or free conversation with Yamato.

Mr. Yamato was an interesting character. He clearly enjoyed chatting with internees to practice his English. We could not tell whether his occasional disparaging remarks about Oura were deliberate, an attempt to win trust and invite information about the escape, or whether they were simply the result of a loose tongue. Once talking with Nellie McKim, Yamato referred to Oura by his first name, Kogoto. (Nellie told Mom that *kogoto* means "scolding.") Although we never heard Yamato use his first name again, Oura would continue scolding the committee. During one of his frequent conversations with Uncle B, Yamato explained that Oura was more interested in teaching us how to "live humbly" than in feeding us. Oura certainly succeeded in keeping us hungry.

Commandant Oura was obsessed with formalities—especially the practice of bowing. On one occasion, he gathered a small group of children to the flagpole and demonstrated to us the proper way of bowing to him and the guards. We listened, followed his lead, and then broke out giggling. A disgusted Oura walked away. His most unpleasant feature was an unabashed hatred of Americans. Oura made frequent references to Americans' yearning for wealth and their disrespect of the poor. Nellie translated his favorite description of Americans as "greedy elitists."

Some weeks after Oura took charge of Camp Holmes, another English-speaking soldier joined the Oura-Yamato team. His name was Masaki. Like Yamato, he served as an interpreter and was the acknowledged scriptwriter of Oura's dictates. Both Masaki and Yamato became regular passersby of the barracks area, stopping frequently to practice their English with internees, often focusing on pronunciation. Noticeably, both felt more comfortable in their conversations with patient women and children. Yamato, particularly, shied away from the men, except for the respected Uncle B. The trio of Oura, Yamato, and Masaki remained with us throughout the rest of our internment.

Complicating the difficulties we experienced with hunger and sickness, Typhoon Felicia, with winds exceeding 90 mph, swept through central Luzon. It was by far the most severe storm I had ever experienced. The roof of our Goat House tried hard to go airborne. Dad's valiant efforts to hold down one sharp-edged, flapping corner of the tin roof saved it from blowing away but left him with badly lacerated hands.

After the winds subsided, torrential rains continued and our little family unit became a shallow pond. The rains persisted for two whole days. We stood in nearly a foot of water as we tried to reach and plug leaks in the roof. Dad discovered that whittling sticks to sharp points and jamming them into the holes in the roof stopped most of the dripping water. Hewing the sticks was my job.

Alas, Mom's spirits dipped and her legs, too painful for walking, prompted Dad's decision to return to barracks living after less than two months of family togetherness in the Goat House. The girls returned to barracks Number Two while Dad and I settled into our former bunks in barracks Number Three. Our delightful neighbors in the Goat House, the Whitfields, survived the typhoon and managed to remain in their little private cubicle.

Felicia came close to demolishing the camp garden. Much of the garden on the embankment next to the men's barracks—meticulously fashioned and tended by Joe Smith and his team of gardeners—was washed away in the storm. Many of the men, including Dad, frantically labored to salvage as much produce as possible. I chased after yams as they tumbled down the embankment into a river of mud. The garden was the primary source of sustenance for all of us, including the Japanese guards, and Dad applauded the guards' efforts to help save it. He told me that their interest in saving it was a good sign.

"Why?" I asked.

He responded, "If they are hungry too, we will all fare better."

Felicia passed. One late afternoon, I was sitting on "my stump" behind the Nunnery when a twin-engine plane made an unusually low pass over Camp Holmes. I clearly saw movement in the cockpit and began to whittle a small likeness of the plane out of a nearby pine bough. My rough carving was near completion when a Japanese guard ambled down the steps leading to the hospital. He strolled toward me and looked over my shoulder. I was surprised when he reached down and took my carving. The guard stared at it for a moment and then grabbed my knife and walked back toward the hospital. I was more afraid than sad, fearing punishment. I said nothing about the incident to Mom or Dad, only telling them a couple of days later that I had lost my knife. I saw the same guard several times thereafter, but never dared ask him for the knife nor did he offer to return it.

Wezer also saw what we learned later was an American P-38. She told me about her race to the middle barracks to tell one of the elderly men about the plane. He was a daily benchwarmer by the dining room door. Wezer said his response was so negative that "I felt like he had slapped my face"; he had only snarled at her statement that "an American plane just flew over us." She imagined that the old man had become numbed by past rumors that never panned out.

The next day, P-38s returned to the sky, flying low in a tight formation. They were clearly visible from the parade ground and easily distinguished from Japanese Zeros. As the foursome of "twin-cigars" roared over Holmes, Aunt Leora stood amazed with other smiling women on the parade ground. Mary Dyer was moved to hum "The Star-Spangled Banner," as the planes made a second pass directly over us. The women nearby joined in. Shortly, the humming turned to singing. Both the air show and the daring songfest trumpeted confidence as our fears of retribution began to dissipate.

Oura stood by the guardhouse looking up at the gleaming stars under the wingtips. He, of course, was not enchanted by the planes and became visibly angry at the musical response to the flyover. Yet he did not challenge the women's bravado. The incident heightened Oura's displeasure with the obvious changing tide of the war and our reactions to it. He shared his ire the following morning in a message on the bulletin board. Citing the previous day's behavior, he warned us that such celebrations would not be tolerated.

Uncle B subsequently posted notices in each of the barracks stating that it was inadvisable to wave at low-flying planes from the parade ground, because (1) we don't know if the flyers are aware that Americans are interned here; and (2) we do not want to anger our captors into any action that can be injurious to anyone. Please be cautious.

Without warning, Oura ordered soldiers to stand by the machine guns on the mesa during the daylight hours. All internees obeyed Uncle B's directive to stay off the parade ground during flyovers. In mid-afternoon the following day, two more P-38s were visible in the distance. The guards sent a message by releasing a round of machine-gun fire from their foxholes toward the planes. Dad described their volleys as "shots at a flying sparrow from a BB gun."

On an evening following the P-38 flybys, a number of very vocal men boasted that U.S. soldiers would parachute into camp before Christmas.

Bets were made on the exact time of the drop. One of the woodcutting crew, also citing the flyovers, expressed what many were eager to believe, "They were messages to 'Mr. Jap.' See if Oura stands on the parade ground looking up when the chutes start to drop."

Even with growing cases of malnutrition, the flyovers lifted spirits. Those sightings certainly affected Mom. She credited her rekindled energy to the passing of Felicia, a healthy husband, smiling children, and the booms of antiaircraft explosions around Lingayen Gulf. We had long awaited those sounds and the sight of puffballs over the gulf that meant misses for the Japanese antiaircraft fire against U.S. airplanes. The message was simple: America had not forgotten the Philippines or us!

In the ensuing weeks, American plane sightings became commonplace, mostly over the gulf. Angered by continued—although subdued—excitement, Oura did nothing more to seek food from the outside. The devastated garden became our sole food source. Because the guards also needed food, Oura ordered them to help with garden chores. Our bodies managed to function each day, running more on fumes of excitement than on nourishment.

I loved listening to the deep hum of unseen P-38s as they approached the mountains surrounding camp. When the hum became a buzz and the planes appeared above the mountaintops, they roared over Camp Holmes like an orchestra's closing crescendo of bass drums. I often wondered if those pilots knew who stood below them.

Christmas 1944

The emotional and physical strain mounted over the waning days of December 1944. I felt it in every group encounter and conversation. Discussions at soup time or around the poker table lacked humor, energy, and laughter. The barracks card players appeared to be just going through the motions. There was little conversation and none of the usual jocular insults tossed at one another. Bridge games were canceled. Efforts at optimism were forced. Camp was rife with tension, but not from any recognizable cause. Naturally, the desire for food was uppermost on everybody's mind. There was a hollowness in the air. Most everyone tried to focus on staying the course, but the periodic P-38 sightings became the only thing that helped keep hope alive.

Two days before Christmas, we were startled by Oura's order that the guards were to confiscate all knives. Even our guards felt ill at ease with the order. They were extremely anxious during their sweep through the barracks, taking knives from everybody. They did not confiscate Mom's treasured bamboo spreader, however. Aunt Leora, not usually one to feel pressure, had no knife. But she told Mom that watching the collection process made her wonder what Oura was going to do. "Will we live to see the end of the war?" she asked Mom. Many questions were in our minds, but there were no answers.

Only mothers of young children went through the motions of preparing for Christmas. I remembered the joy of receiving Red Cross packages a year earlier. Their contents were nearly depleted in most cubicles. The temptation to eat the remaining items often won out over consideration for the future. One year after receiving those cartons, Christmas 1944 found many families with only empty boxes on their shelves.

Mom spent considerable hours counseling depressed women, pressing hard to nurture a bit of optimism. Although she continued to suffer, her athletic instincts to win drove her to make each hour as positive as possible—to be an example for those around her. Her resolve had been strengthened, of course, with the gift of her dear Walter in March. He was not one to show or admit pain. Mom followed his lead and quietly tried to pass on his example to her friends and her children.

Compared with most women, my mother was tall—about five feet seven inches at the start of the war—second only to Cleo Morrison. Mom weighed one hundred sixty-four pounds at the time of the war's outbreak. On the Nancetorium scale, she weighed ninety-four pounds in mid-December 1944. In contrast, I entered Brent in December 1941 weighing sixty-one pounds and had actually gained weight; I was up to sixty-four pounds on Dr. Haughwout's scale on Christmas Day 1943. By Christmas 1944, though, I had dropped to sixty-one pounds. Postwar statistics showed that the amount of weight loss per individual was not as great for internees in Santo Tomas compared to those in Baguio. Most American women in our camp weighed less than one hundred pounds at the conclusion of our prison years, many as low as eighty pounds. Adult men weighed somewhat more at the conclusion of the war, slightly over one hundred pounds on average, but their total weight loss was greater than that of the women.

The food from Baguio ceased coming into camp on December 20. We learned through Uncle B's devoted house girls that Filipinos in Baguio also were suffering from extreme hunger. The last delivery of rice that entered camp appeared to have been scraped off a warehouse floor—it was filled with stones, sand, and moving things. No one complained about weevils in the rice at this point. Tired hands had given up on picking them out, and those critters simply became part of each serving. Few noticed their presence in the meager offerings. Bananas, a fairly consistent staple throughout our internment, were rarely seen in the dining hall. Mr. Ream's banana machine sat idle.

A typical day's menu in December 1944 consisted of a small cup of rice for breakfast and a banana, if available. During one breakfast, I recall eating a banana in its entirety, skin and all! Lunch was a partial bowl of soup, sometimes little more than flavored warm water with a few floating yam leaves. Dinner was usually soup. On a good day, a bit of taro root was added to a nibble of rice. Chef Alex called taro "potato," but to me taro was a poor sticky substitute for potato. If meat were available, a mere bite completed the day's rations. Thankfully, some yams had survived Felicia's downpours, and these were an additional and vital food source for all—internee and guards alike—for the duration of our days in Camp Holmes.

On Sunday, Christmas Eve, Dad delivered the sermon for the ecumenical service. Sensing everyone's shifting moods—ranging from moments of hope to moments of fear or despair—Dad spoke of the trying days ahead. He charged us to lock our hands together to make tomorrow and the next day better ones for all of us. Christmas, he told us, has opened the door for giving, not material things, but gifts of reconciliation. In addition, he gently reminded those gathered, "Enmity of the enemy is the inevitable product of war and the everlasting enemy of Christian friendship. We can accomplish the tasks to win the peace in our world and peace in our hearts only with love."

In her book *Forbidden Diary,* Natalie Croutier wrote of "Walter's fine sermon." Dad's closing thoughts were only positive. He told us that very soon our camp family "will be going out to freedom and community obligations; to a life where *rights* should be less important than *duties.*" The grand amen of the service came as we stepped out of our chapel and looked up at the shining American planes zooming overhead. A threesome of fighter planes emblazened a huge "V" over Camp Holmes. That victory sign gave us more strength to face the days ahead than all the taro root we could swallow.

In the days leading up to Christmas, I had found myself longing only for food, hoping that the special day would deliver it. Hundreds of others shared my feelings. When the dawn of Christmas Day broke, however, an atmosphere of depression filled the dining room. Little had changed. My Christmas morning treat was an extra spoonful of rice in my coconut shell bowl—and a shared banana.

Dutifully, I accompanied my family to listen to Uncle B's Yuletide sermon. We sang traditional carols and Uncle B referred to the days ahead as the "final chapter" of our prison life, a fitting message for a Christmas Day that otherwise was clouded with gloom. His words lifted my hopes and encouraged us all to hold on. Stepping outside after the service, his message was amplified as we again looked up to see P-38s fly overhead. The roar in the sky also stirred the few remaining ducks and chickens beneath the chapel. Their noisy "applause" at the sound of those P-38s lent a staccato edge to the music above us.

In the afternoon, I stood next to Mom, watching American planes conducting war maneuvers over Lingayen Gulf, I shared my excitement about the Christmas flyovers with her. They confirmed that we were in America's sights and that very soon we would live Uncle B's final chapter. That evening, Uncle B, the Whitfields, and our family made a Christmas dinner outside the Goat House from our meager food supply.

For some unidentifiable reason, the energy generated on Christmas Day quickly faded away on December 26. I did not understand the sudden letdown. Somber stares and pained faces reflected widespread tension. I thought to myself: Had yesterday only brought bad dreams for today?

The men seemed less affected physically. They kept hoping for a parachute drop over Holmes, and the flyovers fueled those dreams. We learned from Uncle B that afternoon that General MacArthur had landed on Leyte. It turned out to be old news, but it was fresh news in Camp Holmes. The men were convinced that the general's first business would be to free all imprisoned Americans and that the daily flyovers were a message for us to be prepared for their arrival.

The mood vacillated between hopeful anticipation and fear among the women in barracks Number Two. A significant number of Mom's friends remained depressed. One woman, with whom Mom conversed frequently, spoke about our inevitable death in Holmes if America interfered with the "Asia for Asians" principle. On the bright side, others, including Dr. Skerl, Nellie McKim, and Uncle B—having met with Oura in the morning—seemed more upbeat about the days ahead. Their positive outlook came from "reading between the lines" of their conversations with Oura.

Later in the afternoon Dad, Derek Whitmarsh, and I saw Uncle B cross the parade ground, walking faster than usual as he headed toward the men's barracks from the guardhouse. It looked like he had important news. Dad stood in front of the barracks where he was calming Derek and me after another scuffle. As Uncle B approached the three of us, he said, pointing to Derek and me, "You two have better things to think about right now, and it isn't rolling over each other on the ground . . . besides, it's the day after Christmas. Try to be more loving of one another." Then he paused and added, "It's also time to pack. In two days we're going bye-bye."

Then Uncle B turned to Dad and told him about Oura's pronouncement that all of us will be leaving our "lovely" Holmes this week. Uncle B said, "I know not why, or where or how—only that the move is coming." He urged Dad to pass the word. "By the way," he added with a smile, "please excuse me from playing bridge tonight." Dad joined Derek and me in a handshake. Almost instinctively, we patted each other on the shoulder.

Dad sent me off to share the news with the girls, but they already knew. So, too, did the other women. Nellie McKim had told them that everyone would be going somewhere very soon. The consensus guess was that we were headed to Manila. Those familiar with Manila prayed we would not go to Fort Santiago, renowned for its torture chambers dating back to the days of Spanish rule. The other options we knew about were Santo Tomas and Los Baños, the overcrowded civilian prison camps, and Bilibid Prison. Bilibid had been condemned before the war and partially demolished prior to the Japanese bombings of 1941. Most of the prognosticators in barracks Number Three believed that Santo Tomas would be our new home.

Commandant Oura posted a notice that evening detailing our orders. He did not name our destination, but noted that we would travel in a convoy of thirty-six trucks. Half of them would leave on Thursday, December 28, and the remaining internees would leave on Friday. Updates were posted in each barracks, detailing the space limitations in the trucks and items not to take.

The following morning, December 27, a list was posted with names of those scheduled to depart the next day. Our family was to leave on December 29. Departing families were to be packed and on the parade ground for roll call by 6:00 a.m. both days.

With Oura's permission, the general committee quickly assembled a slaughtering team composed of Chef Alex's staff to kill the few animals remaining in the goat pen—a couple of pigs and the goats—and the chickens from under the chapel. It was a tedious process. Joe Smith and others gathered the remaining yams in the garden to use for dinner that evening and distribution the next day. That evening meal, our last at

Camp Holmes, topped any meal consumed during the internment years. The lights remained on well into the night as families prepared for the move. Only a few got any sleep.

The breakfast line began at 4:00 a.m. on December 28. As promised, trucks started rolling through the main gate and onto the parade ground early Thursday morning. I counted eighteen trucks—not the thirty-six that had been promised. Once the entire camp had completed the roll call routine, Yamato translated Oura's orders.

Three hundred internees, with their personal belongings, were to board ten of the trucks. The remaining eight vehicles were loaded with baggage and any large items (e.g., bedrolls). Some of the guards' keepsakes, including many bottles of sake, were also loaded onto the baggage trucks. Yamato again reminded all that mattresses would be available at our new site of confinement, an indication that Oura knew where we were going. Yet he had told Uncle B that he did not know our destination, except that it was likely to be in Manila.

I watched the loading operation closely. After the carry-on bags were tossed onto the back of the passenger trucks, it looked like there would be no room for people, but close to thirty internees positioned themselves along the sidings of each truck bed. Two guards, armed with rifles, accompanied each vehicle, one rode in the cab alongside the driver, and the other stood in the truck bed with the internees. A taut rope extended from the tailgate to a wooden post attached to the cab, providing a handhold for those who sat on baggage piled higher than the siding.

After watching the first convoy leave, I told Mom that the most comfortable location for her the next morning would be behind the cab, facing the tailgate. From that position, she would be able to extend her painful right leg. Others, observing the loading procedure, also noted the most comfortable locations in the truck bed.

Only as the first trucks pulled out did Oura confirm to Uncle B that we would definitely be going to Manila. Still, he would not say where. Standing next to Dad and me after the trucks departed, Uncle B muttered, "He knows, but he won't say. That makes it Bilibid."

At the front gate, the lead truck turned left and headed toward Baguio. The others followed. With Manila as a known destination, people were more open about being pleased or unhappy with the decision. Those with connections to the city actually looked forward to a move there. Mom and Dad, however, abhorred the idea of going to Manila or anywhere else, thinking Baguio would be the safest of all possible sites in the event of a military conflict.

To prepare for our departure the next day, Dad and I packed our belongings in a matter of minutes. We folded up our mosquito nets. I put my pocket-sized hymnal and small book of poems in a little box. I pocketed the toy car and tank I had carved after losing my original toy cars, around the time Uncle B was abducted as we were under house arrest in Baguio. Then I ran over to visit Mom and the girls in their barracks. They were putting the meager remnants of our 1943 Red Cross boxes in a very small bag. After Oura's notice that mattresses would be furnished at the new location, the girls rolled up their thin sleeping mats and left the mattresses for looters. Our family was now ready for the move.

A Move with a Zig and a Zag

On Friday morning, the early birds lined up at dawn. They boarded the trucks immediately upon their arrival and placed themselves where the cab backrest offered the greatest comfort. Unfortunately, Mom was not one of these. She was not one to compete with friends for a seat, nor was she able to do so. Mom and my sisters situated themselves atop some baggage, which had been piled along the sidings of the truck bed. I hoped one of the men might notice Mom's discomfort and offer her a more comfortable seat, but no one did. Mom suffered miserably, but never once asked anyone to swap places. As our truck passed through the Camp Holmes gate, Dad and I stretched out on top of the baggage in the center of the truck. The thick rope that held the baggage in place also served as a flexible railing and handgrip for both of us.

Our guards signaled us not to wave to Filipinos as we rode through Baguio. Rae spotted her Filipina teacher who had resided in a room in our prewar Burnham Park home, but Rae obediently abstained from waving to her.

The trucks stayed in close convoy as the Japanese drivers negotiated the downhill curves on the Kennon Trail. At every bend, those seated along the sidewalls kept a kindly hand on our legs to thwart our sliding onto them. I held the taut rope with both hands. Sitting atop the baggage seemed fun at first. I could see the small distant barrios and rice paddies and watched Igorots walking along the road to the Baguio markets, skinny dogs in tow. The distant paddies looked like a massive quilt in shades of brown, green, and yellow. When the inclines grew steep and the guardrails along the road disappeared, looking down into the ravines from the open truck bay was frightening. Periodically, I peeked over at Mom, still uncomfortably squeezed against the side of the bed. During that segment of the ride, no one could have swapped seats with her, even if they wanted to.

Near the village of Rosario, the trail became decidedly rougher. Loose rocks and sand covered the hard surface. Whenever the driver applied brakes on the sharp S-shaped curves, the wheels slid on the gravel. The road worsened with each turn. My hands became sore and bloodied from squeezing the tough fibrous rope as my body shifted from side to side around each curve. I noticed Dad's hands also were bleeding.

Loud sighs of relief could be heard as we pulled to a stop in Rosario. The trucks formed a large ring near the town square, a scene that reminded me of a painting in my classroom at Brent depicting circled covered wagons in the Wild West. I wondered where the toilet was, and was told that if I had to "go," to do so inside the circle with the men. The restroom for Mom, my sisters, and the other women and children was the ground outside of the circled trucks. Our guards watched over us to make certain no one wandered away. At first, Mom chose not to get off, hoping that the next stop would afford access to a real bathroom. Dad, however, convinced her that her swollen legs needed movement more than she needed privacy.

As the convoy resumed, road conditions got even worse. Some sections appeared to have been bombed, slowing the drive considerably. To dodge the potholes, our driver had to steer dangerously close to the road's edge. Whenever we neared a cliff that dropped into a steep ravine, Dad beat on the cab roof, warning the driver that he was close to the edge. Dad was the only passenger positioned to pound on the roof with one hand while holding the rope with the other. A man seated below the cab window and weighed down under a stash of belongings, urged Dad to remain by the window to shout or pound on the cab roof. Clearly, he too was afraid we would go over the edge.

Dad could tell from the way the driver kept jerking the steering wheel that he must be fighting off drowsiness, so Dad gladly took on the role of lookout. Every time we approached a curve in the road, he rapped his knuckles against the window or on the roof. The Japanese soldiers did not seem bothered by his actions and made no signal for him to cease his warnings.

Putrid from afternoon heat, the food given to us by the kitchen crew before we left Camp Holmes smelled awful. Taking no chances, Dad had already tossed ours into the bushes. Dr. Skerl warned the others not to risk eating the meat. Indeed, the afternoon heat and motion sickness played havoc with those who had filled their stomachs with the putrid meat. Young children were the first to show signs of food poisoning. One after another, they vomited over the side of the truck. One child, held tightly in her father's extended hands, also managed to pass waste over the side of the slow-moving truck. Only the low clouds blocking the scorching after-noon sun softened the pallid looks of despair and discomfort.

When the road straightened and we coasted to a stop near Binalonan, I felt tremendous relief. It was already mid-afternoon. The Japanese offi-cer in charge of our convoy moved from truck to truck announcing that the stop was for "toilet only." Again, there were no toilets in the immedi-ate vicinity. For the women, "toilet only" translated into a short walk to a nearby banana grove, a rather thin veil of privacy.

Dad and I crawled off the tailgate first and assisted others off the truck. He engaged the two guards in sign language to ask the condition of the driver. Surprisingly, one responded in understandable English. He told us that the driver had not slept since he drove the first group from Camp Holmes a day earlier. After delivering the internees to Manila, the driver had immediately returned to Baguio for the second run. He—and the other drivers—had a very short snooze in the city before reentering Holmes to take us to Manila.

The Binalonan town plaza, only a stone's throw from the trucks, was declared out of bounds. The guards watched our movements closely, per-mitting only a couple of women at a time to walk to the grove of banana trees—their designated potty stop. The few bananas hanging on the trees were unfortunately out of reach. The men did their toilet stint on the oppo-site side of the truck, squatting, or standing. It was an ugly scene. On the men's side of the truck, we were watched over by a lone, rifle-toting guard standing in the truck bed, one foot on the siding. Milling about, a safe distance away from the parked trucks, a few Filipinos stared in awe at our presence. They disappeared quickly whenever a Japanese soldier moved in their direction. The villagers clearly feared Japanese soldiers.

Mom's toilet experience near Binalonan turned out to be a signifi-cant moment in her life. After struggling, even with Dad's help, to get down from the truck, she walked with noticeable pain to the banana trees. Wezer, Rae, and a guard walked with Mom toward a very sparse grove of trees. The guard graciously focused his attention on the surrounding trees to give them privacy. When done, my sisters quickly returned to the truck. Mom and the guard walked more slowly behind them. Slowly, the soldier stepped a few paces away from Mom, raised his rifle with bayonet attached, and cut several bananas off a high-hanging sleeve. The guard peeled back one of the bananas, walked over to Mom, and handed it to her, motioning for her to eat it. She did. Mom then thanked the guard with a slight head bow. He bowed in return. His generosity and kindness touched her immensely, and this uplifting moment energized her to "hang on" in the hours ahead.

Our quick "toilet only" stop turned into a four-hour layover. No one knew why the long wait, whether it gave the drivers a chance to sleep or wait for a fresh crew. In either case, the delay was most welcome.

Eventually, an officer came by and ordered everyone to unload his or her belongings from the truck. No reason was given. At dusk, we reloaded our possessions onto a different truck. Once on board, we again waited. The rest of the convoy had long since departed. I was hot and extremely hungry. Then once again we were ordered off the truck.

To keep us going, Mom opened our next-to-last can of Red Cross Spam. It was a huge treat and an energizer and carried us through the sleepless night hours and into the next morning. In an effort to distract us from the heat and the long delay, Mom told us the story of our last trip through Binalonan. The others enjoyed listening, too. She recounted our family vacation trip to Baguio on Good Friday of 1941, with a stop in Binalonan where we saw thousands of Filipinos watching a reenactment of Jesus' Crucifixion. The Filipino performers playing Roman soldiers drove real nails through the hands of the young man acting the role of Jesus. Mom reminded us that many men in that area vie for the honor of being the chosen Jesus in the annual Lenten celebration. Her message was a simple one: discomfort and boredom on a truck was far better than hanging on a cross with nails through your hands.

The long layover outside Binalonan seemed to restore our energy and our driver's wakefulness. As we readied to embark, the guard seated in the cab came to the back of the truck and motioned for Dad to get off. "Walter, Walter!" Mom cried out in panic. The guard ordered him into the seat in the cab next to the driver and he then took up Dad's position by the rope in the truck bed. Looking through the cab window, I could see that the driver was pleased to have my father next to him. I told Mom that Dad was still on board, just riding with the driver. Although not a Roman Catholic, Mom crossed herself in relief that Dad was still with us.

The air turned sultry as we approached the flatlands north of Tarlac. A strange line of vehicular and walking traffic all headed northward fascinated me. Gripping the rope that stretched down the middle of the truck bay, I managed to hoist my body atop the baggage. From there, I could easily peer over the sides. Japanese troops by the thousands were walking in the direction from which we had come. Almost all carried guns at their sides or across their shoulders. Interspersed with the foot traffic were a few horse-drawn *calesas* (carts) laden with a variety of things: food, rifles, large bags, and even one monkey. But most of the *calesas* were pulled by Japanese soldiers with straps around their chests. The carts were covered with palm branches or banana leaves, probably to camouflage them from U.S. warplanes. I was so entranced with what I saw that I broadcast the sights "play by play" to Mom and my sisters tucked in the truck bed.

As darkness fell over the road into the city of Tarlac, my focus remained on the troop movements. Motorized transport was clearly in short supply in the Japanese Army. Very few trucks passed and each of those carried standing soldiers packed together in the truck beds. The scene reminded me of deliveries of live chickens to the Baguio markets.

The number of foot soldiers passing by seemed endless. Most of them appeared too exhausted to pay any attention to a towheaded boy lying atop a pile of junk on a truck headed in the opposite direction. I thought how much I would hate to be one of those soldiers moving supplies and equipment in darkness.

As night fell, our driver negotiated the potholed roadway without headlights, either out of courtesy to his comrades moving northward or in an attempt to be less visible to aircraft above. With Dad seated beside the driver, I felt far less fearful that we would run off the road. I was also happy that the full moon rising between passing clouds improved visibility of the road.

Dad could see what I was watching, but his focus was on the driver and the road. His most vivid recollection of the journey was that it called for considerable conversation, "all one-way and all in English." Dad played interviewer, asking the driver questions like "Where are all the hikers going?" "Why are they not riding?" "Did you see the fellow carrying a monkey?" "Is the monkey a mascot or tomorrow's lunch?" Not one question, of course, was answered. However, Dad did receive acknowledging smiles, which confirmed the driver's alertness. Only once while he played copilot did the driver veer off the road—more to avoid hitting a pair of soldiers pulling a cart on the wrong side of the road than because of drowsiness. Fortunately, the area was relatively flat, and our driver swung easily back onto the road as passengers in the truck bed shouted.

At Tarlac, a small city halfway between Lingayen Gulf and Manila, we came to a stop under a full moon in a cloudless sky. Given the northerly direction the Japanese troops were heading, the gulf appeared to be their destination. Weeks afterward, we received confirmation that American troops had landed on Luzon at Lingayen Gulf, the site of initial confrontations between American and Japanese forces.

We spent too long waiting around in Tarlac. Since we were next to a city park, I plopped down on a concrete bench looking over hundreds of Japanese soldiers sleeping on the ground. Only a few of them were patrolling the streets surrounding the park. I saw no Filipinos. It seemed odd not to see them milling in the streets, and I wondered where they had all gone. It was a mystery to me.

Dad soon came over and sat next to me. I asked him about the Filipinos. He said, "They probably were scared away by planes bombing the trail." Then I asked why we had not seen any American planes since we left Holmes, where we saw them almost daily. Dad responded. "Perhaps those pilots know we are traveling and don't want to scare the trucks off the road." That thought must have crossed other minds as well, but I did not hear anyone else talking about the sudden absence of planes.

I discovered the answer to my questions only years later. Joe Smith in his unpublished account, "Three Years in the Fish's Belly," tells of a chance postwar meeting between his wife Winnie and a young man named Calvin Hanks at the First Christian Church in Covington, Kentucky. Hanks had been a P-38 pilot who regularly strafed the Kennon Trail in December 1944. His conversation with Winnie revealed that Hanks and his fellow pilots had been grounded for three days in late December because an enemy bomb had destroyed their gasoline storage area, so for the time being they had no fuel to fly. It seemed an amazing coincidence that the days our convoy traveled the Kennon Trail happened to be the same three days the planes were grounded. Hanks assured Winnie that he had known nothing about our convoy.

On the outskirts of Manila City, we encountered many more potholes in the road. Groans in the truck increased in volume with each jolt. Even in the reasonably clear night conditions, the driver could not avoid every pit in the road. Jerking along over the deep ruts caused everyone tremendous pain and discomfort. One elderly woman finally cried out, "Oh God, we truly are being prepared for a hellish death!" Prior to the war, the drive from Baguio to Manila along the Kennon Trail was referred to as the "Road to Hell." Nothing had changed.

Soon it became obvious that our weary driver was lost. We had passed the same buildings a couple of times. We had been separated from the rest of the convoy since our first stop near Binalonan, so the driver's confusion was understandable. At around 2:00 a.m., I told Mom that I thought we were entering Manila. "Yes," she replied, "I can smell it."

As we entered the city limits, the driver stopped the truck. With a farewell salute, he signaled for Dad to return to the truck bed. The driver's original soldier-companion once again joined him in the cab, and Dad climbed atop the stack of baggage as we drove into the city. Occasionally, he whispered our whereabouts to Mom who had become partially obscured by the stuff that had shifted over her. Dad and I relaxed our hold on the rope as the truck crawled slowly through the eerie dark city devoid of functioning streetlights.

Finally, the driver pulled to a stop in front of a gate flanked by high gray walls. He blinked the headlights, and with each flash of light, I could see that the sign above the gate read "Bureau of Prisons." A few exhausted children had overcome their discomfort and were sound asleep, but the adults were all wide awake, looking like mummies with their eyes glued to the grim sign above. Each, I am sure, wondered as I did what the next days might bring. Dad had not needed to read the sign; the gray walls told him exactly where we were. He looked at me with a reassuring smile and said, "Young man, your Uncle B was right—'tis Bilibid."

An internee (Cleo Morrison) inspects the names on crosses lining Bilibid's walls. They mark the grave sites of Bataan death-march survivors who died there during internment. (Courtesy of the National Archives)

Bilibid Prison

Dec. 1944–Feb. 1945

Through the Gates to Hell

Nearing three in the morning, the grating sounds of steel gates opening slowly confirmed our arrival at dreaded Bilibid Prison. Our driver inched the truck backward through a narrow passageway bisecting an intricate network of steel-barred cellblocks. I wanted very much for the wheels not to stop and hung onto a wish that he would reverse direction and take us somewhere else, anywhere else. My wish sprang from the horrible reputation of Bilibid. I had heard many tell of Filipinos imprisoned in Bilibid prior to the war who were said to have been starved, tortured, or put to death. After backing up for a few minutes, the driver braked in front of a large building. Only one light illuminated the entry to the structure, giving it the appearance of a one-eyed sea monster lying on the ocean floor.

A couple of men tossed the baggage to the ground to make room for the human cargo to exit. Our journey, staying seated in cramped quarters for long hours, buried under piles of bags and bedrolls, had taken its toll on everyone. Mom stood contorted, like the letter C and needed assistance to get to her feet. Her badly swollen ankles looked like a pair of fire hoses, and her first steps required the support of both Dad and me.

After gathering our few belongings, we followed a guard's flashlight beam. He pointed the light in the direction of an undistinguished contraption on the grounds, which he called the *benjo* (toilet). Nearly our whole family crowded around it, only guessing how to use the facility. Once indoors, we followed the guard's beam up a stairway to the dark second floor of what once was the prison hospital. We noticed that most of the prone bodies, which had arrived much earlier, were lying on mats under mosquito nets. One wide-awake woman greeted us with a limp wave. We were the last to arrive and made every effort to arrange our thin mats, blankets, and bags by a stairwell without disturbing others.

Before lying down, we draped netting over our mats to fend off mosquitoes. The netting succeeded in keeping out most of the flying pests, but not the crawling variety. Lying on the mat, I felt creepy crawling insects on my feet and legs. My discomfort and my thoughts fought my desire to sleep. Because of our late arrival in Bilibid, we had not had time to seek out the mattresses Oura indicated would be provided. How fortunate we were! In the morning, we learned that the first internees to arrive found the mattresses filthy. They were infested with insects and stained with blood and diarrhea from former hospital patients. The advice given to us by those who had arrived earlier was simple and pointed, "Do not use the mattresses."

I woke early and simply lay on the floor slapping my legs and staring at the concrete above. As I waited for others in my family to stir, I watched four rats scurry around our mats. It was December 30. I very much wanted someone to accompany me to the outdoor privy. Dad woke first and rose from his worn mat on the floor. He lifted his chin in my direction—his silent signal to follow him. I hoped we could take a banana with us, but we had eaten all of our food except the last can of Spam and two bananas.

We had made a brief stop at the outdoor *benjo* after our predawn arrival, but in the darkness, I did not grasp the trick of how to negotiate the strange structure. In the daylight, Dad and I could see there were two troughs, each roughly twelve feet in length, separated by a bamboo thatch partition known in the Philippines as *sawali*. The men used one side of the partition and women the other. The early arrivers told us that the gender partition was put in place only when much confusion after their arrival had necessitated a quick fix. The toilet appeared to be crudely constructed by hand, probably by American soldiers and sailors who Dad told me had once occupied the compound. A hastily created *sawali* screen had been unrolled to surround three sides of the toilet, providing a scant measure of privacy for both genders.

The v-shaped troughs were nothing more than two narrow strips of galvanized roofing slanted downward at an angle of about fifteen degrees and flanked by a board on each side, which provided footing for those using the toilet. A metal drum, which appeared to have been cut diagonally in half, hung at the high end of the trough and slowly filled with water from a running faucet. When the drum filled, the weight of the water upended it and poured water into the trough, thus flushing the waste downward and into a pipe feeding an underground sewer. Using the toilet simply required placing your feet on the wooden slats astride the trough, squatting, and doing your thing while fighting off flies.

I watched the procedure for a couple of minutes to get the idea of how it worked. I thought it was a clever design, but it did lack privacy. Over the next few days, I discovered that looking down on other squatters from a vantage point at the high end of the trough was not a pretty sight. However, I preferred it to being at the low end where I became the victim of splatter when the drum emptied into the trough. From the top, the squatters below looked like a lineup of frogs, each ready to jump! The toilet scene was not for the modest, but very soon modesty lost out to necessity. As Dad and I left the *benjo*, Mr. Yamato, Oura's talkative English-speaking interpreter, intercepted us. He had arrived with the first convoy out of Holmes and began to inform us of the rules we must follow. His litany seemed to have no end, so Dad finally interrupted him, saying, "The walls look like they will take care of the rules."

The morning light revealed the ominous tall concrete walls all around our compound. Dad stood still for some minutes, looking over the layout of the compound and the building in which we had spent the night. It was a dungeon denuded of doors, window coverings, and roof. Then he said, "This old tub may be our prison today, but someday it will be our fortress." I did not understand his words at the time, but a month later I did.

Near the *benjo* were two shower stalls, both surrounded by more bamboo thatch partitions. There was no roofing over the stalls, so privacy was limited. Second-floor dwellers commonly peeked out their windows to check on shower availability. Not surprisingly, the shower stalls were more often visited after sunset. A nearby metal sink was the only spot for washing clothes, dishes, faces, or brushing teeth. It was convenient to have the three watering sources close to each other, but the dampness of the area, as Dad predicted in our walk around, created a haven for hordes of mosquitoes, especially during the warm twilight hours.

As we continued our stroll inside the high walls, Dad wondered aloud if Bilibid had once been home to Dr. Brokenshire. He wanted to discover,

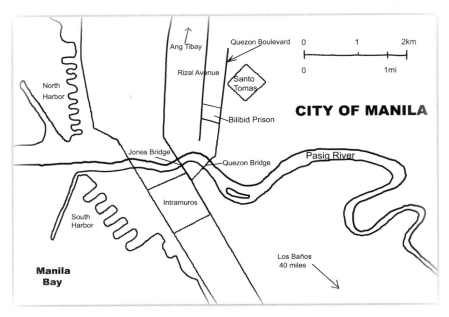

Sketch overview of Manila.

if possible, clues as to the whereabouts of Doctor B. Dad had surmised that he might have been captured or killed in Bataan or Corregidor. While interned in Santo Tomas, Dad had been told that most survivors of Bataan and Corregidor had been incarcerated in the old Bilibid Prison and at Cabanatuan.

Dad was determined to locate Doctor B, if possible. We spent nearly an hour scanning names on the long line of crosses along the two walls that converged at the northeast corner of the prison compound. Dr. Brokenshire's name was not among them. Dad did recognize one name, that of a naval officer Brokenshire had often mentioned in his prewar messages to us. The last two crosses in the long row revealed freshly inscribed dates, one was as recent as December 1944. This indicated that American soldiers had been imprisoned in our compound not long before our arrival. The curious Japanese guard standing in a nearby turret watched us as we scanned every cross. He actually exited his small enclosure to stare down at us as Dad reached up and touched indentations in the wall where bullet holes left evidence of probable POW executions. Those bullet holes were frightening.

Dad continued to show his curiosity during our walk around the full inner perimeter of our new home. We noticed two square window-shaped areas sealed off with thick wooden planks on the north and west walls. Dad guessed that they had been venting gates, like ones he had seen often during prison visitations in Davao. Those boarded square holes in the wall would play a significant role in our lives a month later.

As we headed back to our quarters, we again came upon Mr. Yamato. This time, he revealed to Dad and me that American prisoners, soldiers, and sailors—all survivors of the Bataan march—remained imprisoned in the cellblock directly across the wall from our own. That news totally surprised Dad. Coincidentally, Uncle B joined our brief conversation, and then Yamato moved on.

Thereupon, Dad informed Uncle B of our neighbors across the wall. Uncle B, who arrived with the first convoy and continued to be the general committee chair, was shocked to learn that some of the Bataan survivors were close by. Dad then raised the possibility of meeting with the leader of the American POWs. He very much wanted to learn more about Brokenshire and meet with him if he were alive. Uncle B agreed to ask Commandant Oura for permission for Dad to enter the military POW cellblock. "Don't count on it, but I'll try," he promised. Dad understood that it would not be the first request Uncle B would make of Oura. The first plea, of course, was for food.

After our long walkabout through the entire compound, Dad and I returned to Mom and my sisters. They all wondered where we had gone and were curious about what Dad and I had seen and heard. We shared what we learned through conversations with Uncle B, Mr. Yamato, Chef Kaluzhny, and others wandering around the compound: life will be quite different from what we knew in Holmes.

"You'll be happy to know that there will be no roll calls and that we will be together as a family in our present little area," said Dad. He continued to report that our duties and chores soon would be assigned by Uncle B's committee, some very similar to what we had at Holmes, but there would be no wood crew or garbage detail.

In our absence, Mom and the girls had swept our spot on the floor, killed a bowlful of bugs in hot water, and tidied up the area where we had slept. It was located adjacent to a stairwell, which led up to what once had been a third floor. They had already shared some bites of banana and we did the same. Smiling, Dad reminded me, "Eat it slowly. You'll feel more full."

Mom shared the good news that we would eat some meals with our dear friends, Norman and Evelyn Whitfield, on an open-air balcony next to where they bedded down. Over time, the balcony served as a gathering place for friends to kibitz in the evening. It also offered a partial view of Santo Tomas and a lookout onto much of the city of Manila.

After eating bites of our banana, my sisters and I walked with Dad up the stairwell to the roof. There, he noticed some narrow steel rods and scraps of wood scattered about, remnants of the destroyed cells on the third floor. Dad picked up two metal rods about three feet in length and bent them over his knee into two U-shapes. A day later, the scraps became supports to a stool with a wooden seat. Jerry Crouter gave us a similar stool, which provided our open-spaced cubicle a touch of comfort.

The next morning, I followed David Bergamini around the inner perimeter of the compound. He was a few years older than me and a lover of mathematical figures. David began measuring, by strides, the length, and width of the compound. His estimation was that our prison confines were approximately two hundred feet wide and almost six hundred feet in length. The former prison hospital building, now our home, was about fifty by two hundred feet. I credit David with my first lesson in computing square footage.

During our early days in Bilibid, we spent much of each day trying to discover ways to soften the hardness around us. Naturally, Bilibid required changes in our manner of living. Most of the social arrangements that took place in Holmes (e.g., performances, schooling, lectures, bridge games, baseball) had ceased. For me, life in a walled enclosure like Bilibid was extremely claustrophobic. In the Baguio camps, there was room to play baseball and to run. Whatever suffering Camp Holmes had wrought upon us now seemed minuscule compared to this "hellhole of a place," as Jerry Crouter labeled the prison.

Bilibid was devoid of space and fresh air. Food was sparse. Rice, bean curd residues, and occasional yams were the most common foods brought into camp. Food was handed out in the morning and late afternoon from the small kitchen located between our quarters and the east wall. We lined up with bowls in hand. When Mom was too ill to walk down the stairs to the kitchen, one of us was permitted to carry her ration of food to her. We followed the routine of two meager meals each day, living our lives a day at a time. We often shared evening meals with the very generous Whitfields on their balcony. (Mom continued to hold onto the last can of Spam from the 1943 Red Cross package.) My parents had confidence that some food would be provided, however poor.

The extremely hot days and the putrid, damp, and fly-infested areas wore out our civility and our health. Those who were depressed expressed their misery by their silence. Spirits may not have been broken, but drawn faces revealed demoralized internees headed in that direction. Hunger pangs intensified with each passing day. Signs of panic could be detected in the rude and selfish behavior of a few women. Their actions were not intended to be hostile, but were instinctive expressions of anxiety at the dire food shortages. What would happen to families if the food lines closed entirely, a real possibility, was a question in everyone's mind.

Coinciding with our very real fear of starvation, the new commandant arrived. His name was Ebiko. Interestingly, Oura continued to lurk in the background. He was rarely seen, but was regularly blamed by Ebiko whenever he was pressed by demands from the committee for food.

Outside food deliveries had almost stopped. Ebiko tried to purchase rice from the Filipinos with Japanese yen (the currency at that time). However, the Filipinos, sensing a Japanese defeat, which would make the yen worthless, resisted selling bagged rice to Ebiko. But they did accept cash from him in exchange for rice leavings gathered from a nearby *bodega* floor. When those leavings were delivered, Chef Kaluzhny informed Uncle B that they were so infested with weevils as to be unsuitable for consumption.

Realizing that Japanese currency had no value, Ebiko told Uncle B that if an internee had connections to someone living in Manila who had avoided imprisonment (e.g., a German or Italian), he would grant permission to secure food through those sources. Unfortunately, few prisoners in Bilibid possessed money, since Nagatomi had stolen most of it three years earlier.

Our saving grace was again the Sagada nuns. They came to the rescue with cash—Filipino pesos—to purchase food from the outside. Their generosity also benefited the guard corps. Throughout our internment, the nuns had graciously given money to needy parents with young children. As Mom had often reminded me in Camp Holmes, those nuns of Sagada truly wore angel wings.

With pesos in hand, Commandant Ebiko ordered the purchase of edible rice. Few cared why or where the rice had come from, only that we had some. In their usual modest manner, the generous nuns wanted no plaudits from their prison partners. Unlike Oura, Ebiko seemed to try to accommodate the almost daily demands placed upon him by a most persuasive Uncle B.

Within a week, it became apparent to Ebiko that there were real food shortages across the city. But as he became preoccupied under a growing awareness of the approaching enemy, he put aside further efforts to import rice, yams, or any other food.

Because almost everybody had eaten the last of their vitamin-rich Red Cross foods, cases of malnutrition became widespread, severe, and clearly visible. Adults, particularly, felt body aches caused by the lack of nourishment. Mom suffered far more than Dad did. Yet her strong will prevailed. Dad applauded her drive to pull her family through the war, calling it "Mom's missionary madness."

Our thoughts turned inevitably and endlessly toward food. Father Sheridan, a very caring man, stood out in Bilibid as someone always trying to support others through their struggles. He did so with gestures as inane as a joke and a pat on the back or as powerful as counsel and prayer to inspire strength and hope. I bumped into Father Sheridan one evening on the way to the *benjo*. In his usual uplifting manner, he said with a smile, "Curt, you know that pretty soon you will be having dinner with Uncle Sam. For now, think only of eating *balut*." We both giggled at that suggestion—*balut* is a foul-smelling fertilized duck egg considered a delicacy by many Filipinos, but inedible in the minds of Westerners. His message was simple. Live today now. Live tomorrow when it comes. And keep a smile on your face. It was good counsel.

Rooftop Lookout . . . Look Out!

Later that night, eyebrows raised, and hopes soared upon hearing what sounded like antiaircraft fire and seeing subsequent smoke balls. Could it be that Americans were coming to the rescue? The explosions in the background also seemed to touch off a furious scolding I received from a weary mother, upset that I tripped over the leg of her sleeping child on the way back to my mat from the privy. I asked Mom why the woman was so grouchy. Mom reminded me of a story she used to read to us about early settlers who circled the wagons when puffs of smoke, a warning of danger, appeared on the horizon. "This evening, we, too, experienced sights of smoke in the sky . . . only we call it antiaircraft fire. Now everyone is circling their wagons. Do tiptoe carefully, as she asked."

Despite our hardships, we children still had the energy to play games of tag or Mother May I. Rae was the tag champion, since no one of her age group could catch her. Aunt Leora, who was a surrogate mother to Rae while Mom was bedridden, liked to boast of my sister, "That girl seems to run on empty."

To find places to play without toilets, grave sites, or lots of people, Rae and I, along with our friends, frequently climbed the "stairway to the stars." It was Mom's name for the concrete stairwell near our cubicle that led to the third story. Once a hospital ward for Filipino prisoners, it became our play area. The entire roof and segments of the third floor walls had disappeared with the partial demolition of the old prison prior to the war. That project was interrupted by the Japanese bombings of December 1941. Hence, the concrete floor of the third story remained and became our playground.

Ten days after moving all of the Holmes POWs to Bilibid, we heard gunfire in the Quezon Boulevard area of Manila. The rooftop over our quarters grew busier with each exchange. All of Rae's tag play stopped, a relief to many parents worried about children running on the rooftop. Racing after balls on a surface with large gaps in the perimeter walls was extremely dangerous. Indeed, we shied away from those spaces for fear of a long fall.

As the gunfire exchanges progressed into visible street fighting, the rooftop came to resemble a crowd at an athletic event. From that vantage we could observe the flights of American bombers, spot snipers in church steeples, and watch the looting of shops by Filipinos on Quezon Boulevard. Intermittently, a group of men spent time crouched behind the remaining concrete perimeter wall watching rifle exchanges between GIs and Japanese snipers operating from upper floors and church belfries. Soon attention focused on observations of American bombers dropping ordnance on various Manila targets.

Almost as if God had sprinkled optimism over Bilibid, the daily formations in the sky suddenly enlivened hopes that our "days of hell" were numbered. The airplane sightings brought no food but they did inject energy into the dispirited. The mere presence of the planes patrolling the skies above Manila brought hope to some, fear to others. Still, the aircraft could not have arrived at a better time. My friends and I took great pleasure in counting the planes and guessing the number of aviators in each one.

Morale lifted. We began once again to reach out to each other. Having few material goods to share, a smile, a story, or a moment of counsel sufficed. Kindly gestures were infectious and lent strength to the weak. Clearly, the hunger pains and sickness felt by so many for so long had eased. It was as if the Bilibid tribe had seen the distant smoke and knew that it soon would materialize into freedom.

Amazingly, Camp Bilibid had become a team. We remained a hungry team, but we pulled together in a way that made each hour a livable one. When anger flared, it was directed more at our captors than toward one another. Most conversations centered on happenings in the sky and the growing sounds of mortar fire nearing our enclosure. The pessimists of yesterday, who had predicted that we would someday be lined up against the walls and shot, now leaned toward optimism.

Father Sheridan, a long-time baseball fan, cautioned our small gathering at an early morning Mass on the last Sunday in January: "We've a good chance to win this game of survival. Let's do nothing in the few days ahead to err in words or deeds to either anger or energize our enemy. We've come through eight innings. Now we must keep our calm right through the ninth." His words lent me strength and courage. Others also left the service buoyed with power to pass strength onto others. I noticed that during the times of greatest stress and hardship we pulled together the most; when conditions bettered, individuals quickly found fault with the little things. Such was the pattern.

Moments in the Military Cellblock

Almost three weeks had passed since Dad asked to meet with a leader from the cellblock across the wall from our quarters. Dad still hoped to gain information regarding Dr. Brokenshire from the men there who had endured the Death March. Uncle B's behind-the-scenes persistence finally got Dad his wish. Translator Yamato informed Uncle B that Commandant Ebiko would allow, "Mr. Tong, for a few minutes only," to be escorted through the gate to talk with the American military leader. Ebiko cautioned that this would be the *only* request he would grant for an internee to speak with the military POWs, though earlier, and grudgingly, Oura had granted Father Sheridan permission to give last rites to an ailing Catholic chaplain in the military compound.

At the designated time, I accompanied Dad to the gate, hoping to catch a glimpse of Dr. Brokenshire as it opened. The guard, assuming we both had permission, ushered us into the compound. There Yamato met us. He signaled for me to accompany Dad. The building holding the American GIs appeared more a hospital ward than a dormitory. Almost all of the men we saw as we walked down the corridor behind Yamato were lying or sitting on cots. Most had sallow staring faces and sunken ribcages. One POW, the only one I saw standing, winked at me. A couple of the men tried to smile. One wiggled two forefingers toward me—sort of a wave—but most had blank, stonelike faces.

Although Dad held little hope of actually meeting with Dr. Brokenshire, he did study each face in the long corridor on the chance that he might recognize "Doc." We did not spot him in that cellblock, but there was a second one. Yamato led us to the very end of the corridor where two men, probably officers, were seated on a cot awaiting Dad's arrival. They had not expected a youngster to be with him, but welcomed both of us and graciously apologized for having no goodies to offer. It was apparent from their skeletal features that goodies had not been a part of their lives for a long time. The men wore only loincloths; their upper bodies were bare and showed multiple scars on their backs, suggesting that they had experienced hard times. Only one man spoke.

With Yamato standing only yards away, both men chose their words carefully. Dad sensed their hesitation to talk about anything besides Dr. Brokenshire. Because Yamato had told us that our time there would be brief, Dad posed his questions in a manner that elicited short responses, mostly yes or no.

In a few words, the leader told Dad that he knew Brokenshire and praised his work at Bilibid, but his recollections of dates seemed dim. He thought Dr. Brokenshire had been first interned at Cabanatuan before being reassigned to Bilibid to help with the severe medical needs at the prison. The other soldier nodded confirmation.

Yamato then stepped toward us, indicating that it was time to go. Dad reached over, touched the hands of both men, and thanked them before we followed Yamato to the gate. Dad regretted not having asked their names.

Hopes Point Skyward

Only days after our move from Camp Holmes to Bilibid, I watched two American planes fly over Manila. Those planes, mere specks in the sky, were likely observing Japanese troop placements or specific defense locations in the city. There was no antiaircraft fire. After seeing the thousands of soldiers moving north as we were trucked to Bilibid, I imagined there was no firing because the Japanese Army had fled Manila.

Soon thereafter, I watched as huge bombers in formation filled the skies. Just as the P-38 fighter planes had buoyed our hopes at Camp Holmes, the regular appearance of B-24 bombers promised an answer to our prayers that the end of our imprisonment might come soon. We had no way of knowing their targets for certain, but Mr. Crouter—who believed he knew what was what—surmised they were zeroing in on the Japanese planes at Clark Field and smaller airstrips north of the city. We did not see any Japanese warplanes challenge the B-24s, so we guessed that the incessant bombings of the airfields had obliterated much of Japan's capability to retaliate.

I found watching the strings of bombs falling from the B-24s on the city and listening to the echoing booms to be a surreal, chilling experience. Those bombing raids initiated the near total destruction of Manila.

During those early raids, almost everyone gathered on the prison grounds or the rooftop to watch where the planes were headed and listen to their deliveries of destruction. Mothers held their children high, pointing excitedly toward the sky.

Dad and I watched the flyovers from the rooftop. One morning, the smooth roar of engines was interrupted. The sky surrounding the formation suddenly became dotted with puffballs—the explosive aftermath of antiaircraft fire known as "ack-ack." Clearly, some Japanese forces remained in Manila. When a trail of smoke began pouring out of one of the planes, we knew it had been hit. Seconds passed. The wounded plane dropped slowly, and then slanted away from the formation. Moments afterward, four parachutes drifted downward and out of sight as the plane tumbled toward earth. A very visible and audible explosion tore the fuselage and tail section into aerial debris, scattering it all over the city. Silently, we returned to our cubicles. I fought back tears as I descended with Dad.

I had a hard time sleeping that night as images of death filled my mind. I replayed the scene through the night hours, but I could not change reality. The sequence of events that day left behind a haunting picture. The initial sightings of the planes had so stirred our hearts in Bilibid, each one beating rapidly with patriotic pride as we took in those beautiful planes in formation. Minutes later, our hearts had been broken.

The bombings continued, however. Fearing more tragedies, many chose not to watch the flights overhead again. Stepping onto the roof from the stairwell two days later, I heard a woman moan loudly "Oh, no!" I looked up to see another bomber struggling from a direct hit. With smoke trailing, it remained in formation for a short while, giving me hope that it would return home safely. Then flames suddenly emerged from the underbelly and the plane began a downward tumble. I prayed for parachutes to drop. Only one appeared. The parachute was so close that I could actually make out the aviator, hands raised, holding the chute strings as he dropped toward the streets below. As he neared the ground, his arms fell to his sides and his body went limp. He had been shot. I immediately sought out my father. I found Dad by a second floor window. He, too, had witnessed the event and embraced me. No words were needed. He understood my sadness.

At sunrise the next day, we heard a dull drone and looked up to see nine specks in a cross formation flying over the same area. They appeared to be paying tribute to their fallen comrades. My tears flowed freely as Father Gowen explained the significance of the flying cross passing overhead.

A chronic fatalist in camp, recognizing that the formations were clearly targeting nearby Intramuros (commonly called the Walled City by Westerners), predicted that our walled prison itself would be a target soon. That notion had not crossed my mind before. But his words added another worry to my thoughts.

As each day passed, the bombs fell closer to Bilibid and the surrounding structures along the Pasig River. The closer proximity of the raids indeed caused anxiety in camp. We could only pray that American intelligence experts were aware of our position.

When a couple of days passed with no bomber sightings, I asked Uncle B if America was giving up. "No," he replied, "it means that our foot soldiers are coming to town." It turned out that they had already arrived in the northern outskirts of the city, near Valenzuela.

When hot shreds of shrapnel and phosphorus fell into our compound for the first time, the excitement of seeing the metal fragments in our midst caused my friends and me to race to pick up the scraps. The fragments likely were remnants of exploded shells from tanks in the area. We discovered very quickly that a simple touch of those hot, jagged pieces of metal would cause severe burns. I still bear a small scar on a knuckle as a reminder of those hot fragments. Quickly, we all realized that "sky trash" should not be picked up for hours, if at all. Mom ruled the trash a no-no. But it continued to fall into our confines regularly.

Two imaginative teenage brothers, the Pattersons, capitalized on the metal bits by setting up a tiny workspace in the tin-roofed camp kitchen. There, they took the debris gathered over several days, boiled it to liquid on the wood stove, and then poured the liquid into a mold they had shaped out of wood. The product resembled a small lead toy car.

One day, I followed them to the kitchen to observe the procedure, eager to make a car of my own. I watched closely as they poured the hot fluid into the mold, and then clamped it shut. After some time, they decided it had cooled sufficiently to remove it from the mold. I asked, "Is it hot?"

"You tell me," replied one of the brothers.

Holding the "car" between two bamboo sticks, he poked the hardened lead against my bare chest. It was excruciatingly hot, and the car-shaped brand on my chest remains my most notable memento of a form of experiential learning in a very different kind of schoolyard.

As days passed, the novelty of picking up jagged scraps diminished. I became far more absorbed in watching the increased military activity on Quezon Boulevard, only a long stone's throw from our rooftop. While observing thousands of Japanese troops moving northward from Manila a month earlier, some pundits aboard our truck had surmised that those movements meant that Manila would be left an open city, and so a safer place to be interned. We discovered within days, however, that Japanese resistance in Manila remained extremely strong. From all sections of the city, especially in and around Intramuros south of the Pasig River, enemy antiaircraft fire was incessant. The Japanese also set fires to slow American troop advancement from the north. Clearly, they had an all-out strategy worked out to defend Manila.

As the American raids over the city intensified, our rooftop was officially ruled out of bounds for long stretches of each day. Commandant Ebiko reminded Uncle B, "We must protect you."

"Thank you for caring," responded Uncle B, somewhat sarcastically.

In some ways, Ebiko's order reflected the reality of our situation and supported Uncle B's periodic reminders to parents to caution their children about third-floor activity. Yet, he also knew that Ebiko's order was intended to free the roof for the guards to use as an observation post. They regularly visited the rooftop in the late afternoon. If my pals and I were there, a guard would nonchalantly signal us toward the stairway, rarely with any rebukes or threats. After awhile, they totally ignored us.

Watching the battles raging in the nearby streets and boulevards of Manila had become a daily routine in my life. On Ebiko's orders, the guards appeared on the rooftop more frequently. One of them we called "Tojo." He seemed intent on showing off his less-than-perfect English by directing us off the roof with a loud, "No, no, *kiken!*" (No, no, danger!), and then followed up by ushering us to the stairway. We learned quickly that he was lenient, just gruff, and following orders. If we ignored him, he said nothing—he had done what he had been told to do. He was telling the truth. The roof had become very dangerous as the exchanges of rifle and machine-gun fire moved closer to Bilibid.

Only the damaged walls of what had been the third floor served as any form of cover. But those weakened structures were penetrable. The wide-open areas on the rooftop also exposed our movements to several vantage points outside the prison walls. A lofted grenade or well-aimed howitzer could easily be directed to the unprotected rooftop. Japanese snipers had taken over the upper floors of almost all the nearby buildings. Church steeples, we discovered, were favored locations from which to fire machine guns and rifles or heave incendiary bombs. My parents soon agreed with Tojo and declared the rooftop out of bounds for me. Still, a number of men continued to observe the surrounding activity from the roof. They paid no attention to Tojo or the other guards.

The guard corps of our camp was armed only with rifles. Never, however, did I see any of them fire on American or Filipino targets from the roof. They must have known it would have been suicidal to do so. On one of our later clandestine rooftop visits, Ward Graham and I watched what appeared to be several Japanese soldiers standing in the box-like belfry of a church across the street from our compound. Mr. Crouter was crouched next to us. The moving figures in the belfry appeared to be shielding themselves from the volleys of rifle, machine-gun, and artillery fire in the surrounding streets. From our rooftop perch, I observed the gunfire between American foot soldiers and the Japanese snipers. I felt like I was watching a movie or a play. The fighting was extremely loud but difficult to follow. Then, suddenly the exchange of fire stopped as though a dark curtain fell in the middle of a theatrical performance. Mr. Crouter led us down the stairwell to the chow line. As we parted, he softly said to us, "I hope that what we saw was the final scene and that there won't be a replay tomorrow."

January 29

The final days of January brought a time of living the extremes. We fought off depression, pain, and starvation, yet were buoyed by what was happening outside our prison walls. Some saw death as our final chapter, but more of us pictured ourselves riding the waves under the Golden Gate Bridge. Misery was pushed to the side by signs of hope—the sounds of low-flying planes were met with fear and joy. Those planes not only diverted our attention from our woes but also alarmed every enemy soldier in Manila's hideouts. Days afterward, those hideouts became direct targets.

Following Don Zimmerman's short chapel service on January 29, Mom and I visited with a woman who had not been able to attend the service because she did not have the strength to rise from her mat. In pain and completely lethargic, the woman wished only for death. She refused food. To buoy her spirits, Mom shared with her news of the American troops in the city. Those words brought only a shadow of a smile. Speaking softly, she said, "God bless each one of them." She was one of several adults too weak from malnutrition to share in viewing the goings-on outside our walls.

The daily presence of American troop activity above and around Bilibid generated both excitement and apprehension for us, but it infuriated Ebiko and Oura. Oura, who we had not seen for some time, suddenly reappeared. He ordered all of us to remain inside our building with all windows closed, cutting off air circulation and making quarters extremely stuffy. The next day, Oura told Uncle B that he had ordered that no more food or medicines would be brought into Bilibid. Uncle B was incensed and went to Commandant Ebiko's office by the entry gate to protest these deprivations. Ebiko told him that Oura was no longer in Bilibid; he had simply disappeared. Hearing that news, Uncle B himself authorized the opening of the windows. Ebiko laid out no additional orders and the guards focused their attention on the rooftop.

January 30

The ear-splitting sound of two very low-flying planes woke me that morning. They sped across the city toward Manila Bay in tight formation. Within minutes, they reversed direction, crossing the Pasig River in an easterly path. Two other fighter planes simultaneously followed a similar flight pattern, but flying north/south. This back-and-forth parade of air power continued until mid-morning. Of course, there was much speculation in Bilibid as to the meaning of these low flyovers. We heard no bombs fall, nor antiaircraft firings. Their low altitude, no doubt, precluded a Japanese response. But the flyovers lent credence to my belief that we would soon be free. "The Americans are coming," announced my very excited sister Rae to anyone who would listen.

February 1

When Mom's calendar flipped to February 1, life in Bilibid moved too fast for me to track all the details. Dad had to rein me in, sensing that my explorative instincts might get me into trouble. The new soldiers who had joined the guard corps made Dad uneasy. That afternoon we went up to the rooftop together. He was curious and wanted to check out American infantry foot traffic around the buildings on Quezon Boulevard. Even from the high vantage point, we could hear much more than we could see. Staccato rounds of gunfire were exchanged between GIs hidden on the west side of Quezon Boulevard and Japanese snipers in the upper floors of buildings across the street. The boulevard was empty. The two guards walking slowly around the rooftop paid no attention to our movements.

For some reason, following minutes of eerie silence, a Japanese soldier ran out onto Quezon Boulevard, and then bent over as if to retrieve something. A crescendo of rifle fire suddenly erupted and the soldier collapsed in the middle of the road, his hat still on his head. Again, silence followed. Dad ushered me down the stairwell. Mom was not happy that I had seen a soldier shot. Yet it paled with what Dad and I were to encounter later.

February 2

In the forenoon, with Dad beside me, we slowly followed Japanese guards to the rooftop. Again, they paid no attention to us as we joined a cluster of men and older boys peeking around the blasted walls toward activity on the boulevard. I noticed immediately that yesterday's corpse remained on the boulevard, but without boots and cap.

I returned to the roof with Mom and Aunt Leora in the afternoon. They were curious about the condition of the church outside the north wall—a structure they had admired for some time. I could not help but notice how Mom struggled walking up the stairs. She held Leora's arm, even while on the roof. The sounds of gunfire between Japanese snipers in the belfry and unseen American troops were intermittent. Bilibid's giant walls hid much of the action from our sight. Dad and I returned to the second floor soon afterward. The dead soldier on Quezon Boulevard had been dragged to the curb and was now naked except for his underwear. Clearly, needy Filipinos had found a use for his clothing. Dad, speaking to no one in particular, commented that the scene we observed told a story of human behavior when life's struggles with stress and starvation dictate our actions.

At suppertime, Uncle B joined our family and the Whitfields for an early meal on the north balcony, adjacent to the Whitfield bed space. The last remnants of food from our collective Red Cross "goodies" highlighted the evening meal. Since the adults had a lot to talk about and wished to converse freely, Mom excused my sisters and me to join the Crouters in what would be one of the last evening get-togethers with them.

Later, I learned that most of the adult talk on the balcony centered on what was going on outside the walls. Mom, ever the interrogator, and fully aware of Uncle B's recent conversations with Ebiko and Yamato, wanted to know what the Japanese response would be when U.S. troops unlocked the prison doors. "Will they plan to fight to the end inside the walls?" she asked. "Or, will they pull out of Bilibid without confrontation? Or worse, will they spitefully leave the arriving American forces with a burial detail?"

Uncle B dismissed the last option immediately. "I think we're lucky," he said. "Ebiko holds no anger toward us. He is consumed with his own worries right now."

Uncle B's best guess was that the Japanese garrison would disappear before our troops took the prison.

February 3

The American soldiers—preoccupied with sniper activity and excited Filipinos and having no familiarity with the area around Bilibid's walls—were totally unaware of our presence only yards away. Separated from the GIs' activity by the huge walls, we followed their movements as best we could through breaks in the rooftop walls. At the same time, inside we were suffering. Dysentery was rampant. A number of the elderly were at death's door. Yet our courageous doctors, suffering themselves, moved from cubicle to cubicle assisting as best they could.

Nellie McKim talked regularly with Yamato. She even approached a few passing guards in an effort to understand the turn of events they were now facing. Never had Nellie's gift of language been so beneficial to Uncle B than during his interactions with Commandant Ebiko in Bilibid. Uncle B relied heavily on her judgments of possible Japanese actions toward us.

In the late afternoon, the Japanese guards began to clear the rooftop of internees eager to watch the activity outside. At some risk, a surge of impatient men had charged back onto the roof anyway. Luckily, the guard corps simply ignored them. Very few women joined the surge to the rooftop, most abstained to stay with their children. The excitement spread to those unable to manage the stairwell. Taking turns, the ones who could climb up hustled back down with news of the events occurring outside. Their reports were so invigorating that even some of the bedridden found the strength to sit up and listen to the play-by-play accounts of the fighting around us.

Dad, allowing his own boyishness to take over, decided to see the action too. Calming Mom, he took me to the rooftop with him. Dodging the scattered shreds of hot shrapnel, we positioned ourselves with a cluster of men at a spot by the north wall. The rooftop was crowded with onlookers mesmerized by the action outside—gunfire, mortar fire, yells, explosions, and planes overhead. I could see and hear the bombardment destroying structures alongside Quezon Boulevard. Then I heard voices rising from the area immediately outside our walls. I could not make out what was being said, but knew the language was neither Tagalog nor Japanese. It was exciting to hear American voices so close by.

What Mom later called "The Last Supper" took place on the Whitfield balcony. Norman led the commentary of the day's happenings for the girls. He explained the probable roles of each low-flying plane and suggested that the Filipinos milling around our compound were taking foolish chances. As he talked, I watched an empty stool move on the concrete floor like it was performing a tap dance. I thought we must be having an earthquake.

Evelyn Whitfield peeked over the balcony to see what was causing the vibrations. Sensing something unusual, she dashed off to look out other windows. Soon I heard what sounded like a drumroll in an orchestra performance. Moments later, Evelyn spotted the source of those deep rumbling sounds. Racing through the building she shouted, "American tanks! American tanks!" Those words triggered excitement and bedlam in all quarters. As Evelyn relates in her book *Three Year Picnic,* "A cry tore from my throat—for rolling down Quezon Boulevard, a few blocks away, were enormous tanks—and they were firing at the buildings along the way."

All that night, sounds of war engulfed us. Mom worried about the raging fire lighting up the sky, which sprinkled red embers into our compound. She felt trapped. In severe pain, she remained awake throughout the night, so she could rise periodically to check out the status of the fires around us.

Mayhem reigned that night in Bilibid. Parents and children ran about, responding to the sounds outside our prison walls. Others yelled at them to "stay down!" Guards, oblivious of our movements, carried what looked like jars up the steps, probably to throw at targets across the wall, and then returned for more. Around midnight, committee members ordered us not to go outside. They told us to cover the windows on the second floor and to move to the first floor for safety. Parents raced upstairs for bedding so that their children might sleep in the crammed quarters of the first floor. Only the few bedridden remained on the second floor. Doctors worked through the night to comfort the ailing. Uncle B encouraged everyone to remain calm and to give the guards free use of the stairwells. For the first time, I could actually hear bullets pinging against the walls and window shutters. It was a miracle no one was shot. I occasionally relive memories of that ugly night in my dreams.

February 4

In the predawn hours of the next day, Mr. Yamato entered our compound. He tiptoed around the smoking phosphorus on the grounds leading to our quarters and passed through the maze of waking bodies. Others, standing about, were already rehashing the sights and sounds of the night before. Yamato had become quite attached to Uncle B, Evelyn Whitfield, Nellie McKim, and others on the committee, and he wanted to wish them farewell.

At the same time, our kitchen crew was performing nobly to feed us. Before dawn, several had run in the dark from our quarters to the tin-roofed kitchen to prepare soup with whatever they could find to toss into the pot. They could hear shrapnel falling on the tin roof from the battles outside. As I made a morning dash to the privy with Dad, my calloused feet dodged the red embers dotting the grounds. Interestingly, the sounds of bullets striking our building had stopped. Returning to my mat on the first floor, I could see flashes of light leaping from gun turrets, and the subsequent fires on the streets surrounding our prison. I studied the faces of my friends standing by windows as their faces lit up with each explosion. In the morning light, we clearly saw the buildings on Quezon Boulevard all ablaze. So, too, were structures closer to our compound. The scene was surreal, with flames spitting angrily from windows and rooftops all around us. I became deeply uneasy as the fires approached Bilibid, yet felt fortunate to be protected by Bilibid's monstrous walls and the almost constant presence of Dad. He noted that the Americans, Japanese, and Filipinos on the outside—all engaged in fighting or dodging the fight—were far more in harm's way than we were.

At breakfast, Uncle B told us about Yamato's predawn visit and his farewell words. With a sword at his side, Yamato had shared his honest desire to say *sayonara* with fond wishes for our well-being. Uncle B relayed to us Yamato's sincere wish for an honorable death. And he would find it soon, thought Uncle B, knowing that American soldiers nearly controlled the streets surrounding Bilibid. At mid-morning the next day, as Uncle B and Phil Markert were taken by jeep to Camp Santo Tomas, their driver told them that earlier in the day a lone Japanese officer exiting on foot from Bilibid's main gate was shot. "Was he a short man?" asked Uncle B. "He was very short," replied the driver. Very likely the victim was Mr. Yamato.

Since it was a Sunday morning, Don Zimmerman had prepared an informal chapel service on the first floor of the hospital quarters. Attendees, sitting on mats on the floor, participated in song and scripture. Uncle B was called away from the service by a guard who accompanied him to Ebiko's office near the main gate. A major, representing our rarely seen Bataan neighbors, was already in the office. Uncle B had never before met the major, yet they immediately embraced one another. The major's name was Warren Wilson. Ebiko entered moments later and handed each a single sheet of paper with the word "message" boldly written at the top. Ebiko explained that the announcement had been written in English by Mr. Yamato days earlier. Uncle B and Wilson parted, agreeing to meet soon after each one announced the contents of Ebiko's message to their internees.

All who were able to move assembled in the foyer to hear the commandant's official announcement. The first words out of Uncle B's mouth were inaudible. He was so choked up with tears that his words came out in a whisper. Pulling himself together, Uncle B announced, "The Japanese are leaving!" Overwhelmed again, he finally added, "They are preparing to leave us as I speak."

As soon as Uncle B spoke those words, there was a sudden silence. Mrs. Herold placed her finger on her lips and let out a loud, "Shush!" Down the steps came the Japanese garrison, rifles in hand. For a fleeting moment, my attention returned to Major Mukaibo's threat of death at Brent School three years earlier. "This is the end," I thought to myself. Only seconds later, the Japanese garrison marched through the foyer without even glancing in our direction. They continued through the gate toward Ebiko's office and went out of sight.

Then Uncle B read Ebiko's formal message. I was speechless—numb with joy.

MESSAGE
1. The Japanese Army is now going to release all the prisoners of war and internees here on its own accord.
2. We are assigned to another duty and shall be here no more.
3. You are at liberty to act and live as free persons, but you must be aware of probable dangers if you go out.
4. We shall leave here foodstuffs, medicines, and other necessities of which you may avail yourselves for the time being.
5. We have arranged to put up sign-board at the front gate, bearing the following content—

Lawfully released Prisoners of War and Internees are quartered here. Please do not molest them unless they make positive registance. [*sic*]

Following his announcement, Uncle B took the American flag, which some women had constructed in Camp Holmes and kept hidden, and held the flag up for all to see. The first voice I heard was Mary Dyer's. We all joined her in singing "The Star-Spangled Banner," many so choked up that the words would not come out. Mom held my hand, her own quivering badly. As the flag hung from a nearby windowsill, the song "God Bless America" followed. I blushed at not knowing the words.

As Uncle B left our joyful group to meet with Major Wilson, people were embracing one another. All were in a state of absolute euphoria. When the leaders met, Wilson's first words were an urgent command, "Carl, you must remove that flag before it becomes a target." Uncle B hustled back to the foyer and told Mrs. Herold to take the American flag down "Now!"

Returning to the major, Uncle B asked if our respective groups might meet for a military/civilian POW visitation. Wilson explained the condition of his men. He knew that they would love to see new faces, but their state of being called for a much-abbreviated visit, and only with those able to mingle. The two leaders agreed to meet the next morning to arrange a short period for civilian men to visit with his soldiers in their quarters. Given the condition of his men, Wilson asked that no women or children visit, at least not for the time being.

Ambling toward the gate separating the compounds, the two devised a plan to notify American troops outside that hundreds of Americans were inside Bilibid. As they parted, loud noises outside the main gate startled them—the sound of a rifle butt banging against the gate and then a shout in English, "Who's in there?"

Major Wilson yelled back, "POWs!"

"How do we get in?"

Wilson called on two of his stronger men to open the gate.

"I was so happy," Uncle B said, as he recounted the story to us on the balcony that evening. "I didn't know whether to laugh or cry."

We had a story of our own to tell Uncle B. While he was greeting soldiers at the front gate, two GIs had magically entered our courtyard by themselves through "a hole in the wall." Standing inside the wall, rifles in firing position, one of them called out, "Hello!" The shout drew the immediate attention of some women and young girls. After staring for a moment in disbelief at the two profiles by the wall, the women ran like stones shot from a slingshot toward the two soldiers. As Aunt Leora, one of those who first noticed the soldiers described the scene: "There they were, two handsome hunks of humanity. They somehow gained entry by jumping over the wall, running through it, or on angels' wings. No one bothered to ask, nor did they seem to care." It was not important to know their names, rank, or how they got in, only to get as close as they could to hear their voices and to touch them.

Rae and Wezer had been with Aunt Leora and the first throng of women and children to see the GIs' faces. The soldiers were stunned. They had no notion that any Americans were behind the prison walls and were aghast at seeing the women and children. Soon, I joined the human huddle around the soldiers. We all had dreamed of this day. What a thrill it was! Tears welled in my eyes. I sobbed as my sisters and I lived those very happy moments. I had not seen such smiles in a long time. I was so focused on the soldiers that I did not hear or see my dad standing behind me until he placed his arm around my shoulder. I looked up at him; his face was also wet. The only other time I had seen Dad cry was the day we reunited in Holmes—that special day in March 1944. The sight of those two sturdy American soldiers surrounded by a growing crowd of internees prompted Father Gowen, who was standing next to us, to pronounce loudly, "This is like manna from heaven!"

One mother, holding her daughter's hand, was unable to resist contact any longer. She broke out of the crowd and rushed into the arms of the taller GI. Her child hung onto his leg. The mother's head obscured the name on the soldier's chest. She would not let go. The GIs clearly had not anticipated anything like this avalanche of waving arms, tears, and unabashed devotion. They had not seen American women for a long time, and it was clear that being greeted by such a surge of affection was extremely meaningful to them.

Breaking the emotional intensity, one of the soldiers asked, "Where are you from?"

Aunt Leora answered loudly, "I'm from Ohio."

"Me, too!" said the soldier.

"Where?"

"Paris, Ohio."

As the introductions continued, Aunt Leora's new Ohio soldier-friend, Phil, asked Rae where she was from. She stared for a moment, and then honestly replied, "I dunno." (Thinking back, that was a fair answer. I do not think I could have responded differently.)

Minutes later, Father Gowen turned to Dad and me, signaling upward with his eyes at a cloud of thick smoke drifting toward us. The smell of smoke accompanied the darkening sky. Our soldier friends, Phil and Earl, also saw the threatening clouds and turned to head back to their tank outside the wall. Throwing kisses and bidding farewell, they headed toward the wooden barricade in the north wall through which they had entered the compound. Phil called back, "We're from the Thirty-seventh Ohio Division, just outside."

Dad helped several other men reset two thick crossbars over the opening where the two soldiers had entered. The rest of us filtered back to our quarters, each sharing stories about the GIs with those who could not negotiate the walk to the courtyard. Mom, unable to join us outside, giggled with glee at the tales my sisters told her and listened to the rapid-fire stories being shared by others with anyone wishing to listen. For the remainder of the day, we huddled indoors with windows closed to shut out the heavy smoke. Inside, we could hear artillery fire pouring out from tank turrets on Quezon Boulevard. Children held fingers in their ears. Low-flying planes were easily heard but nearly invisible. Naturally, we thought about Phil and Earl who only an hour earlier had filled our hearts with joy. Truly, the war had arrived around our walls. For a short while the angry sounds outside and the dense smoke layer above us quieted the emotions of those electric minutes with the American GIs.

February 5

Smoke continued to engulf Bilibid Prison, but the sounds surrounding the walls had subsided. At a very early hour, I woke up from my fitful sleep to see Mom standing by her mat. She appeared stronger. Without Wezer's assistance, Mom walked down the steps with her daughter to visit the *benjo*. Our family gathered for a brief breakfast together near the more protected south balcony. Uncle B joined us and brought two bananas for Mom. Dad brought several bowls of soup from the kitchen. His blessing was simple but meaningful, "May our prayers on this cloudy day be with those inside and outside our walls whose lives are being challenged by the war surrounding us."

Mom was eager to move about and found her way with Evelyn to a second floor window, still covered with sheets the committee had ordered us to put in place two days earlier. Others joined them by the windows. They, too, pulled down the cloth covers to watch what was happening across the wall. In her book *Three Year Picnic*, Evelyn explained what followed: "We proudly spotted a sniper in a church tower . . . Cold terror clutched us when Peg's face turned white and with a scream she threw herself flat crying, 'There's a sniper in that window across the street—he pointed his gun right at me!'" Mom's sharp cry created a domino effect of bodies ducking below the windows.

The sniper's shot, followed by others, was the apparent cue for the tank corpsmen outside our walls to fire their "heavy hitters" into the church, putting an end to the sniper fire. For the rest of the morning tank fire and GI raids attacked all structures facing the prison. We could see similar confrontations taking place along the boulevard and in the area around Santo Tomas. Buildings were set ablaze. Those fires generated a smoke screen that shut out the sun's rays. Shreds of hot debris fell around the area, much of it landing in our compound. Everyone was urged to remain indoors. Quezon Boulevard, once a beautiful section of Manila, lay smoldered in ruins.

While relieved that Mom was okay, Dad was extremely upset that she had ventured from her mat and allowed her curiosity to overtake good sense. He scolded her for having taken that chance with her life, especially in her fragile condition. It was the first time I had seen my dad show such anger toward his dear Peg. Then he bent down and kissed her forehead. Mom, still shaken from her experience, was grateful for the precautions that followed. Dr. Skerl, covering for Uncle B who was at Santo Tomas meeting with their internee leader, ordered all windows closed and declared the rooftop out of bounds.

Shortly before noon, an American officer, Brigadier General Bonner Fellers, surprised us by strolling into the compound. Dr. Skerl went and met him. My eyes widened at the sight of a general. His was not a recognized name like MacArthur or Wainwright, but he wore a gold star on his lapel, which from my perspective made him very important. We were amazed that he had come to visit us in the midst of the battle around Bilibid. General Fellers greeted everyone very warmly and promised us that Red Cross packages would arrive in a few days, mail from America would be delivered soon, and General MacArthur would visit Bilibid.

I joined others who followed Dr. Skerl as he escorted the general through the first floor quarters and then to the cemetery along the north wall. On the way, Fellers shook any extended hand and greeted people by name as Dr. Skerl introduced them. I watched as the general stopped at the grave site and excused himself from conversation to bow his head and stand solemnly. All who were there joined him in a moment of silence. His visit was short but meaningful.

By late afternoon, Mom was back on her mat and seemed to have regained her composure after her traumatic sniper scare. She reminded Dad to keep us kids away from the grounds, the rooftop, and all the windows. Shortly before he ordered me to remain in the cubicle with Mom, I had snuck up to the roof with Ward. There, we discovered that the church we had observed before was now lacking the steeple and belfry from which the sniper had fired toward Mom. We also noticed that the sky above Bilibid was so dense with smoke that Quezon Boulevard was nearly invisible.

In the early evening, Dr. Skerl moved through the quarters, announcing that we were to be evacuated soon. Those words took everyone by surprise. Skerl strongly recommended that we take only absolute necessities with us. Dad worked out a plan to help Mom move to the designated meeting site outside the main gate. We flanked Mom, her arms over our shoulders. Wezer carried a thin folder containing Mom's calendar and sketches. Although told not to take accessories with us, and that mats would be delivered to us soon after we arrived at our destination, most everyone placed some valuables in bags to take along. I was amazed at how quickly we responded to the evacuation order. Wisely, Evelyn Whitfield, the aide to the general committee, secured the camp records and carried them with her, since Uncle B was off at Santo Tomas working out details for visitation exchanges.

It was the first time since arriving at Bilibid that we had stood outside the prison walls. All of us gathered on the open ground next to Rizal Avenue, bordering the south wall. GIs were posted around the clearing to keep an eye on activity in the vicinity and to shoo Filipinos away from the main gate.

As we waited for the trucks, we could easily see the reason for our evacuation. A heavy smoke layer completely blanketed Intramuros and Manila Bay. The nearby Marco Polo Hotel was ablaze, and the fire was moving directly toward Bilibid. Sitting on the ground outside the wall, I could feel the heat of the approaching flames, but like everyone else, I remained seated. Army medics carried a couple of the Bataan POWs in their arms. It was heart wrenching to see so many young bodies mere skeletons. They were carried on stretchers to the awaiting trucks and ambulances, and those POWs who could walk helped load their buddies into the vehicles. In minutes they were gone.

The last of the empty trucks pulled up to load women, children, and the few civilian men who were unable to walk. We were told that able men would begin walking until the trucks could return to pick them up. Dad grabbed my hand, saying, "Young man, you're with me." Wezer also offered to walk, but Dad helped her board the truck saying, "Watch Mom."

The fire had already spread to nearby Filipino homes. As we walked, flanked by rifle-toting GIs, windows of buildings along the road opened, and Filipino after Filipino shouted the traditional greeting, "Mabuhay!" It was a joy to see so many Filipinos once again. We had not walked far before the first convoy of trucks returned and loaded all of us aboard.

The ride was much shorter than I expected. Our truck pulled up in front of a large former shoe factory called Ang Tibay, which had temporarily been turned into an army headquarters station. Inside, disarray reigned as mothers tried to situate their children into sleeping arrangements. Most waited for food promised by Army Food Service personnel. The Zimmermans graciously shared with us some goodies they had been handed by GIs.

We were amazed by the marvelous efficiency of our soldiers in moving eight hundred POWs through dense smoke and a still-active battle area. Everyone arrived safely, and the Ohio Thirty-seventh Division truck crews had even delivered our mats and mattresses. I enjoyed watching the GIs visiting with the young women who shared tales of imprisonment. Wezer learned from one soldier that during the Japanese occupation, Ang Tibay had been an airplane engine repair facility. Soon after midnight, our family collapsed for some much-needed sleep. It was a day of lifelong memories—February 5, 1944.

February 6

For me, the highlight of our short stay in Ang Tibay was the bacon and powdered eggs served for breakfast. Mom warned me to go easy on the food, but I gorged on a whole mess kit full of scrambled eggs. Half an hour afterward, though, I gave my breakfast the heave-ho in a gutter next to a parked tank.

The GIs invited children and teenagers to tour the insides of several armored vehicles parked along the street. A group of fathers joined us in gaping at the innards of two tanks and an amphibian "duck." Our GI guide was quite impressed with the toy tank I had carved at Camp Holmes and still carried with me. Dad later described my joy that morning to his mom, saying, "Ang Tibay was your grandson's heaven."

By late afternoon of February 6, the officer in charge of our care informed Dr. Skerl that we would return to Bilibid after sundown. He said that the fires around the prison had subsided but Filipinos had pillaged the grounds and buildings during the night hours. That unfortunate news caused considerable anxiety, especially among those who had left valuable items or keepsakes behind.

Before our return, Dad sought out the leader of the military POWs whom we had met a couple of weeks earlier at his prison bedside. He enjoyed the opportunity to visit freely with Major Wilson, who told Dad that he had not dared mention his name during our earlier meeting. Wilson reported that Dr. Brokenshire had been removed from Bilibid with hundreds of others in October of 1944. With additional prisoners from Cabanatuan, they were shipped to Japan to serve in forced labor installations. Dr. Brokenshire's ship, the *Arisan Maru*, had been torpedoed northwest of Luzon by an American submarine, unaware that it carried the precious cargo of sixteen hundred POWs. Wilson noted that a few survivors had been returned to Manila, but he did not know if Brokenshire was one of them. Dad kept that account to himself, holding onto the hope that the good doctor might be alive and interned at Cabanatuan Prison.

Sniper fire interrupted our convoy's return to Bilibid. The drivers made a quick U-turn and drove us back to Ang Tibay. We remained onboard the vehicle while a crew of GIs cleaned up the sniper problem, and we were back in Bilibid an hour later. Compared to that eerie December night when we first passed through the steel gates, we entered the prison cheerfully. We knew that Bilibid's confining walls had protected us and given us hope.

It was dark when we arrived, and a blackout in the prison had been ordered for our safety. We could not make out the clutter strewn about our cubicles and had to wait for morning to look for lost items. Few mats remained, so that night the concrete floor served as both mattress and pillow for most of us. A few who had brought pillows with them were spared some discomfort. Still, most accepted the night as a temporary bad scene, given the army's promises of bedding to be delivered within a day.

Just as Dr. Skerl had told us, our quarters had been cleaned out. Mom gave Filipinos the benefit of doubt, suggesting they may have assumed our exodus was a permanent one. Those generous thoughts, of course, did not erase the losses. I rationalized the loss of my two small books, Longfellow's poems and my hymnal, was worth the breakfast I had consumed that morning. Also, I still had my carved toy tank and car in my pocket; I had not played with them for a long time, but I remained attached to them. Thankfully, Mom had her calendar and sketches, which Wezer had taken to Ang Tibay and guarded closely.

For those who had lost items of personal value—particularly camouflaged notes of happenings in prison—the morning light offered little comfort. The remaining personal items lay scattered all over the floor, mostly destroyed. I actually found my Longfellow book shredded, as though ripped apart in anger. I could not imagine why anyone would participate in that kind of destructive looting. Fortunately, a number of our friends who had been keeping diaries had the foresight to take them to Ang Tibay.

As many continued to search for lost items, an army officer came to our barracks and offered sincere apologies for our losses and the mess. He explained that the military police assigned to watch our compound had to leave the prison soon after midnight because it had become too dangerous. Fire had actually scorched the outer north wall and snipers had targeted the military police lookouts on the roof. Uncle B learned days later of two MPs' deaths by sniper fire on our barracks' rooftop. That news tempered our disappointment about lost items. And most folks, even those who lost valued items, eventually concluded that the delicious meals of K rations made up for their losses.

Hours after our return from Ang Tibay, Mrs. Moule alerted me at the outdoor sink that the looters had likely broken the water main. The only water available was from two holes that a couple of men had dug during the night hours following our return. She cautioned me against brushing my teeth with the water and warned "don't drink it." I chose not to brush my teeth at all and went upstairs to tell my family to stay away from the water. The groundwater attracted flies, and within days diarrhea, dysentery, and dengue fever would again descend on the camp.

Fortunately, military medics soon brought clean water, medications, and two army doctors into Bilibid. They answered many urgent needs. Within hours, food was delivered to our confines and ordnance personnel began making repairs. The military presence gave everyone a feeling of security and confidence.

Amid the morning chaos, we were informed that General MacArthur would make a visit within the hour after he finished talking with the emaciated soldiers across the wall. Any who wished to visit with him and his coterie of aides were to meet by the main entryway to the barracks. When the general arrived, Uncle B graciously greeted him. He tactfully chose not to usher MacArthur through the trash-covered barracks. Men, particularly, were anxious to see him. I could not help noticing how their poorly clad and skinny bodies stood in sharp contrast to the well-dressed leader of the American forces in the Pacific Theater. Even my "husky" dad looked emaciated next to the robust MacArthur.

The general understandably spent most of his visit with the survivors of the Bataan Death March. I imagined that seeing their skeletal bodies made him lament having left them behind in the trenches of Bataan and Corregidor following his escape to Australia. MacArthur promised to evacuate us as soon as possible and expressed his deep regret at not being able to do so immediately because of the extended fighting that continued throughout Manila.

Waiting and Watching

Days after MacArthur's visit to Bilibid, our lives assumed a holding pattern. It was like treading water. We vacillated between feeling joy at having survived and an irresistible urge to go home. When darkness fell each day, we were reminded that our Bilibid home with its vast ugly walls was truly a beautiful and safe sanctuary. The fighting around and above us was incessant. The Japanese had not given up. In a strange way, coming back from Ang Tibay to the fighting around us was like a return to normalcy. Happily though, we felt our soldiers' arms around us.

Artillery fire continued near Camp Santo Tomas and explosions erupted along the Pasig River and around Intramuros. The Walled City must have presented our troops the same degree of difficulty the Japanese faced as they tried to secure Corregidor in the spring of 1942. The clamor from holed-up enemy strongholds in Intramuros and responding tanks on the ground and planes overhead continued as Japanese forces held onto Manila south of the Pasig River. The exchange of fire was especially heavy during the evening hours, and much of it could be heard passing over Bilibid.

Idle days inside the walls prompted some parents to think about setting up classes for the children. Those who had taught at Holmes found it difficult to mount the energy for such an undertaking, however, so the idea died quickly. I found that the hours of inactivity gave me time to talk to our attending GIs and even play catch with them. For some unknown reason, I frequently thought about my grandma, Nana Tong. Would she soon be living with us and making rhubarb pie? Was she alive? A host of other questions crossed my mind, too. Would we be living in America or in Davao? How does a war end? Will it ever end? What if it does not end?

Leading up to the war, Dad had little patience with MacArthur for his apparent indifference to the swelling numbers of Japanese men pouring into Mindanao. He felt much better about the general after his Bilibid visit. Dad was pleased that MacArthur, after mixing with the ghostly figures of the survivors next door, had ordered them evacuated as soon as possible. They sorely needed that immediate attention, and the general provided it. By mid-February, they were gone.

We had hardly known the Bataan survivors, but they had been our comrades and quiet disciplined examples of endurance and fortitude. Having returned with us from Ang Tibay to the protective walls of Bilibid, their final evacuation was a drama our entire internee community witnessed. As they slowly exited the place they had known as hell, some stretched their emaciated arms over the shoulders of medics, others lay prone on canvas stretchers. Each was gently placed in an army ambulance or a truck bed. It was difficult to imagine that they had once been stalwart sons, brothers, husbands, or fathers. I felt both remorse and joy at seeing them leave. Wezer and I stood next to Dad and shared finger waves with the once robust defenders of Bataan as they departed to freedom. Our internee friends standing nearby could not easily disguise their tears—many wept openly at the poignancy of the scene. The exodus was quick and organized. Major Wilson brought up the rear and gave each of us a friendly salute as he walked out of sight. Wilson had told Dad that the men were headed to tent hospitals behind the battle lines, and would eventually be flown to Honolulu for hospitalization.

As soon as Wilson and his men had departed, we learned that Camp Santo Tomas, only blocks away, had been shelled by enemy troops and suffered casualties. A few in our camp, including Dad, Evelyn Whitfield, and Father Sheridan, had once been imprisoned there and had close ties to many of the Santo Tomas internees. They were naturally concerned to learn of their comrades' situation. The news from Santo Tomas was yet another reminder that Bilibid's walls, though confining, were our primary line of defense against the war raging around us. The next day, we learned that seventeen deaths and many serious injuries had occurred at Santo Tomas. Theirs was a truly tragic turn of events, just as we all harbored dreams of freedom.

The battles and fires around Bilibid continued, but not with the same intensity as before. It was clear that the enemy had stored munitions in hospitals, churches, schools, and even under our own quarters before the American invasion. Those hidden stockpiles of armaments slowed MacArthur's takeover of the city. We were extremely fortunate that the munitions hidden under our quarters never ignited.

During the early days of MacArthur's drive into central Manila, I felt exhilarated as I watched the battles around us. But those feelings changed radically when news filtered into Bilibid about the huge numbers of American lives being lost. Each day it seemed that we heard yet another tragic story.

At dawn on February 16—eleven days after our liberation—a very low-flying Japanese Zero bombed the tank positioned outside Bilibid's north wall, killing four. We had come to know those men of the Thirty-seventh Ohio Division from their periodic visits inside our walls. Phil was one of those men killed. Rae was not the only one to sob at that news. The days afterward were solemn, indeed. Mom continued to meet with a number of her woman friends to lend them moral support. After learning of the soldiers' deaths, one aging couple voiced doubts about our finally gaining freedom, much less a return to America.

Toward the end of the month, the intense sights, smells, and sounds of the war had largely moved on to other sections of Manila. Concern in

Bilibid turned to the thousands of Filipinos being held hostage inside the seemingly impenetrable Intramuros. And we all realized that the U.S. military's gaining control of that city within walls would determine how soon we could be transported home. We could not move until the fighting had finished.

Our GI friends told us that a huge number of Japanese corpses had been piled outside our walls. We never actually saw the bodies, but in the Manila heat, the smell of death filtered into our quarters despite the thick walls that separated us from the horrific scene. Even after the corpses were removed, the vile odors remained for a couple of days. I felt lucky I did not have to see the source of the stench.

At nighttime, many of us returned to the rooftop lookout to watch and listen to the fires and explosions still lighting up the sky to the south around Intramuros. Our viewing was more a routine to eat up time than driven by a wish to watch buildings burn.

Recurring sicknesses continued to plague many. The elderly and young children were most vulnerable. Fortunately, army medics were quick to respond and assist our weary corps of doctors with sorely needed medicines. "Those men are heaven-sent," Dr. Skerl told Dad and me as he attended to Mom's continued problems with dysentery.

Our growing impatience for a quick return to America was put aside when the battle for the Walled City again drew us to the rooftop. With Dad and my sisters, I saw the walls of Intramuros blown open by U.S. tanks, which allowed Filipino hostages to flee by the thousands. Many, though, were killed in the salvos. Apparently satisfied that Filipinos who could escape had done so, the Americans sent teams of dive-bombing fighter planes to take over the fight. For days, they formed lines in the sky. Peeling out of line one by one, each plane dove toward the interior of Intramuros, some with guns blazing, others unloading strings of bombs. Our rooftop was like an outdoor theater, offering no obstructions to the aerial ballet going on nearly a mile away. The number of American casualties grew steadily as the U.S. Army fought to gain command of Intramuros.

Our Sad Loss of the "Bs"

February 22 turned out to be a mini-VJ Day for Uncle B and twenty other friends of ours who were the first internees designated for return to America. That morning an American soldier drove his jeep from Santo Tomas into the Bilibid confines and asked to see Walter Tong. Dad was standing next to Uncle B as he prepared to depart Bilibid, when the soldier handed him an envelope. It was from Frank Cary. Dad immediately opened it and shared the message with Uncle B as he boarded the bus.

I was torn between sadness at losing my dear father figure of the war years and joy in the knowledge that he would soon be in the embrace of his family, who had yearned for him these three long years. Uncle B and I shared a long hug and teary farewell. He was put on the first plane to fly to Leyte and from there boarded a ship to the States.

Minutes after Uncle B's departure, Dad called our family together on the north balcony. There he shared with us the news of Dr. Brokenshire's death. It was as though Mom, my sisters, and I had been smacked in the head. Learning about the loss of Dr. B so soon after Uncle B's departure was more than I could bear. I sobbed on my mat that night until exhaustion won out.

Mom's loving tap on my shoulder awakened me the following morning to what she called "a new day." In a hushed tone, she asked me to walk with her to the north balcony. I could tell she wanted to talk with me without waking my sisters. Still distraught with the knowledge of Dr. B's death and Uncle B's departure to America, I anticipated more sad news. Instead, she shared with me that a fellow internee and our close family friend, Marjorie Patton, would be giving birth "any minute now." That news brightened my day and helped soften the sorrows of yesterday.

Marge hoped for a son. Dad had kidded her, suggesting the boy's name be Rokuro, after Commandant Tomibe. (The Pattons were among the first to take advantage of Tomibe's family unit living arrangement in Camp Holmes and so conceived a child.) Marge delivered Richard on February 23 by caesarian section in a U.S. Army field hospital on the outskirts of Manila. The chosen name was Richard, not Rokuro, but was widely accepted as the English version of Tomibe's given name.

In Search of Johnny Oesch

Only days after Uncle B's departure, Dad and I learned rather quickly that feeling free and being free were two different realities. For some days following our return from Ang Tibay, American forces were too occupied with fighting a determined enemy to monitor us. They had neglected to assign an officer to oversee our comings and goings from Bilibid. Naturally, most internees were eager to explore the city around us. Unable to resist the desire to explore the damage done outside Bilibid and to make contact with friends in Santo Tomas and other areas of the city, a small number of internees planned, on their own initiative, to seek out acquaintances. Dad was one of those.

An officer of the Ohio Thirty-seventh Division had told Dad that Santo Tomas had been freed. Dad also knew that the Japanese shelling there had killed seventeen civilians, and this fact set his determination to visit that camp, where he had resided for four months earlier in the war. He was most eager to see Frank Cary and learn about the other Mindanao internees.

He was also very anxious to track down an Australian woman, Ada Oesch, and her son Johnny, a mute child with whom I had played during visits to his home to Padada, Mindanao. Dad wanted to determine whether they were living, and if so, to check on their welfare and needs. Locating them was a high priority for him. Johnny's father had been murdered by aborigines at the Oesch plantation home before their internment in Davao. At about the time Dad was transferred to Holmes, Johnny and his mother were released from Santo Tomas into the custody of German nuns in Manila.

Determined to locate the Oesches, Dad and I walked out the front gate of Bilibid several days after the Japanese had shelled Santo Tomas. He thought my presence would be meaningful to Johnny. Outside the gate, we stopped to look back at the entryway in the daylight. Except for the two turrets that flanked the main gate, it appeared unchanged from what we saw seven weeks earlier when we had first arrived at the prison from Baguio. Both towers were now badly pockmarked from fresh rifle or machine-gun rounds, possibly during an exchange of fire when our Japanese guard corps had fled.

With a map in hand and the approximate location of the German nuns' convent fresh in his mind, Dad led me toward the Pasig River. He knew that their shelter was on the south side of the Pasig, east of Intramuros. Once we located the nuns, Dad hoped to assure himself that Ada and Johnny would be safe by moving them to a protected zone like Santo Tomas. Walking toward the Pasig, we found the north side of the river relatively quiet; the GIs seemed in control and were pacing the area just to ascertain that basements, culverts, and other potential hiding places were devoid of snipers. But Dad did not realize that the area around Intramuros was still a war zone.

The most direct route to the convent was to cross the Quezon Bridge, but when we arrived at the bridge, we discovered it impassable. The midsection of the span was gone, and only a few of the support pillars remained. We were horrified to see the wide calm Pasig River camouflaged by acres of flotsam and hundreds of dead Japanese soldiers in the shallows. The air was rank with the stench of the dead and debris. For a few moments, I thought about our family picnic on a lovely grassy knoll above the Pasig in 1941. Now, it was a river of mud and blood. The memory of that scene and scent still often invades my dreams.

Dad and I spotted a team of Seabees busily setting up a pontoon bridge across the river. One of them did a double take in response to Dad's voice. He told us that the Quezon crossing would not be completed for hours and added that only the Jones River Bridge was passable, so we had to walk farther.

The north side of the river appeared to be free of gunfire exchanges. There was no visible sign of U.S. or Japanese troop activity. But when we reached the Jones Bridge, an astonished military policeman stopped us. Looking directly at Dad, he blurted, "Sir, you are in a war zone!" Unabashed, Dad began to explain his plan to the MP and the location of the convent.

Impatiently, the MP interrupted, "Japanese snipers remain active on the other side, next to the Walled City." When Dad described his search for a woman and her child, the MP backed off slightly, respectful of Dad's mission. Nonetheless, he urged Dad not to proceed and to return to Bilibid, the "safest place in town." Dad persisted, so without further argument, the MP escorted us across the heavily damaged Jones Bridge to the south side of the Pasig River. As we crossed, Dad asked him how the hundreds of floating bodies got there and how they were to be removed. The MP responded curtly, "Bulldozers and a landfill up river, after we secure this f——g zone." I did not need a translation, having been exposed to similar adjectives by the card players at Camp Holmes. Dad did not ask any more questions, but I was sure he had many on his mind.

Two MPs received us on the south side of the Pasig. One of them was the tallest man I had ever seen. I read his name tag: Cummings.

"You want to be here? Are you sure, sir?" Cummings asked, and Dad nodded. Without a word, Cummings signaled for us to follow him and led us quickly along the buildings. He stopped a moment as if listening for something, then again motioned for us to follow. I braved a question of Cummings, asking if he was an officer. "I'm better than that," he answered with a chuckle. "I'm a corporal."

Suddenly, we heard sounds of machine-gun fire a block or so ahead of us. Cummings quickly ordered us into a narrow alleyway between two buildings and told us to stay under the fire escape. At the alley exit, he turned and cautioned us, "Stay right where you are." We did not move. Cummings disappeared in the direction of the gunshots. We remained in the alley for what seemed a long time. Dad broke the silence with an uncharacteristic apology. He admitted to having made a mistake in coming. I felt his deep concern for me; shielded only by a steel fire escape in an area fraught with danger and a long way from the shelter of Bilibid.

More than twenty minutes passed and Dad became impatient. I could tell he was thinking about running back to the bridge. I wondered if he shared my worry that Cummings had been hurt and would not be returning. Then suddenly Cummings reappeared in the alley. He was out of breath and holding a bloodstained sword. Cummings matter-of-factly handed the sheath-covered saber to Dad and said that the guys up the street had just shot two snipers in a culvert and that there may be more in the area. "You must return, sir," said Cummings, adding only that his buddy told him to give the man the sword and "send him back to Bilibid."

Dad had no desire for the sword and asked the MP to give it back to his friend. "Your friend earned it," he told Cummings.

The corporal responded, "Those guys have a bunch of swords already. Sir, let's go while we can."

Dad and I followed Cummings to the Jones Bridge and across the river to the safer side. He and Dad shook hands, and the gigantic man patted me on the head as we turned to leave. Then we rapidly walked back to the protection of Bilibid's walls.

I felt nervous carrying the sword through the main gate, but a freshly assigned MP did not mention it as he motioned us through. His presence added to our sense of safety inside the walls. As Dad and I walked down the long dark corridor leading to our north compound, I noticed what appeared to be a dog on a leash led by a GI at the far end of the passageway. I pointed it out to Dad and he nodded, confirming that he, too, could see it.

As we neared the soldier, Dad blurted out, "My God, my God, no!" The GI stopped in front of us, blocking our path forward. He turned to his newly trained "pet," and ordered loudly, "Say hi, Joe; hi, Joe." Attached to the leash was a Japanese soldier with his hands and feet on the concrete floor. The leashed soldier did not respond initially, but when the GI jerked the leash pulling his arms off the floor, the prisoner spoke in his Japanese accent, "Hi, Joe." The grinning GI looked shocked when Dad grabbed and and, without another word, stepped around the two and briskly continued toward our compound.

Dad was sickened by the GI's abuse of the Japanese prisoner. Given the upbeat mood in camp, Dad chose not to bring up the issue with others and told me as we entered the compound to "Keep that one in your noodle." For sixty years, I did.

Mom greeted us with relief and a touch of anger. Dad did not share with Mom the details of our outing. Weeks later, he casually described our day by simply telling her, "We couldn't get to the convent." Adding with a smile, "We only met up with some Cummings and goings."

Two days passed. An internee couple accompanied Dad and me on another sojourn outside Bilibid, this time to Camp Santo Tomas. Our walk took us due north over an area of the city fully under American control. Dad knew the way and we arrived at the camp in about forty minutes. The streets were in disorder, but quiet. Many buildings were mere shells—victims of tank mortars, B-24 bombings, and fires. Some of the fires had been set by the retreating Japanese. A powerful smell of smoke lingered. The entry gate at Santo Tomas was also monitored by military police, their manner more formal. One sentry stepped forward and asked, "Bilibid?" Dad nodded, and they opened the gate. A few steps farther, we showed another MP our ID cards issued to us after our return from Ang Tibay.

Santo Tomas, the largest civilian internment camp in the Philippines, had suffered heavy loss of life in the recent attacks; its main building had sustained considerable damage from Japanese shelling. Dad managed to locate a number of his former Mindanao internee friends and discovered that others had been sent to the Los Baños camp months earlier. Dad found Frank Cary relatively well, but extremely thin and suffering from beriberi. I stood spellbound as I watched the two men tearfully embrace each other for a long time. I had never before seen such a bond between grown men. They spent almost an hour talking.

I joined a group of youngsters who had gathered on the stairway in front of the main building. They were talking with two playful GIs who seemed happy to be in the company of adoring children. They shared an abundance of chocolate with each of us. A couple of days later, we learned from a Santo Tomas visitor to Bilibid that a GI had been shot accidentally in Santo Tomas on the same stairwell where I had received chocolates. The accident involved a four-year-old child whom the soldier had allowed to hold his pistol.

At Santo Tomas, American troops had already begun the process of unearthing boxes (coffins) of buried internees. Frank Cary told us that the coffins would be reburied in a large cemetery on the outskirts of Manila. As we prepared to return, a jeep driver offered us a lift back to Bilibid. We happily accepted his offer. As he drove us toward the exit gate, he stopped and asked if we wanted to listen to a small military band. Without hesitation we agreed.

Most of the Santo Tomas camp family had gathered near the main gate to listen. We stayed seated in the jeep as the band tuned their instruments and began to perform. I saw tearful eyes and some salutes amid the throng of internees. American soldiers gathered nearby to listen to the band's farewell song. When the music to the words "Oh, say can you see" began, Dad placed his hand on his chest and nodded me to a standing position. I followed his lead, and once again saw tears roll down his cheeks. The music and a happy Dad made this a memorable day for me.

Dad experienced another moment of joy when Frank Cary rushed to the jeep before we departed. Frank had managed to arrange for Dad, Mom, my sisters, and me to be driven by jeep the next day to the convent where he thought Johnny and Ada were located.

My parents were relieved when we found the Oesches. Johnny, nearly naked but with a pillow under his head, was asleep on the bare concrete floor, surrounded by filth. With the help of a Filipina nurse, my parents arranged for the Oesches to be moved to a nearby church anteroom. Days later, we said our farewells to Ada and Johnny as they left to join extended family in Brisbane, Australia, on a routine military flight. Their exodus was evidence that planes were now flying out of the country and gave us hope that our turn would come soon.

*After liberation, my sisters and I stand with the Culpeppers and Vinsons
on the rooftop of Bilibid as Manila continues to burn, 1945.*

CHAPTER 7

Homeward Bound

Feb. 1945–April 1945

. . . .

Up and Away

The last days at Bilibid toward the end of February raised us to spiritual and emotional heights. Our dreams of returning to America seemed close to becoming reality. Almost daily new lists of individual and family departure dates were posted. Postings allowed time for preparation and the swapping of future addresses with dear friends. Those of us still waiting stayed upbeat, knowing that our turn would come soon. I was in no rush to depart.

The gradual shrinking of the camp population, coupled with a refurbished toilet scene, imported clean water, and regular deliveries of those delicious K rations had greatly improved our standard of living in Bilibid. The regularly delivered army K rations were my idea of paradise, though most of the GIs we came to know were less fond of them than I was. In a two-week period, I gained five pounds. I was given a new pair of shoes and a khaki shirt by army ordnance. Our high walls, once claustrophobic, felt protective—like concrete guardians. The world outside the walls had also become safer with each passing day, so we were able to visit with Filipino friends and fellow POWs in Santo Tomas. What more could I ask for?

On February 24 our family was listed for a March 2 departure. Words cannot describe Mom's emotional response to that news. She stepped quietly away from those around her at the posting board and stood aside to privately shed tears of joy. Mom spent our last week organizing our meager belongings and sharing loving farewells. I felt like we were leaving family behind.

On occasion, I would think about America, a place that was only a blip on my memory screen. I wondered about where we would go, what grade I would attend in school, and whether I would ever see my friends Reamo, Ward, and Bedie again.

I had not anticipated the tearful feelings I experienced saying good-bye. On the March morning of our departure, I realized my three-year journey through Camps Hay, Holmes, and Bilibid had been filled with love. I had always imagined that I would feel only joy at leaving Bilibid. But even my last visit to the latrine was filled with nostalgia as I walked up to the top and tipped the barrel to splash its full load of water down the chute for one last time.

A gathering of those still waiting for their departure dates watched as our family and others boarded the truck. We had shared confinement for over three years in three different prisons, but my journey through those years had not only shown me fear and hunger, it had created strong ties to the many who had shared my days through the war. Standing by, I saw a host of "aunts" and "uncles"—an extended family, not in bloodlines but certainly in love lines. Each, at one time or another during our intern-ment, had been like a parent to me. Seated in the truck bed between Mom and Dad, I hid my tears from the supportive hand-waving internees. As we departed, very abruptly those years became history, those faces my angels. To this day, I bless them for their caring guidance and affection. I am forever grateful, more than words can ever express. They were truly family, and the few still living continue to be even though we are scattered "from sea to shining sea."

The truck drove slowly through the prison gate and on to Rizal Avenue. Our soldier-driver told us that our Japanese guard corps had met death on that avenue as they fled Bilibid a month earlier. As we passed through the barrios on the outskirts of Manila, many Filipinos waved their farewells. Then we entered the gate to Nichols Field. Several airmen and Filipino *cargadores* helped us up the portable ladder into a waiting C-47. I had never been in an airplane before and was surprised to see how much space there was inside the fuselage.

We followed instructions and dutifully sat down in the line of padded bucket seats extending along both sides of the military transport. All of us had a lap-and-shoulder seatbelt draped over us and a parachute hanging above. A crew member showed us how to use the parachutes. As an air force staff sergeant demonstrated to Mom how to attach herself to the chute in an emergency, she jokingly commented, "Don't spend too much time with me, I can't even imagine jumping into the Visayan Sea!" Little did she know at the time how close she would come to doing just that. Within minutes, we were in flight.

After being airborne for just ten minutes, the thumping sounds of antiaircraft fire again brought us fear and anxiety. Dad held tightly to my sisters' hands, and I squeezed Mom's. Through a small window in the fuselage I could see the explosions, which looked like round gray sponge balls in the sky. Our plane was clearly the target of ground fire coming from an area south of Manila the Japanese still occupied. Everyone on board stoically sat still despite the rough ride—no screams, no tears. I watched the girls across from me tense up with each explosion, either closing their eyes or staring ahead in disbelief. One mother ritually exercised her rosary beads with a soft murmur. Minutes later, all went silent except for the drone of our transport. Then we heard an announcement from the cockpit, "We are out of the danger zone. You have been good troopers. Please relax and we shall be landing in Tacloban (Leyte) within the hour."

On the Beach at Leyte

A relieved group of families stepped out of "Mama Mia," the name emblazoned behind the crew chamber of our plane's siding. Several medics greeted us on the tarmac and asked about our needs. Dad pointed to Wezer's ear, since she had developed an earache during the flight over the inland waterway. For my sisters and me, and all the other children, that first airplane ride had been a memorable one.

After the medics finished their work, we were trucked across a roadway lined with damaged coconut palms to a beach village outside Tacloban. It was the location where General MacArthur had waded ashore months earlier. After being tagged with identification badges, we gathered on the beach for instructions and our housing assignments. Apologies accompanied the announcement that men would be trucked to a location several miles away. Women and children would stay in large army tents perched on wooden platforms close to the beach. Coconut palms served as massive umbrellas over our tents, and we had an unobstructed view of the harbor. Portable latrines were located behind the row of tents. Since most of the children in our group were girls, I felt as though I had returned to the women's barracks in Camp Holmes. We were told that the men would be driven back to our beach site daily and that soldiers were camped along the beach near our tents.

I had a hard time sleeping my first night under the tent. For long hours I replayed the happenings of the last two days. The rhythmic slapping of the waves eventually helped put me to sleep. At daybreak, I wandered out to the beach and noticed that a couple of large ships had dropped anchor in the harbor during the night. I wondered aloud if one of those ships would take us home. A sailor sitting near me on the beach answered my question by pointing to the largest ship in the harbor, which sat alone at anchor several hundred yards from shore. He told me it was a battleship awaiting repairs. The sailor was from San Diego and quickly became my naval instructor. He chatted nonstop about where he had been in the Pacific. None of the names meant anything to me, but I did memorize several special words he said would be useful after I boarded our ship: "bow," "stern," "port," "lee," and "bridge."

When Wezer stopped by, "San Diego" became more interested in talking with her. He asked her, "What's your favorite movie?" When she told him she had never seen a real movie, only a "Popeye" cartoon in the Davao theater years ago, he could not believe it. He looked even more bemused when she admitted that she had never heard of a movie star named Hepburn.

Soon, Rae joined us and asked me to go with her to look for seashells. I happily left Wezer behind with the sailor. While we were beachcombing, Rae found a starfish to show our mother. Mom placed the starfish in a jar of water next to Rae's cot. Two days later, its scent eclipsed its beauty, and Rae put it in the tidewater, hoping to restore its life. She and I watched it float away.

While waiting for our assigned ship to America, we lived in our beach tent home with twelve other women and children for almost a week. Most of our days were spent visiting with GIs who, like "San Diego," ambled our way, curious about life in a Japanese prison. Wezer, Rae, and I loved walking with the GIs to the PX where they would treat us to candy bars or green coconuts. I especially loved the coconuts. Sitting on a beach and sipping coconut milk through a straw was my new idea of paradise.

One extremely hot day, Wezer and I got Dad's permission to play catch with a beach ball in the "shallow water only." Neither of us could swim. We alternated between tossing the ball around in the shallows and sitting on the sand to watch a submarine and a destroyer edge into the busy harbor to anchor. Shortly before time to get into the chow line, I saw our beach ball floating out in the water. Instinctively, I ran to retrieve it. As I reached to grab it, the ball jumped farther out of my reach, so I lunged for it but only secured it for a moment. When I tried again, I felt a surge pull me down and away from shore. I tried to doggie paddle toward shore, but only sank again and swallowed water. I rose to the surface and yelled, "Wezer!" She had already screamed in panic as a soldier walked by. The soldier, fully clad in uniform, kicked off his boots and sprinted into the water. Swallowing water, I was panic-stricken. Suddenly I felt strong arms around my chest, and a hulking man quickly towed me to shallow water.

By the time he had carried me ashore, a medic and my frantic mom had arrived. I do not know what they did, but I am alive today thanks to that random act of heroism by my dear rescuer, Frank Magelky, from New England, North Dakota.

Whitecaps and the USS *Admiral Capps*

On the afternoon of March 8, we learned that we would be boarding ship the next day. I woke on our departure day, first at 3:00 a.m., and then at 4:00 a.m. Each time I thought about almost drowning, the floating beach ball, my sister Wezer, and the man who saved my life. I would miss my new friendship with Frank. I thought about Dad, too, and hoped that he would arrive with the other men in time to board the ship back to America with us.

Dawn could not come soon enough. I repeatedly reached over and peeked through the canvas door flap to see if our ship was visible in the harbor yet. I could not see it in the dark overcast night. My last peek, though, revealed what looked like a huge whale on the black sea with a hundred yellow eyes peering toward shore. After guessing the ship was in, I fell asleep. Before I had truly awakened, I fell back into a dream mode, revisiting Bilibid and the giant Corporal Cummings, and envisioning a huge ship cruising slowly under the Golden Gate Bridge, with all of our relatives waving their greetings from the bridge.

At 6:30 a.m. a bugle sounded, and I heard Dad's voice outside the tent singing to us, "Rise, shine, see God's glory." I was out in a flash and the girls soon followed. Anchored in the harbor was the "whale." Painted in white behind the port bow was its name, USS *Admiral Capps*. That had to be our ship. Its broad deck was aflutter with white-capped sailors attending to preparations. Other families had assembled on the beach, all staring in excitement at what was to be our floating home.

Frank came on the scene suddenly, calling "Hi, Tongs." He hugged my parents and asked if he could take my sisters and me to the GI mess tent for breakfast. They happily obliged and then set about organizing our few belongings for the trip to America. Following breakfast, Frank had to attend to his assignments, but not before answering my question about his role as a soldier. With a big smile, he said, "I'm a staff sergeant in the 129th Infantry and I pull people out of the harbor." I sobbed as he left me, but we promised to see each other again someday, and in fact Frank and I remained in touch for years. Our last visit was at his farm in the Dakotas in the summer of 1973. He told me then that a strong undertow was common at Leyte and that command should have had a guard present with the children on the beach.

By late morning, almost all assigned POWs, including some from Santo Tomas, were motored out to the *Admiral Capps* aboard several modified LSTs (Landing Ship Tanks). After our water taxi was safely secured to the *Capps*'s belly, Dad and I climbed up a taut rope ladder on the port side to an open gateway about ten feet above the water. The girls rode up on what looked like a huge park swing. We had been informed earlier that the men would be quartered in the hold, several floors below the cabins to which women and children were assigned, but families would take meals together. Gathered on deck, each of us was presented with a life vest and instructed in the inflation procedure. Then everyone was led to their assigned quarters. My wish to be with Dad was denied by the officer-in-charge.

I did not understand why Dad could not be quartered with us in the cabin, but discovered on my first visit to the family lavatory why men were separated from their families. I pleaded with Mom to be housed with Dad in the hold. "You'll stay where you've been told," she said. "You can visit your dad in the hold in the evening or on the deck after supper." Having to use the toilet and lavatory for the women and children upset me. The only women in the ship's crew were nurses, and they had their own lavatory next to the infirmary.

Soon after ten o'clock that evening, the *Capps* nudged toward open water. A destroyer escort led the way. A second destroyer followed off the right stern. The loudspeaker reached all quarters with a list of orders: lights on deck would be turned out at sundown and no smoking would be permitted until daybreak. Those orders were repeated daily. For evening entertainment, most women and children played cards or worked on a variety of puzzles made available in cabins, always with shades covering portholes. The men in the hold had no lighting restrictions, since their quarters were below water level.

Wezer again became my scout on evening toilet runs. But the facility was in almost constant use, and since the showers and toilets were situated in an open bay, I eventually conceded to a pee can in our cabin for night-time, saving "other matters" for my trips to the men's hold. Only twice did Mom insist on my braving the women's shower scene because "you just plain need a bath!" I made a habit of joining Dad down below in the evenings with my toothbrush in hand. We chatted together and talked with friends about events of the recent past and about what our return to America would be like.

Several times a week, boxing matches between the sailors—carried out with a referee in a real ring enclosed with a rope—would take place in the hold. I attended almost all of them. Each bout lasted three rounds and was judged by three preassigned sailors. Most boxers had friends who coached them and wiped down their sweaty bodies between rounds. On those rare occasions when blood was drawn anywhere on a boxer's head, the referee stopped the bout and declared the blood-free combatant the winner. The stifling heat below decks did not slow the shouts of encouragement or friendly boos if the sight of blood stopped a fight. The bouts had a spirit of fun to them. Unlike most of the viewers Dad did not bet on the contests, but as a former college boxer he enjoyed watching them.

A couple of times each day, postings informed us of our approximate location and sea conditions. None of us knew our ultimate destination, but Mom hoped it would be San Francisco. Several days after departing Leyte with our destroyer escorts, we awoke and noticed the ship was not moving. The *Capps* had dropped anchor in a place called Manus. Two men Dad called the "port pundits" had all the answers as to why we were there. One Santo Tomas internee said that at Manus we would pick up wounded GIs and food. The other predicted a long stay for repairs. As it turned out, neither guess was correct.

A navy medic stepped out of the infirmary to chat with my folks as we stood on deck after supper. The medic had lost his brother in Bataan and had wished for an assignment in the Philippines. He had not seen Bataan but did make it to the Philippines for a one-month stint in Leyte. I asked him if Manus was an American territory. Smiling, he said "No, we only rent the harbor." He excused himself for a moment and said, "Don't go away." He was back in a minute with a map and delighted in showing me the island of Manus, describing the port as the "guardian of the dinosaur." He told me, "The dinosaur is New Guinea, south of Manus." Running his finger around the border of New Guinea, he made clear the shape of a huge reptile. Then, before excusing himself, he told us that when we woke up again, "You'll see nothing but the Pacific and two destroyer escorts." He was absolutely right. I was thrilled that we were really heading home this time.

For days after leaving Manus, the *Capps* followed a zigzag course behind the lead destroyer. The pattern, we discovered, was a routine procedure to make Japanese torpedo attacks difficult. As we neared the equator, excitement mounted. When the *Capps* crossed that invisible line, eager internees lined up to receive a commemorative souvenir from the captain. It was a grand celebration.

Waking the next morning and seeing no destroyers but only the open sea for the first time since departing Leyte gave me chills. I feared that enemy submarines could be stalking our ship from below, awaiting an opportunity to send the *Capps* to the ocean floor. Dad joined me on the deck and noticed my look of concern. He must have read my mind since he told me how happy he was for us to be out of the war zone. I felt relieved.

Dad led me to breakfast where we mingled with some sailors eager to hear about prison life and the kinds of cruelty the "Japs" had imposed on us. I really enjoyed visiting with the crew; it helped the days pass more quickly. The words "Japs" or "Nips," slang we avoided using in prison, were commonplace on board ship. Initially the expressions took me by surprise because Mom had trained us to speak otherwise. By habit, I responded to queries about our captors with the more respectful word—Japanese, "Some Japanese were mean, some were not," I told them.

I found it interesting that the servicemen in the hold wanted to trade war souvenirs. Dad had kept a considerable number of monetarily worthless wartime Japanese paper pesos, and he gave me a stack to give to sailors who wanted to swap souvenirs. On one occasion, Mom asked me what the soldiers gave me for the pesos. "A Hershey bar," I responded. I received no more pesos! Mom thought that pesos might be nice gifts to family in America, but empty Hershey wrappers would not.

Wezer fell ill with seasickness and an ear infection in our second week at sea. She stayed in sick bay for one or two nights, attended to by a gregarious sailor with a quick wit. When I visited Wezer, I was happy to see her laughing so heartily again. The medic kidded her about his nickname, Gig, which in military parlance means demerit. She never asked him whether Gig was a given name or one earned from lapses in military decorum. Some years later, Wezer recognized his face on a movie screen, where he played the role of one of *The Three Musketeers*. His professional name was Gig Young.

Riding the Waves to Pearl Harbor

It seemed to take forever for the *Capps* to plough from Manus to Pearl Harbor. Understandably, the length of the voyage was extended because of the zigzag path the ship took through the dangerous waters of the Pacific. Dad and I learned from an attending officer that our ship was named after Rear Admiral Washington Lee Capps, who served with the U.S. Navy during the Spanish-American War in the Philippine Islands.

After crossing the equator, we did not hear any messages from the bridge until the morning of April 1 when the captain announced that we would arrive in Honolulu that afternoon. Mom giggled at the announcement. "Don't believe it," she said. "Today is April Fools' Day." But her internee friends seemed to believe the announcement, and after lunch they swarmed the deck, eager to catch a glimpse of Pearl Harbor. Right on schedule, the outline of Oahu appeared. Oohs, aahs, and big smiles appeared on faces eager to see land again. Mom admitted to being the fool. She then called our attention to a far-off aircraft carrier anchored well away from our path to the harbor. I could not make out the name on the bow, only that it was floating with a severe list.

The harbor scene was like a carrier sick bay. As the *Capps* cruised slowly into Pearl Harbor, two more carriers loomed like a couple of crocodiles in a fishpond. They were immense. One, obviously very damaged, was severely atilt. We could only see a few sailors moving around on the slanted deck. A Santo Tomas internee, peering through borrowed binoculars, identified the distant carrier as the USS *Franklin*.

We learned from a *Capps* medic that the *Franklin* had been severely damaged and almost sunk after taking direct hits from bombs and kamikaze strikes on the carrier deck in the Pacific, east of Japan. Over seven hundred crew members had lost their lives.

The other carrier, almost directly in our path, showed no list. The *Capps* slowed to a near stop as we pulled parallel with the largest ship I had ever seen. Hundreds of sailors, bedecked in white regalia, stood facing us in formation, but at ease on the carrier's deck. All at once, they snapped to attention and raised their hands in a formal salute as the *Capps* eased by.

I joined the throng of internees standing by the railing, waving to the saluting sailors. I looked at Mom. She was sobbing. Dad, too, showing a tear, was moved by the military greeting, and commented guiltily, "I think we owe *them* the salute."

We remained in the harbor for a couple of days, never leaving the ship. During our time in port, I saw a number of military officers come aboard to check on the condition of some of the more seriously ill folks, removing several for hospitalization in Honolulu. Officers also interviewed some of the internees, usually the least healthy. Mom was one of those. She parlayed all questions about her health to her pet response, "I'm fine."

Finally, we were oceangoing again. When the captain made the formal announcement, "Next port is San Francisco," all shared cheers and tears.

At Last, the Golden Gate

After what seemed like endless wave watching, I finally saw the dream of all my dreams come into sight—the Golden Gate Bridge. That bridge was one of our symbols of freedom during the war years. It looked absolutely majestic! The relatives of many passengers on board stood on the Golden Gate along with hundreds of curious onlookers. Many waved signs, some with names I recognized. Over the din of yells from the bridge above and announcements coming from the ship's loudspeaker below, I could faintly hear a recording of the national anthem. I felt like a huge period had been placed at the end of a very long sentence.

Our days in port were spent filling out legal forms and purchasing clothing and shoes with an allowance of money distributed to everyone. The allowance did not quite cover all our family's needs. Therefore, Mom continued to be a skinny WAC (Women's Army Corps) for a number of days, wearing the uniform given to her in Leyte. Most of our camp friends quickly departed to join their respective families across America. Our family, however, remained in a hotel while Dad and Mom communicated with the American Board offices and with our family on the East Coast. The board had received no word of our arrival date, so we had to delay travel plans eastward for a few days.

By the time we boarded a train bound for New York, I felt as though Bilibid and the events of the war were part of a past age. It was a strange feeling, probably the result of the many new faces I'd seen and conversations I'd had over recent weeks.

Our first night on the train, I replayed the day-by-day happenings of the past month in my head. In early March, we left Bilibid aboard a truck, then we boarded a plane, then a ship, and finally a train.

I woke the next morning as we crossed the Sierra Nevada Mountains and made a short stop at Reno. I received many geography lessons as I watched the ever-changing landscape pass by. A woman who was going to Salt Lake City, which our conductor called "Mormon Town," told me about the unique Salt Lake and the "world's best skiing" in the nearby mountains. The following day I stared in awe at the snow-covered Rocky Mountains. Even more excitement awaited me on the eastern plains of Colorado.

The train conductor, who had become my friendly tour guide during the long hours of travel, invited me to join him at the back of the caboose as the train sped through an expanse of scrub plain, void of homes, trees, or anything perceptibly interesting. He told me, however, that I was to make a delivery at a special spot. We waited a long while, just chatting. Then, looking at his watch, he handed me a rolled up newspaper and said, "When I say 'bow-wow,' toss it as far as you can." Moments later, a small dog the conductor had named "Spot" ran into view.

"Bow-wow!" he yelled, and I let the newspaper fly. Spot quickly picked it up in his jaws and headed off on a run. I was flabbergasted! Where had the dog come from? The conductor did not know; he guessed it was someone's pet. It routinely met the passing train to fetch the newspaper.

"How did you know where to meet Spot in the middle of nowhere?" I asked.

"I look at the clock," he said. "I've been doing this for four years. The pup is always waiting for the train two hours and fourteen minutes after we leave Denver. If we are running a little late, Spot sits there and waits for us."

I could not wait to tell my sisters about Spot. But I stayed with the conductor and looked over the railing as I listened to another of his stories about travel across the western plains. Suddenly a loud crackling sound interrupted us and then there was a pause. An announcement came across the speaker system that a forthcoming news report would be delivered shortly. The speaker system remained silent for long minutes. The conductor quietly led me back to my family compartment, bidding my parents, my sisters, and me farewell.

Together, our family listened for the announcement. "This won't be good news, Walter," Mom predicted. Then very clearly these words rang out, "I am sorry to report that President Franklin Roosevelt died three hours ago in Warm Springs, Georgia."

Mom and Dad stared at one another in disbelief, torn by grief. It was mid-afternoon on April 12, 1945.

Dona nobis pacem

Afterword

Our return to American soil allowed me to resume the life of a normal child and suppress my worst memories of the war. Yet I never forgot the compassionate Commandant Tomibe of Camp Holmes, and when I had the opportunity to visit Japan I contacted him. Our several meetings, the last while on sabbatical with my wife and son in 1982, confirmed his character and reminded me why he had had such a huge impact on me both as a child-internee and as an adult.

As we rode the train to Nara with Tomibe, he shared the account of his last eighteen months in the Philippines. In early January 1945, he and a group of soldiers got separated from the Japanese infantry in southern

*Here former Commandant Tomibe is standing with me
outside his Kyoto home during happier days in 1982.*

Luzon and set out for the mountains northeast of Baguio. There they fought off starvation and the hateful Filipinos for months. Suffering severely, Tomibe attempted suicide in a mountain stream in late August 1945, but he was denied death by his comrades and the group struggled southward. They were captured south of Baguio and sent to Laguna as war prisoners in September. In March 1946, Tomibe was ordered to Manila to face the War Crimes Tribunal. Manila-based Father Sheridan spoke to the court on his behalf, and a group of the Holmes internees—including Dad, Uncle B, and Nellie McKim—wrote supportive letters. Tomibe was freed and returned to Japan in August 1946.

Tomibe revealed to us that he had known the whereabouts of the two young men who escaped on 4/4/44, but he did not act on that information because he knew he "would have to kill them" if they resisted capture. Tomibe also knew about the radio hidden in the camp hospital and had agreed with Phil Markert (holder of the radio) that he would not interfere so long as Phil shared the newscasts with him. Both men kept their word.

In addition to the story of his capture, Tomibe gave us transcripts of the writings he had prepared for the memorable 1977 reunion with Holmes internees in the States. Regrettably, coaching responsibilities at Williams College prevented me from attending, but at the Presidio in San Francisco, my parents, sisters, and nearly two hundred internees offered Tomibe Rokuro their sincere gratitude for his humane and caring ways during their internment. The outpouring of love, tears, and forgiveness to the 65-year-old former commandant was unique and overwhelming. I'm certain that no other enemy commandant of World War II has been so honored on American soil.

Tomibe had a strong affection for children in particular, and one of my most vivid memories of him at Camp Holmes was at a children's party that he patterned after the traditional Japanese celebration of the Emperor's Birthday. On April 29, 1944, he invited all the children to the parade ground. He personally handed me—and every child—a banana. To his utter surprise, since it not a practice in Japanese culture, we each thanked him and shook his hand individually. Tomibe's speech at the Presidio in part read: "I have come to make independent decision according to my own thinking way. . . . I must confess that it was the children who were in the Baguio Camp 33 years ago and who attached so much importance to every one's free will that gave me this lesson."

Tomibe's thoughts on friendship and peace have been inspiring. As he departed Camp Holmes in 1944, he gave a handwritten message to Jim Halsema that was intended for us all:

> You are a young man supporting your fatherland. I am like you. We have become friends here, but if the fate of our countries demands, I am sure that we will confront each other bravely. Yet with the dawn of peace, our friendship will be deeper than before.

Tomibe's resolve to build friendship and understanding continued as he reflected on Camp Holmes in a letter he wrote to Father Sheridan on his seventy-first birthday:

> A warm relationship of brotherhood, a real friendship was born between people of enemy countries. The environment was inhumanly cruel; a life of imprisonment without freedom; a life of starvation and death. Yet each man's spiritual strength was gallant enough to endure everything with a conviction that his mother country would one day win victory.
>
> Forty-odd years have passed since then . . . [I] worry that after a few years the brotherly relationship that was nurtured in the Baguio Concentration Camp for Enemy Aliens might die out.
>
> I regret very much now that I did not make more effort to transplant this seed of friendship to the next generation. I feel very badly about it. . . I would like to bequeath or leave behind for the next generation something and I am seriously thinking about and reflecting what that something will be.

Since Tomibe's death on September 26, 1983, we have maintained ties with his wife, Shizue, son Hajime, and daughter-in-law Hiroe. Additionally, we continue to nurture our family connection with our Davao friend Matsumoto Katsuji, through Koizumi Hanako, his great-granddaughter in Yokohama. In this way, I believe we are living Tomibe's wish to "transplant this seed of friendship to a new generation."

Bibliography

"Biography of Dr. Mukaibo." *Aoyama Courier,* 1 Dec. 1981: 2.

Cary, Frank. *Letters from Internment Camp, Davao and Manila 1942–1945.* Ashland, OR: Independent Printing Company, 1993.

Crouter, Natalie. *Forbidden Diary.* New York: Bert Franklin and Co., 1980.

Eschbach, Carl B. "The History of the Japanese Army Concentration Camp #3." 1950. TS. Collection of Curtis Whitfield Tong, Williamstown, MA.

Halsema, James J. *Bishop Brent's Baguio School.* Baguio: Brent School Inc., 1987.

Heimke, Betsy Herold. *Bring Cup, Plate, and Spoon.* Laguna Vista, TX: River Road Press, 2008.

Hendricks, Kenneth C. *Shadow of His Hand: The Reiji Takahashi Story.* St. Louis: The Bethany Press, 1967.

Hind, R. Renton. *Spirits Unbroken.* Berkeley, CA: The Howell-North Press, 1946.

Mansell, Donald. *Under the Shadow of the Rising Sun.* Nampa, ID: Pacific Press Publishing Association, 2003.

Marshall, Cecily Mattocks. *Happy Life Blues.* Clinton, MA: Angus MacGregor Books, 2007.

Mary Hilary, Sister. *Ten Decades of Praise.* Racine, WI: The DeKoven Foundation for Church Work, 1965.

Miles, Fern Harrington. *Captive Community: Life in a Japanese Internment Camp, 1941–1945.* Jefferson City, TN: Mossy-Creek Press, 1987.

Minear, Richard H. *Victors' Justice: The Tokyo War Crimes Trial.* Princeton: Princeton University Press, 1971.

Moule, William R. *God's Arms Around Us.* New York: Vantage Press, 1960.

Ream, John F. "An Interview with Lt. Col. Herbert Swick." *Military magazine. http://milmag. com/2009/02/an-interview-with-lt-col-herbert-swick/. Accessed 27 April 2005.*

Scaff, Marilee. "Excerpts from Scaff letters, 1941." Manuscript in the collection of Curtis Whitfield Tong, Williamstown, MA.

Smith, Joseph M. "Three Years in the Fish's Belly." Self-published, 2004. Collection of Curtis Whitfield Tong, Williamstown, MA.

Sobeck, Katie Ream. "What Did the Children Do?" 2004. Manuscript in the collection of Curtis Whitfield Tong, Williamstown, MA.

Stevens, Fredric H. *Santo Tomas Internment Camp, 1942–1945.* New York: Stratford House, Inc., 1946.

Taylor, Harry and Miriam. *Edge of Conflict.* Camp Hill, PA: Christian Publications, 1993.

Tomibe, Rokuro. "Baguio (Philippine Islands) Concentration Camp: Aftermath Report – Part II." *The Asahi Shimbun,* Feb. 1977.

———. "Record of Baguio Camp Home in the Philippines: Secret Story on the End of the War." *The Asahi Shimbun,* 13 Feb. 1977.

Whitfield, Evelyn. *Three Year Picnic.* Corvallis, OR: Premiere Edition International, Inc., 1999.

About the Author

After the war, Curtis Tong attended Newton High School (Massachusetts) and Otterbein College (Ohio) on an ROTC scholarship. He then served as an officer in the United States Air Force for three years. After leaving the military, Tong taught and coached at Bexley High School in Columbus, Ohio, while earning his master's degree from Ohio State University. He then returned to Otterbein as professor and basketball coach, during which time he also served as school-board chair and completed a PhD in education at Ohio State University. In the early 1970s Dr. Tong moved on to Williams College in Massachusetts, where he coached men's basketball and women's tennis and served as physical education director. After ten years at Williams, Tong became athletic director, physical education department chair, and creative writing instructor at Pomona College in California. He is the author of *Off the Bench: A Perspective on Athletic Coaching* (1991).

As a teacher on sabbaticals in China, Japan, and the Philippines, Tong was able to broaden his perspective of his World War II experiences. Now retired, he resides with his wife, Wavalene, in Williamstown, Massachusetts, where he spends time writing, serving his community, competing in regional tennis tournaments, and keeping up to date with his three children and seven grandchildren.

Production Notes for Tong | *Child of War*

Cover design by Julie Matsuo-Chun

Text design and composition by Jansom
    with display type in Bernhard Modern Std
    and text type in Adobe Caslon Pro

Printing and binding by Sheridan Books, Inc.

Printed on 60 lb. House Opaque, 500 ppi